Praise for
Lord, Renew Your Wonders: Spiritual Gifts for Today

Renew Your Wonders is a description of the charisms done, "from the field," that is from their practical exercise and in their often amazing and unexpected manifestations. It tells what most of the time the author "has heard with his own ears and has seen with his own eyes" and has been instrumental for. All this makes the book a reading which can edify the faith of all and contribute to the theological understanding of the charisms and to their discernment in the life of the Church today.

> —**Fr. Raniero Cantalamessa, OFM Cap., preacher to the Papal Household**

Renew Your Wonders is an excellent book. While reading it I was convicted by the Holy Spirit that I wasn't really "earnestly desiring the spiritual gifts." I repented and am now. Thank you Damian for the great care that went into the book and the even greater care that went into the spiritual journey that led to it and still continues. Your ministry and teaching is a great gift for the Church.

> —**Ralph Martin, STD, president of Renewal Ministrie and director of graduate theology programs in the new evangelization at Sacred Heart Major Seminary**

Drawing upon over twenty-five years of experience in worldwide ministry, Damian shares not only what he has come to know about the *charisms* but, more importantly, what he has seen. This book provides a wealth of teaching about the charisms or charismatic gifts highlighted in 1 Corinthians 12. It is well researched, drawing from Scripture, Church tradition, and the wisdom of the Fathers and saints. The teaching is accompanied by clear, practical guidance, encouraging people to move in the charisms. The testimonies alone make this book exciting and engaging. The book provides a strong witness to what we have seen the Lord do in the power of His Holy Spirit, and it also encourages us to be expectant for what is still to come.

I highly recommend *Lord, Renew Your Wonders* as a rich resource, a practical teaching manual, and a t'

> —**Michelle Moran, form   tholic
>   C   CRS)**

As a medical doctor, I have had the privilege of witnessing some of the healings, signs, and wonders at Damian's events, and there were cases in which I was able to obtain the medical documentation afterward. In this book, you will find encouragement, hope, and guidance that will enlarge your vision for the supernatural, so that you can embrace the fullness of your Christian inheritance.

—Borbála Tobisch, MD

Damian Stayne has helped people for many years to yield to the supernatural works of the Holy Spirit. This book offers you the same opportunity. The stories will inspire you, and the teaching will guide you. You will grow confident that the Holy Spirit will empower you to proclaim the kingdom of God with power.

—Neal Lozano, founder of Heart of the Father Ministries and author of *Unbound: A Practical Guide to Deliverance*

Damian Stayne's teaching on spiritual gifts is in line with orthodox Catholic theology. My exposure to his ministry is very positive, and God does accompany his preaching with signs and wonders. I hope that this book will encourage the spread of the use of spiritual gifts for the upbuilding of the Body of Christ in the life of the Church and her mission.

—Fr. Francis Martin, STL, SSD, renowned Scripture scholar and professor emeritus of New Testament at the Dominican House of Studies, Washington, DC

Damian Stayne takes readers into the heart of the mysterious workings of the charismatic gifts of the Holy Spirit in the life of the Church, ancient and modern, Eastern and Western. *Lord, Renew Your Wonders* offers a joyful affirmation of the continued supernatural nature of Christ's presence in his Church through her saints, clergy, and laypeople. Indeed, we have received a reliable guide on how to be open to receiving and growing in these charisms in our own ministries for the building up of the Church. A delightful read!

—Fr. Kyrillos Ibrahim, St. Paul American Coptic Orthodox Church, Los Angeles

In July 2012, the Alleluia Community had the privilege of hosting Damian and his Charism School as well as a citywide healing and miracle service held at the local Augusta University. The spiritual results of his seminar and the accompanying healing service were something like pouring gasoline on a small fire. We experienced a new level of passion and love for Jesus, a deeper grace of personal and community prayer, and truly a fresh outpouring of the gifts of the Holy Spirit. Damian and his ministry to us were an unmistakable movement of the Holy Spirit in our midst. On behalf of the Alleluia Community, Damian, I want to sincerely thank you for your ministry and for your excellent book.

—**Robert Garrett, moderator, Alleluia Community, Augusta, Georgia**

As a clinical psychologist, I have researched many charismatic and healing ministries, and I have personally witnessed present-day signs, wonders, and miracles in Damian Stayne's ministry. The examples he provides from his own ministry, as well as the ministries of others, make the theology of the spiritual gifts come alive. The author is careful to point out that mission and holiness go together and that effective ministry is grounded in love and a sense of community. Reading this book will spiritually nourish, bless, and inspire you to step out in faith to exercise the gifts that are the inheritance of every Christian.

—**Dr. Fernando Andre Leyva, clinical psychologist**

Damian Stayne's new book, *Lord, Renew Your Wonders*, is amazing. A great book for Catholics and Protestants, it is biblical as well as full of testimonies from church history and contemporaries. Damian speaks at our training school each year. I highly recommend Damian and his new book.

—**Dr. Randy Clark, President of Global Awakening**

This is a book of fire and life, soundly rooted in Scripture, Christian tradition, and Church teaching. With wit, wisdom, and good sense, Damian Stayne offers a compelling corrective to the tendency among Western theologians, ministers, and churchgoers to decouple kerygma from charism, preaching from power. The result is a book ablaze with life-changing testimony, a book full of hope and challenge, a book that I found daunting to pick up, hard to put down, and impossible to forget.

—**Dr. Anthony Towey, STL, director of the Aquinas Centre for Theological Literacy, St. Mary's University, London**

One of our foremost teachers and practitioners in the gifts of the Holy Spirit, Damian Stayne shares his experience of promoting and using these charismatic gifts all over the world. Thousands have been healed through his ministry, but it is equally exciting to learn of the vast numbers inspired, equipped, and launched into this vital work themselves through the Charism Schools, initiated and widely presented by Damian and members of the Cor et Lumen Christi Community. *Lord, Renew Your Wonders* contains a wealth of teaching and experience in the exercise of the spiritual gifts. It is, in my opinion, essential reading for all of us.

—Charles Whitehead, former President of International Catholic Charismatic Renewal Services (ICCRS)

Damian Stayne has written a profoundly approachable survey of the charismatic gifts that takes into account not only biblical teaching on the subject, but also patristic witnesses, hagiographical material from both Western and Eastern Christian sources, and contemporary experience. As can be expected, the book is written primarily from a Roman Catholic charismatic perspective, but—uncharacteristically for such writings—it includes material on such important personages as St. Seraphim of Sarov, St. Simeon the New Theologian, the Desert Fathers, and the twentieth-century holy man, Coptic Pope Kyrillos VI. There are references to non-Catholic Western Christians with particularly striking gifts as well. Thus, the author presents a truly ecumenical survey, grounded in official Catholic teaching.

But the book's value does not end there. The author provides an always humble account of his own journey of discovering, growing, and maturing in the charismatic gifts, as his international ministry of healing has grown over the years.

Thus, *Lord Renew Your Wonders: Spiritual Gifts for Today* is not only a descriptive survey of the charismatic gifts in the Christian history of both East and West, it is also a step-by-step guide in how to receive and grow in these gifts. Its teachings should be widely read and applied by the Churches. Damian Stayne presents an optimistic view of the outpouring of the gifts of the Holy Spirit that not only confound but also convert those skeptical and even inimical towards the saving gospel of our Lord, God, and Savior Jesus Christ.

This book should be included in seminary requirements, and should be widely disseminated among the laity, so that it may further the renewal of confidence in the Lord's spiritual gifts in today's world.

—**Fr. Andriy Chirovsky, Mitred Protopresbyter S.Th.D, founder of the Metropolitan Andrey Sheptytsky Institute of Eastern Christian Studies at the University of St. Michael's College, University of Toronto**

This book brings to mind the words of St. John Paul II: 'Whenever the Spirit intervenes, he leaves people astonished. He brings about events of amazing newness.' Lord, Renew Your Wonders is filled with amazing testimonies of the new things God is doing through the gifts of the Holy Spirit. Yet, as Damian Stayne compellingly demonstrates, these new things are actually a rediscovery of what belongs to the normal life of the Church. His book will inspire and challenge readers to greater faith in the God who loves to do extraordinary things through ordinary people.

—**Dr. Mary Healy, professor of Sacred Scripture at Sacred Heart Major Seminary, Detroit, and a member of the Pontifical Biblical Commission**

I am delighted to commend this powerful book. The narration of personal anecdotes, rooted in the teachings of the apostolic faith, encourages Christians—including those of the Catholic, Protestant and Orthodox traditions—to nourish their faith. With clarity, wisdom, and honesty, Damian emphasizes the need to use the spiritual gifts of the Holy Spirit to build up the Church and gives us practical guidance on how to operate the supernatural gifts. I very much recommend this as a must-read for all Christians.

—**Fr. Soji Olikkal, Sehion International Ministries, Syro-Malabar rite, Kerala India**

Lord, RENEW YOUR WONDERS

Spiritual Gifts for Today

DAMIAN STAYNE

Published by The Word Among Us Press
7115 Guilford Drive, Suite 100
Frederick, Maryland 21704
www.wau.org

22 21 20 19 18   2 3 4 5 6

ISBN: 978-1-59325-323-3
eISBN: 978-1-59325-500-8

Scripture quotations are from the Revised Standard Version of the Bible—Second Catholic Edition (Ignatius Edition), copyright © 2006 National Council of the Churches of Christ in the United States of America. Used by permission. All rights reserved.

Scripture texts marked "NRSV" are from New Revised Standard Version Bible, copyright © 1989 the Division of Christian Education of the National Council of the Churches of Christ in the United States of America. Used by permission. All rights reserved.

Quotations are taken from the English translation of the *Catechism of the Catholic Church* for the United States of America (indicated as CCC), 2nd ed. Copyright 1997 by United States Catholic Conference—Libreria Editrice Vaticana.

The theological adviser for this book was Carmelite theologian Fr. Christopher O'Donnell, Professor Emeritus of Spirituality at the Milltown Institute of Theology and Philosophy, Dublin, Ireland.

Cover design by David Crosson
Cover art: "The Raising of Lazarus" by Mount Tabor Studios, Holy Transfirguration Monastery Monks of Mount Tabor, Redwood Valley, California. Used with permission.

Made and printed in the United States of America

Library of Congress Control Number: 2017942648

Acknowledgments

This book would not have ever been possible without the spiritual and practical input of others, both in its writing and in the years that preceded it.

First, I wish to honor my dear parents, whose love I never doubted for one moment of my life and who passed on to me the assumption that the Christian faith is something utterly central and radical. I wish to honor a Catholic layman, Myles Dempsey, whose love of the Church, life of prayer, and powerful deliverance ministry helped me enormously in my early years after my adult conversion. I also wish to thank Charles Whitehead, who encouraged me and was the first to give me a platform from which to minister in spiritual gifts, at a major conference. I especially wish to honor Fr. Chris O'Donnell, O Carm, my spiritual guide for more than twenty years. He is a man of great wisdom, learning, and holiness, without whose patient guidance and kindness I would have never grown to enjoy so many unmerited graces in my life.

I feel I must also honor so many of the Church's canonized saints, whose extraordinary example of loving supernatural ministry in the spiritual gifts made my heart burn with zeal: St. Peter, St. Paul, many of the Desert Fathers, St. Patrick, St. Francis of Assisi, St. Vincent Ferrer, St. Seraphim of Sarov, St. John of Kronstadt, Pope St. Kyrillos VI, and St. Pio of Pietrelcina. I also wish to honor many of great holiness from the charismatic and Pentecostal streams who have gone to the Lord—such magnificent Christians as Smith Wigglesworth, Maria Woodworth-Etter, and John G. Lake, whose outstanding holiness and faith for miracles was so inspiring.

I want to acknowledge a real debt to the early pioneers in the Catholic Charismatic Renewal, who showed me that God was doing these things in the Catholic Church in our time: Francis MacNutt, Sr. Briege McKenna, Fr. Bob de Grandis, Fr. Michael Scanlan, TOR, Fr. Rufus Pereira, and Fr. Emiliano Tardif, among others. However, it was through the ministry of John Wimber, and his teaching that all Christians can be involved in the ministry of spiritual gifts, that I experienced a major breakthrough, especially in the area of physical healing. In the area of prophetic ministry, I am indebted to Graham Cooke for his brilliant teaching on prophetic gifts.

While much of this book comes from my teaching and training materials researched over many years, it took the help of many patient people to make it into a book. I owe a great debt of thanks to my lovely son, John, who convinced me this book must be written and generously donated more than fifty hours to help me reshape the material. Duncan Mitchell, a brother in our community, helped in corrections in matters of language and style and sat advising me as I painfully chopped the book down to a reasonable size.

I owe particular thanks to my editor, Patty Mitchell, whose determined patience and editing skills brought this book from its first desperate state to something ready for publication. I want to thank my lovely daughter, Miryam, for her constant encouragement and belief that this book was "the will of God." I wish to express my sincere gratitude to all the dedicated members of my community, Cor et Lumen Christi, who prayed regularly for me and encouraged me as I was writing.

Finally, I want to honor and thank my darling wife, Cathy, who persistently exhorted me to persevere. She has carried me in prayer, supported me through all my highs and lows, and stood by me faithfully in this ministry for over twenty-eight years as I made foolish mistakes and witnessed the glory of God.

Thanks to you all.

Damian Stayne

Contents

Acknowledgments 3

Foreword 11

Introduction 13

Chapter 1: The Spiritual Gifts 17

    Charisms are not natural gifts 19

    Jesus: The Pattern for Our Christian Life............................ 22

    Jesus' vision for charismatic disciples 22

    The early Church was committed to the charismatic gifts...24

    Spiritual Gift in the Early Centuries of the Church.............. 25

    Spiritual Revival 30

    A historic breakthrough 32

    Pope St. John XXIII and the Second Vatican Council 33

    Recent popes on the charisms...34

    Moving from Theory to Encounter 37

    Love or spiritual gifts, which is more important? 38

    One gift each? 38

    Only for "the mature and holy"? 39

    Giving people time and space to grow 40

Part I: The Prophetic Gifts 43

Chapter 2: The Theology of Prophecy and a Short History 44

    Jesus as Prophet 45

    Jesus as *the* prophet...46

    Jesus' use of prophetic knowledge and

    the reading of hearts 47

    Prophecy in the New Testament Church 48

    Examples of Prophecy from Church History...................... 50

    St. Pio of Pietrelcina 53

    Prophetic gifts in the Orthodox and Coptic churches 54

    Prophetic gifts in the Pentecostal and Evangelical

    Charismatic tradition 57

Chapter 3: The Practice of Prophecy Today 59

    Inspirational prophecy 61

    Revelational prophecy...61

Sharing God's Knowledge, Heart, and Wisdom...................... 62
    Sharing God's knowledge 63
    Sharing God's heart...64
    Sharing God's wisdom 65
How Does Prophecy Come?.. 66
Three Elements of Prophecy... 68
Effects of Prophecy 69
    Restore dignity and self-respect 69
    Bring correction or warning 70
    Reveal sin..71
    Provide an agenda for prayer 71
    Bring an anointing to preaching 72
    Evangelize 72
    Identify gifts and callings 73
    Bring healing, praise, and perseverance in battle 74
Cautions Regarding Prophecy 75
    Self-control in prophecy 76
    What if it's strange?..77
    Youth is no disqualification 78
Growing in the Word of Knowledge Gifts............................ 78
    Receiving names 80
Preparation for Prophecy 81
    Ongoing exposure to prophetically gifted people 82
    Prayer..82
    Meditation on God's truth 82
    Praying in tongues..82
    Praise 83
    Desire to prophesy 83
    Expectation...83
    Thanksgiving 84
    Rejoicing over others' successes......................................84
    Honesty...84
    Motivation..84
    Reflection..84
    Purity 85
    Repentance 85
A Model for Ministering.. 85
    Delivery...86
    How to respond to prophecy 87

An Extraordinary Story of Prophetic Guidance..................... 88

Part II: The Healing Gifts.. 93

Chapter 4: The Theology of Healing and a Short History........... 94

Jesus' Ministry of Healing 96

The New Testament Church: A Model of Proclamation with Healing Power 97

Healing in the History of the Church 98

Healing in the Orthodox and Coptic traditions...............100

Healing in the Pentecostal and Evangelical charismatic tradition 101

Healing Ministry Today.. 102

An exercise of the kingly anointing 103

Chapter 5: Physical Healing 106

Why do we often resist praying for physical healing? 109

Is there a place for suffering?..............................111

Growing in the Gift of Healing 112

Laying on of hands and other gestures 113

Words of knowledge 114

Explicit orders or words of command 118

Acting in faith 120

Other Ways Healings Can Happen............................. 121

Healings at a distance.....................................121

Healings after the event....................................122

The use of material things in healing 123

Healing through hearing a testimony 124

Prayer for those unable to cooperate 125

Healing in the streets and public places 126

People being healed without expecting it 127

Healing through visions and visitations 128

Healings from watching a film or TV 129

Healings and medicine working together......................129

No physical change, but everything works anyway 129

Repeated prayers..130

A miracle for a friend 130

Children being used in healing 131

Healing through forgiveness 131

Healing of animals 132

Developing Compassion.. 133
Our Basic Model for Prayer for Physical Healing 135
Chapter 6: Liberation from Evil Spirits 138
Deliverance in the History of the Church 139
The writings of the Fathers..140
Moral theologians 142
Gifted saints and lay people 144
Deliverance and exorcism in the Coptic and
Orthodox traditions 145
Deliverance and exorcism in the Pentecostal tradition......146
Deliverance Today... 147
Deliverance of believers..148
Weapons in deliverance 149
Holiness in deliverance...150
Physical healing through deliverance 150
Deliverance from mental disturbance 151
Multiple deliverances 152
Degrees of Demonic Influence 152
Demonic Temptation 153
Affliction 153
Oppression..154
Obsession..154
Bondage or infestation 154
Possession 155
The Importance of the Word of Command 156
How to tell when the spirits have left 157
Prayer for Deliverance: Several Approaches 158
Deliverance prayer model 1 159
Deliverance prayer model 2 161
Deliverance prayer model 3 162
Chapter 7: Inner Healing.. 165
Common Elements of Inner Healing 168
The root lie...169
A Model for Inner Healing Prayer...................................... 170
Part III: Other Spiritual Gifts.. 171
Chapter 8: Discernment of Spirits 172
The Role of Discernment of Spirits.................................... 173
Discernment of spirits for prophecy 173

Discernment of spirits in spirituality..................................173
Discernment of spirits in ministry....................................175
Discernment of spirits in prayer ministry........................175
Discerning mysteries...176
Discernment of good and evil in unexpected places.........177
Having new eyes in discerning ministries.........................178
Discernment in discipleship 179
Discernment of spirits in deliverance ministry 180
Growing in the Gift of Discernment of Spirits.................... 181
Chapter 9: The Gift of Tongues 182
Speaking Known Languages Miraculously 182
Praying in Tongues.. 183
Tongues as jubilation..184
Beyond human structures 184
Praying without ceasing 185
Prophesying in Tongues.. 186
Tongues can facilitate the other gifts 186
A Deeper engagement in the Mass..................................... 186
Chapter 10: Faith 188
The Power of Faith 188
Steps for Increasing Our Faith 190
Chapter 11: Miracles.. 193
Power over the Elements 196
Manifestations and miracles of fire..................................197
Extraordinary Healings 198
Metal healings..198
Healing of blood 200
Tumors vanishing...201
Paralytics walk...202
Power over the Body 203
Extraordinary fasts...203
Levitation 204
Raising the Dead 205
Multiplications 206
Manifestations of Glory 208
Transfigurations 208
A glory cloud 209

Chapter 12: Ten Keys for Growing in the Anointing 212

    1. Absolute conviction 212

    2. Hope and desire 213

    3. Faith 213

    4. Prayer and fasting 214

    5. Purity 214

    6. Family 215

    7. Humility 216

    8. Detachment 217

    9. Community 218

    10. Love 218

Conclusion 220

Damian Stayne's Ministry and Cor et Lumen Christi 221

Recommended Reading 222

Foreword

Cardinal Peter Turkson
Prefect of the Dicastery for Promoting Integral Human Development

Two episodes in my ministry make me want to draw particular attention to this book of Damian Stayne and to recommend it to clergy and the laity for reading.

Participating in the first Synod on Africa on the *New Evangelization* as a newly ordained bishop (1994), it struck me already then how much both the universal Church, and so the Church in Africa, needed to revisit the role and place of *signs and wonders* in her evangelizing mission. Evangelization refers to both the mission of Jesus and its continuation in the Church in the power of the Holy Spirit. The mission of Jesus took the forms of his ministry of the Word of God and the ministry of signs (miracles); and the inseparable relationship between the two ministries was not lost to Peter. For Peter, then, Jesus was "*a man accredited by God through signs and wonders which God himself performed through the works of Jesus*" (Acts 2:22).

Having entrusted his mission to his disciples, he promised them the gift of the Holy Spirit, through whom Jesus continued to remain in their midst, confirming their own ministry of the Word with signs and wonders (Acts 4:29-30). Thus, when Peter healed the paralytic who begged at the temple gate and the crowd wondered how he did it, Peter said: " *. . . and the faith that is through Jesus has given him this perfect health in the presence of all of you*" (Acts 3:16ff.). The Church of the Apostolic age appeared not only to have kept the mandate of her Lord and Master to "*preach the Gospel to the ends of the earth*" (Matthew 28:19; Mark 16:15), she carried out this mandate (mission) also through the ministry of the Word and of signs, like her Lord and Master.

Later, in the post-Apostolic Church and especially in our day, the presence and the place of the ministry of signs, as the confirmation of the risen Lord to the mission of his disciples, has lost both emphasis and prominence, as if it is a ministry that was meant to characterize only the nascent Church. But if the ministry of signs constituted credentials for Jesus of the Father's anointing and authorship of his mission, so must it be for the Church, the Bride of Christ, even in our day.

When I talked about this at the Synod, a Synod Father retorted, "*We cannot **force** the hand of God.*" I concurred with him: we cannot force the hand of God, but we can always **pray** that Jesus glorifies himself in our ministry and believe that this is possible! Indeed, Jesus promised it!

The second episode was a meeting of clerics, religious, and laypeople to discuss ways of making the Church attractive and relevant for young people. I observed at the meeting that we have to find ways of *celebrating the charisms of the Spirit* in our Churches. And the immediate question was "What do you mean?" When I answered that we need to celebrate the *spiritual gifts of Jesus and his Spirit* in our liturgies—the gifts of healing, prophecy, teaching, administration etc., namely, all the endowments that Jesus bestows on the Church *"to build it up!"* (1 Corinthians 14)—there was silence.

The Charismatic Renewal and several individuals, religious and lay, have sought in their various ways to awaken the Church in different parts of the world to the reality and necessity of the ministry of signs in the evangelizing mission of the Church and the bestowal of bridal gifts: *the gifts of the Spirit*, by Jesus on his Bride, the Church. The present book, *Lord, Renew Your Wonders* by Damian Stayne, is an addition to the *multitude of witnesses* of the abiding presence of the Lord's Spirit in his Church and a useful contribution to the discussion of the charisms of the Spirit in the Church in our day.

May its reading lead the reader to invoke the outpouring of the Holy Spirit on all in the Church today!

INTRODUCTION

We live in an amazing time. In the past century, the Lord has been renewing the place of the spiritual gifts, which had for some centuries become quite a rarity in the body of Christ.

When I first heard of spiritual gifts, I was highly cynical. I could believe such things might be possible among the saints but not among ordinary people. I remember watching a clip from a healing service broadcast on British TV when I was eighteen, before my adult conversion. It showed people being freed from their crutches and various ailments. I thought to myself, "Well, only a fool would believe that's real!" How ironic, considering what God in his mercy is doing in my own life and that of my community, Cor et Lumen Christi, today, as we proclaim God's word with healing, signs, and wonders.[1]

For many people, the spiritual gifts remain a mystery. Either they don't believe in the possibility that they can be practiced among ordinary Christians, or their experience of them has been weak and therefore dismissed as of no real significance to the Church and her mission. However, there have been many people ministering effectively in spiritual gifts, especially since their fresh outbreak in the Catholic Church in 1967. Some have developed famous ministries that have become accepted across the Church. Even so, in many countries, it is not common to see the spiritual gifts operating among ordinary people in a very powerful way.

In the last few years, there seems to have been a shift. In 2009 a prophecy I gave entitled "On the Threshold of a New Season" was printed in a British Catholic magazine. In 2010 Pope Benedict came to England and prophesied almost the exact same words, declaring that we are "at the threshold of a new age."[2] In that article, I shared my belief that we were approaching a new season in the Church that would be characterized by humility, unity, and faith for miracles. I wrote that I believed we would cross that threshold by 2014.[3]

---

1. In 2010 Cor et Lumen Christi was recognized by the Vatican as a full member of the Catholic Fraternity which is an international Private Association of the Faithful of Pontifical Right.

2. Pope Benedict XVI, speech at Westminster Abbey, September 17, 2010, http://www.thepapalvisit.org.uk/Replay-the-Visit/Speeches/Speeches-17-September/Pope-s-Ecumenical-Celebration.

3. *Good News Magazine*, May/June 2009.

Over those few years, 2009 through 2014, beautiful acts of humility have been demonstrated by both Pope Benedict and Pope Francis, which amazed the world. There were also extraordinary developments in unity with many churches in relation to the papacy and an increased manifestation of supernatural activity in many churches and ministries. God seems to be speeding things up, pouring out in greater power healing, prophetic, deliverance, and miraculous gifts.

Joshua was given the privilege of crossing into the Promised Land before the rest of his people. He was able to taste the abundance of gifts and blessings awaiting Israel across the Jordan in Canaan. This was the place where the Israelites as a people would experience the fulfillment of God's promises and where they would become a sign to the nations. On his return, in spite of the serious challenges, Joshua was utterly convinced that the people of God could inherit the promises God had made to them (Numbers 14:7-9).

This is my conviction about the spiritual gifts today. God has made the most amazing promises to believers in the New Testament, and I believe he desires to fulfill them. The world is waiting to see a Church that ministers as Jesus did, in supernatural power with humble love and joy. Our heavenly Father is inviting his children to take up their inheritance. My hope is that this book will encourage and convince you that every Christian is called to minister supernaturally in the spiritual gifts, so that the words of Isaiah will become increasingly true of the Church:

> Arise, shine; for your light has come,
>   and the glory of the Lord has risen upon you. . . .
> Nations shall come to your light, and kings to the brightness of your
>   dawn. (Isaiah 60:1, 3, NRSV)

Although this book contains a good deal of teaching that I have been presenting for the last twenty-five years, it is not a training manual as such. Detailed material and practical training can be received by attending one of our conferences on the spiritual gifts (the Charism School, Healing and Empowerment School, Prophecy School, and so forth). I have chosen to emphasize two areas, the prophetic gifts and the healing gifts, not because I devalue the other spiritual gifts but because these two areas of the supernatural are those emphasized in the prophecies of the messianic age by Joel and Isaiah. A third section on the other spiritual gifts—discernment of spirits, the gift of tongues, faith, and miracles—is also included, as these gifts are by no means less important or desirable. All spiritual gifts are vital to the vigor and dynamism of the Church.

This book has many quotes from the Bible, saints, theologians, and Church documents, so that the reader can have a sound basis for embracing and exercising the spiritual gifts and a source for explaining and justifying their place in the Church today. By contextualizing these gifts within the great tradition of the Church, I believe that many people will be reassured and helped to lay down their suspicions and embrace a new openness to the value of spiritual gifts in the lives of believers today, for the good of the Church and her mission. My hope is that others who are familiar with spiritual gifts will find greater understanding and inspiration to persevere and grow. I have chosen to include a large number of stories and testimonies that illustrate the teaching and bring it to life, so as to build up faith and give glory to the Lord. As Peter and John declare, "We cannot but speak of what we have seen and heard" (Acts 4:20).

Although I am a committed Catholic, I pray that this book will be a help and encouragement to all Christians. My hope is that it will enlarge your vision of the great place spiritual gifts have had in the history of God's Church and of the extraordinary age of grace into which we are moving. I hope, as this new season unfolds, that this book will inspire you to allow the Holy Spirit to fan into a flame your desire for spiritual gifts and a new level of faith for what is possible through their exercise in God's Church and your life today.

Before we get started, I want to share a revelation that had a profound effect on me. Once in a prayer meeting, I experienced speaking out in a language I had never learned, as the apostles and disciples did on the day of Pentecost. As I spoke, I did not know what I was saying, but the woman next to me, who was a linguist, told me immediately afterward that I had been speaking in Spanish. The phrase I had been saying was "We can know nothing except what God reveals to us." And it is true that unless the Lord gives us revelation in our minds and hearts, any real life-giving knowledge and understanding about the things of the kingdom will elude us.

Before every talk I give, I invite those in attendance to pray for "a spirit of wisdom and revelation" (Ephesians 1:17) that will cause the material to be life changing and empowering. I would like to invite you to do the same right now. Let's pray with St. Paul that "the God of our Lord Jesus Christ, the Father of glory, may give you a spirit of wisdom and of revelation in the knowledge of him, having the eyes of your hearts enlightened, that you may know what is the hope to which he has called you, what are the riches of his glorious inheritance in the saints, and what is the immeasurable greatness of his power in us who believe, according to the working of his great might" (Ephesians 1:17-19.)

CHAPTER 1

THE SPIRITUAL GIFTS

Make love your aim, and earnestly desire the spiritual gifts.
—1 Corinthians 14:1

Those who are truly disciples, receiving grace from him, perform
[miracles] in his name for the well being of others, according to the gift
which each one has received from him. For some truly drive out devils,
so that those who have thus been cleansed from evil spirits frequently
believe [in Christ] and join themselves to the Church. Others have fore-
knowledge of things to come; they see visions and utter prophecies.
Others still heal the sick by laying their hands upon them, and they are
made whole. Yes, moreover, the dead even have been raised up
and remained among us for many years.
—St. Irenaeus[1]

The testimony above of St. Irenaeus of Lyons (AD 130–202) is a description of normal Church life in his century. He is referring here not to the deeds performed by the saints with a capital *S* but rather the deeds of ordinary Christians who, filled with the Spirit, believed and lived out the promises of Christ.

Can you imagine your parish or community regularly experiencing such amazing manifestations of the Holy Spirit? The early Church prayed, "And now, Lord, look upon their threats, and grant to your servants to speak your word with all boldness, while you stretch out your hand to heal, and signs and wonders are performed through the name of your holy servant Jesus" (Acts 4:29-30). Could we dare to make this same prayer for an increase of the supernatural and miraculous in the Church today?

Yet a prayer for greater wonders is exactly what Pope St. John XXIII expressed in the first line of a prayer he asked the entire Church to pray leading up to the Second Vatican Council: "Renew your wonders in this our day as though for a new Pentecost."[2] Pope John XXIII's prayer is a cry

---

1. St. Irenaeus, Against Heresies, book 2, chap. 32, par. 4.
2. Pope St. John XXIII, Apostolic Constitution Humanae Salutis, 23, convoking the Second Vatican Council, given at St. Peter's Basilica, Rome, December 25, 1961.

to God that he wanted echoed in the hearts of all the faithful, to reestablish today what should be normal in the Church in every age.

The gifts that St. Irenaeus lists above are called "charisms." Today many practicing Christians are familiar with the word, but few know its real meaning or what the Church or the Bible have to say about it.

So what is a charism? "In the Greek language in which the New Testament was written, the word *charis* means 'grace.' So a *charisma* is a gift which comes from God's grace and 'gifts' (plural) are *charismata*."[3] Paul uses this word in five main ways.

First, in a general way, he uses it to refer to any gift that comes from God, including marriage, celibacy (1 Corinthians 7:7), or even deliverance from danger (2 Corinthians 1:10). Second, when speaking of Israel, Paul tells us that God does not change his intentions regarding his *gifts* (Romans 11:29). Third, he uses it when referring to the *gift* of eternal life (Romans 6:23) and the *gift* of justification (Romans 5:15-16). Fourth, he refers to the *gift* Timothy received through the laying on of hands, which is probably the gift of the Holy Spirit himself (2 Timothy 1:6-7). And finally, St. Paul refers to them as spiritual gifts (*pneumatika*) in 1 Corinthians 12:7-10, which are the charisms we will focus on:

> To each is given the manifestation of the Spirit for the common good. To one is given through the Spirit the utterance of wisdom, and to another the utterance of knowledge according to the same Spirit, to another faith by the same Spirit, to another gifts of healing by the one Spirit, to another the working of miracles, to another prophecy, to another the ability to distinguish between spirits, to another various kinds of tongues, to another the interpretation of tongues.

Even though these gifts rely on an intervention of the Holy Spirit and are therefore supernatural, Paul does not seem to suggest that they are rare in the Christian communities and their mission but rather very frequent and normal in the Church.

So important are charisms to the life of the Church that Pope St. John Paul II, on the vigil of Pentecost in 1998, went so far as to state about the Church that "the institutional and charismatic aspects are co-essential."

---

3. David Petts, *Body Builders: Gifts to Make God's People Grow* (Mattersey, England: Mattersey Hall, 2002), 9.

What an amazing statement when one considers that "institutional" includes all the magisterial and sacramental life of the Church. He continued,

> They contribute, although differently, to the life, renewal and sanctification of God's People. It is from this providential rediscovery of the Church's charismatic dimension that, before and after the Council, a remarkable growth has been established for ecclesial movements and new communities. . . .
>
> Today, I would like to cry out to all of you gathered here in St Peter's Square and to all Christians: Open yourselves docilely to the gifts of the Spirit! Accept gratefully and obediently the charisms which the Spirit never ceases to bestow on us![4]

These charisms may be clearly supernatural, such as healing or miracles, or they may, by a supernatural grace, raise natural gifts such as preaching, teaching, or the leading of worship to a supernatural impact and effectiveness unattainable by human abilities alone. Either way, what is distinctive about charisms is that they require a dependence by the believer upon the intervening action of the Holy Spirit for their power and fruitfulness.

Charisms are not natural gifts

My spiritual guide of twenty years, Fr. Christopher O'Donnell, O Carm—who translated *Lumen Gentium* 12, the chapter dealing with charisms, for the official English text[5]—would regularly remind me that the Church, when referring to charisms in these texts, is not referring to natural gifts but gifts that depend upon the intervening action of the Holy Spirit. Likewise, Fr. Francis Sullivan, former head of systematic theology at the Gregorian University in Rome, writes that charisms are "special graces," because they involve "a direct intervention of the Holy Spirit." "[I]t follows that charisms cannot be simply identified with natural talents."[6]

---

4. Pope St. John Paul II, Speech to Ecclesial Movements and New Communities, 4, 5, Pentecost Vigil, May 30, 1998, Vatican.va.

5. Austin Flannery, OP, ed., *Vatican Council II: The Conciliar and Post Conciliar Documents* (Northport, NY: Costello, 1981), 363–64.

6. Francis A. Sullivan, SJ, *Charisms and Charismatic Renewal: A Biblical and Theological Study* (Dublin: Gill and Macmillan, 1982), 12–14. He quotes the term "special graces" from the Second Vatican Council.

The document *Iuvenescit Ecclesia*, issued in 2016 by the Congregation for the Doctrine of the Faith, confirms this view: "A close relationship between the particular charisms (*charísmata*) and the grace of God is affirmed by Paul in *Romans* 12:6 and by Peter in *1 Peter* 4:10. The charisms are recognized as a manifestation of the 'multiform grace of God' (*1 Peter* 4:10). They are not, therefore, simply human capacities."[7]

I believe that the Church and her mission cannot effectively be renewed without a renewal of the charisms and, in particular, the spiritual gifts. Neither can the Church stem the present exodus in the West nor reach a thirsting world with only theoretical or formalized religion. Even our practical acts of love, centrally important as they are, can be dismissed simply as humanistic charity if they do not bear the aroma of the Savior through the power of the Holy Spirit.

Charisms both ignite and reawaken faith. They make Jesus real and dynamic. They grab people's attention and draw it to Christ. As Blessed Pope Paul VI said,

> We cannot but desire that these gifts come—and may God grant it—with abundance. Besides grace, let God's church be able to obtain and possess the charisms. . . .
>
> . . . God grant that the Lord would still increase this rain of charisms to make the church fruitful, beautiful, marvelous and capable of inspiring respect, even the attention and amazement of the profane world, the secular world.[8]

It is not my intention in this book to write about all the charisms the Holy Spirit might give to the Church. Instead, I will look at the spiritual gifts that were regularly manifested in the life of Jesus and the early Church and that St. Paul lists in First Corinthians 12:7-10 above. Spiritual gifts carry a special power to reveal the imminent dynamic presence of the Lord and, for this reason, are referred to as "manifestations of the Spirit" (1 Corinthians 12:7). They personalize the gospel message in a very effective way, giving

---

7. Congregation for the Doctrine of the Faith, *Iuvenescit Ecclesia,* Letter Regarding the Relationship between Hierarchical and Charismatic Gifts in the Life and the Mission of the Church, 4, May 4, 2016, vatican.va/roman_curia/congregations/cfaith/documents/rc_con_cfaith_doc_20160516_iuvenescit-ecclesia_en.html.
8. Pope Paul VI, quoted in Kilian McDonnell, ed., *Open the Windows: The Pope and Charismatic Renewal* (South Bend, IN: Greenlawn, 1989), 8.

people an encounter with the kingdom of God and enabling them to taste firsthand the ministry of Jesus. They had a very prominent role in the communities, ministries, and mission of the New Testament Church and that of the rapidly growing Church in the early centuries after Christ.

All of us accept the fact that we should develop our natural gifts, and an increasing number in the Church now understand that all of us also have charisms from the Holy Spirit, which he wants us to cultivate. So why is it that we seem to balk at the door of the spiritual gifts? In the gospels and the New Testament, the spiritual gifts are the charisms spoken about and aspired for the most, whereas in the Church today, these spiritual gifts are the charisms that are spoken about and aspired for the least! How did that happen? This attitude has no basis in the New Testament or in official Church teaching.

Some people want to put these gifts out of reach by referring to them as extraordinary, but they are only extraordinary in the same way a tribesman from the African bush speaking his native language in England would be extraordinary. When he is in his own country, his language is perfectly normal! The language of the supernatural appears extraordinary in our secular culture, but in our homeland, the kingdom, it is natural.

We are heirs with Christ, so these gifts are not extraordinary for us; rather, they are part of our inheritance. We are also "ambassadors for Christ," as St. Paul tells us (2 Corinthians 5:20). Every embassy is a piece of another country's territory on foreign soil, a place that upholds the culture and traditions and the way of living of the nation that it represents. The Church is the embassy of God on the earth. It is an embassy that God desires would cover the whole world, until everyone is living in the culture of the kingdom and speaking the language of heaven, which of course includes the exercise of supernatural gifts.

When one reads the New Testament and the testimony of the Fathers, it becomes dazzlingly clear that these spiritual gifts made an incredible contribution to building up the Church, causing her to be highly fruitful in evangelization. n estimated 70 percent of all church growth is among Pentecostal and charismatic groups, Christians committed to the practice of spiritual gifts.[9] If we are committed to building up the Church today and engaging seriously in the New Evangelization, the spiritual gifts cannot be ignored.

---

9. See John Wimber and Kevin Springer, *Power Evangelism* (Kent, England: Hodder and Stoughton, 1995), 49.

Jesus: The Pattern for Our Christian Life

It would be impossible to imagine the life of Jesus without the gifts of healing, deliverance from demons, miracles, supernatural wisdom, prophecy, and supernatural knowledge about people and events. Such manifestations in the lives of Christians are a share in God's own powers; they are manifestations of his kingdom on earth. They were part and parcel of Jesus' mission and the fulfillment of prophecy of the messianic age and the age of the Church:

> Then the eyes of the blind shall be opened,
>   and the ears of the deaf unstopped;
> then shall the lame man leap like a deer,
>   and the tongue of the mute sing for joy. (Isaiah 35:5-6)

> And it shall come to pass afterward,
>   that I will pour out my spirit on all flesh;
> your sons and your daughters shall prophesy. (Joel 2:28)

St. Thomas Aquinas writes, "Hence it is clear that *all the gratuitous graces* ['graces freely given,' including spiritual gifts] *were most excellently in Christ as the first and chief teacher of the faith*."[10] And Pope Leo XIII, in *Divinum illud munus* [Encyclical on the Holy Spirit], states, "In Him [Christ] were all the treasures of wisdom and knowledge, *graces gratis datae* ['graces freely given,' including spiritual gifts], virtues, and all other gifts foretold in the prophecies of Isaiah (Isaiah 4:2; 11:2-3)."[11]

Jesus' vision for charismatic disciples

If the Gospels and the Book of Acts had all the references to supernatural gifts removed, these books would be unrecognizable, considerably shorter, and infinitely less compelling! Although such gifts have never completely disappeared, God in his abundant mercy seems to be restoring them to his Church

---

10. St. Thomas Aquinas, *Summa Theologiae*, III, q. 7, quoted in Fr. Pat Collins, CM, *The Gifts of the Spirit & The New Evangelisation* (Dublin: Columba Press, 2009), 57, italics by Fr. Collins.
11. Pope Leo XIII, *Divinum illud munus*, Encyclical on the Holy Spirit, 4, May 9, 1897, vatican.va/content/leo-xiii/en/encyclicals/documents/hf_l-xiii_enc_09051897_divinum-illud-munus.html.

in our day with a new generosity. It is clear from the words of Jesus that he intended believers to inherit supernatural gifts through the outpouring of the Holy Spirit. Some of his promises are extraordinary. For example, in John's Gospel we read, "Truly, truly, I say to you, he who believes in me will also do the works that I do" (14:12).

The context of this verse is a discussion on miracles. Biblical scholars, including the renowned Fr. Raymond Brown, make it clear that the word *works* here includes miracles and supernatural acts performed by the Christian believer.[12] Commenting on this verse, Fr. Brown writes, "Belief in Jesus will bring to the Christian power from God to perform the same works [including miracles] that Jesus performs, because, by uniting a man with Jesus and the Father, belief gives him a share in the power that they possess."[13]

Jesus promised the early Church in Acts 1:8, "You shall receive power when the Holy Spirit has come upon you." The New Testament Greek word that is translated as "power" is *dynamis*, from which we get *dynamite*, *dynamic*, and *dynasty*. It is the word most often translated as "miracle" or, at times, "mighty work," literally, a "deed of power." Therefore the text of John 14:12 can then be understood as follows: "Truly, truly, I say to you, he who believes in me will also do the works [including the supernatural deeds of power] that I do."

Jesus is the model of the Christian life; in the Letter to the Romans, we read that we are to be "conformed to the image of his [God's] Son" (8:29). This is speaking, of course, about our manner of life but also of what is available to us in our ministry to others in the power of the Holy Spirit.

There are three great commissions in the New Testament. First, the twelve apostles are sent out and are given "authority over unclean spirits, to cast them out, and to heal every disease and every infirmity" (Matthew 10:1). Then there is the sending out of the seventy: "The Lord appointed seventy others, and sent them on ahead of him, two by two, into every town and place where he himself was about to come. . . . 'Heal the sick in it and say to them, "The kingdom of God has come near to you"'" (Luke 10:1, 9). Finally, Jesus at the ascension widens his commission to all believers:

---

12. "By the use of the term 'works' for his miracles Jesus was associating his ministry with the creation and the salvific works of his Father in the past." Raymond Brown, *The Gospel According to John*, vol. 2 XIII–XX8, *The Anchor Bible* (London: Doubleday, 1966), 527.
13. Ibid. 633.

"And these signs will accompany those who believe: in my name they will cast out demons; they will speak in new tongues; they will pick up serpents, and if they drink any deadly thing, it will not hurt them; they will lay their hands on the sick, and they will recover."

. . . And they went forth and preached everywhere, while the Lord worked with them and confirmed the message by the signs that attended it. (Mark 16:17-18, 20)[14]

The crucial word in this passage is *believers*. This ministry of supernatural signs and wonders was not only entrusted to a special category of Christians—the twelve and the seventy—but poured out across the Church. Neither are these gifts only promised to experts or very holy people but to all those who believe. That is not to suggest, of course, that expertise and holiness are unimportant; this goes without saying. History demonstrates that those with more expertise and more holiness are invariably more effective and fruitful in their exercise of spiritual gifts. But these are not the fundamental criteria for beginning.[15]

The early Church was committed to the charismatic gifts

It is clear from reading the Book of Acts that spiritual gifts played a critically important part in the effective proclamation of the good news, the building up of the early Church, and its rapid growth. In fact, the very first act of the newborn Church was a supernatural one: speaking miraculously in languages the disciples had not learned. And what is it the Holy Spirit

14. Even though protection against snakes and poison is listed and can be granted, it must be noted that there is no time in the New Testament when these are listed as charisms that one is commissioned to exercise in the life of the Church and her mission, as the others are. They are not to be "practiced" in the same way as prophecy or healing. However, there are numerous examples of this kind of miraculous protection being granted in the lives of holy men and women through the ages.

15. It is common in Catholic writing to refer to Mary as the model disciple. Some assert that, as she did not appear to practice such gifts as healing and prophecy and deliverance from demons in the biblical accounts, these things are quite secondary. However, in all the greatest apparitions of Mary that the Church has affirmed as "worthy of belief," Mary's message of conversion or of affirmation of some aspect of the faith is invariably accompanied by extraordinary prophecy and demonstrations of healings, signs, and wonders. As such, she ministers just as the apostles and the early Church did, fulfilling the commission of her Son.

had them declaring? "The mighty works of God" (Acts 2:11)—his super-natural interventions among the people of God. The supernatural is in the very DNA of the Church!

Twenty-two out of twenty-eight chapters in the Book of Acts, or three-quarters of them, make reference to healings, liberation from demons, prophecies, supernatural knowledge, miracles, or raising of the dead. Charismatic activity through the exercise of spiritual gifts was not only normal among believers in the early Church but widespread and essential to its extraordinary growth and success.

St. Paul gives extensive teaching regarding spiritual gifts, which, he stresses, are highly desirable for the Church's life and mission and not optional extras for those who "like that sort of thing." In 1 Corinthians 14:1, the Church is encouraged to "earnestly desire the spiritual gifts," suggesting something crucial and imperative that must be sincerely and urgently sought. The New Testament Greek phrase used here can also be translated "have zeal for" or "be zealous toward."

The vital role of spiritual gifts in the proclamation of the gospel was deeply impressed upon St. Paul following his failed attempt to convince the Greeks in Athens with clever speeches alone. Having returned to a proclamation of the gospel with healings, signs, and wonders, he was later to write to the Corinthians, "My speech and my message were not in plausible words of wisdom, but in demonstration of the Spirit and of power, that your faith might not rest in the wisdom of men but in the power of God" (1 Corinthians 2:4-5). What do we want people's faith to rest on today? Should we not want what St. Paul wanted?

As individuals and as the Church, both locally and internationally, we have to ask ourselves whether we can honestly say we share the mind of Christ on this subject as expressed in his word. Do we earnestly desire the manifestation of the spiritual gifts in our own lives and in the services and ministries of the Church today? Do we truly consider them as normal to Christianity and their absence as a great loss that must be urgently addressed?

Spiritual Gifts in the Early Centuries of the Church

It is helpful to know that the exercise of spiritual gifts did not die out with the death of the apostles. For four centuries, spiritual gifts were very common in the life and mission of the Church, as we find in the writings of many of the early saints and Fathers of the Church. In this section, I am going to provide many references to spiritual gifts in the writings of significant saints and Church fathers, because it is important to make clear that such references are not isolated but common. They do not express a single opinion here and there but rather reveal a culture of supernatural ministry across the Church that was normal in the early centuries of the Church. These writings offer us a vision and model for today.

Let us begin with St. Irenaeus of Lyons. In his book *Against Heresies,* he reports, "We . . . hear many brothers in the Church who possess prophetic gifts, and bring to light for the general benefit the hidden things of men."[16] And again, as we cited at the beginning: "For some . . . truly drive out devils. . . . Others have foreknowledge of things to come. . . . Others still, heal the sick. . . .Yea, moreover . . . the dead even have been raised up, and remained among us for many years."[17]

St. Justin Martyr, the great apologist, also writing in the first half of the second century, testifies,

> For numberless demoniacs throughout the whole world, and in your city, many of our Christian men exorcising them in the name of Jesus Christ, who was crucified under Pontius Pilate, have healed and do heal, rendering helpless and driving the possessing devils out of the men, though they could not be cured by all the other exorcists, and those who used incantations and drugs.[18]

Tertullian, who died in AD 225, wrote a letter to a Gnostic heretic called Marcion. Boldly confident of the prophetic gifts in the Church, he states, "Let Marcion then exhibit, as gifts of his god, some prophets, such as have not spoken by human sense, but with the Spirit of God, such as have both predicted things to come, and have made manifest the secrets of the heart."[19] And in another treatise he writes,

---

16. St. Irenaeus, *Against Heresies*, in *Ante-Nicene Fathers*, vol. 1 (New York: Christian Literature Col, 1890), 532, as quoted in Bruce Yocum, *Prophecy: Exercising the Prophetic Gifts of the Spirit in the Church* (Ann Arbor, MI: Servant, 1976), 21.

17. St. Irenaeus, *Against Heresies*, book 2, chap. 32, no. 4, newadvent.org/fathers/0103232.htm.

18. St. Justin Martyr, *The Second Apology*, chap. 6, newadvent.org/fathers/0127.htm.

19. Tertullian, *Against Marcion*, book 5, chap. 8, newadvent.org/fathers/03125.htm.

Therefore, blessed ones, whom the grace of God awaits, when you ascend from that most sacred font of your new birth, and spread your hands for the first time in the house of your mother, together with your brethren, ask from the Father, ask from the Lord, that his own specialties of grace and distributions of gifts may be supplied you.[20]

Other Church Fathers who affirmed the place of charisms in the Church include the following:

- Origen (185–254), writing in the early third century, states, "Not a few cures are wrought in the name of Jesus, and certain other manifestations of no small significance have taken place."[21]

- St. Cyprian (c. 200–258) declares in the third century, "Oh, if only you could hear and see them when they [evil spirits] are adjured by us. For they are tortured with spiritual scourges and are cast out from the possessed bodies with tortures of words. Howling and growling at the voice of man and the power of God, they feel the stripes and blows and confess the judgment to come. Come and acknowledge that what we say is true."[22]

- St. Cyril of Jerusalem (313–386) exhorts the newly baptized to welcome charisms as they are baptized: "Let each prepare himself for reception of the Heavenly gift. . . . And now, brethren beloved, the word of instruction exhorts you all, to prepare your souls for the reception of the heavenly gifts [charisms]."[23]

- St. Hilary of Poitiers (300–368), also writing in the fourth century, explains, "We begin to have insight into the mysteries of faith; we are able to prophesy and speak with

---

20. Tertullian, *On Baptism*, chap. 20, newadvent.org/fathers/0321.htm.
21. Origen, *Contra Celsus*, bk. 3, chap. 28, newadvent.org/fathers/04163.htm.
22. Cyprian, Treatise 5, 15, see newadvent.org/fathers/050705.htm.
23. Cyril of Jerusalem, Catechetical Lectures lecture 17, no. 19, see no. 37, newadvent.org/fathers/310117.htm; lecture 18, no. 32, newadvent.org/fathers/310118.htm.

wisdom. We become steadfast in hope and receive abundant gifts of healing. Demons are made subject to our authority."[24]

- St. Theodore of Mopsueste (350–428) declares, "Many heathen among us are being *healed* by Christians from whatever sickness they have, so abundant are miracles in our midst."[25]

- St. Augustine of Hippo (354–430) asserts, "So long as our knowledge is imperfect, the eternal light of the evident truth is made known to us through the many and diverse forms of prophecy."[26] And in his *City of God*, he relates, "It is only two years ago that the keeping of records was begun here in Hippo, and already, at this writing, we have nearly seventy attested miracles."[27]

- St. Gregory the Great (c. 540–604), when referring to the charisms, writes beautifully, "We should . . . consider them as foot-prints of God among us: they fill us with awe and admiration, help us to long for the celestial things to come, urge us to revere the secret counsel of the Spirit who is at the origin of them."[28]

The writings of the Fathers give us a beautiful foundation in the spiritual gifts, which continued in a variety of expressions in the Church.

Throughout the ages, we see wonderful accounts of charismatic activity in the lives of the saints and many of their disciples. We will look at examples in more detail in the following chapters: extraordinary gifts of prophecy, supernatural knowledge, healing, deliverance, and miracles such as multiplication of food, bilocation, nature miracles, and the raising of the dead! These were prevalent in the astonishing charismatic ministries of St. Anthony of the Desert, St. Patrick, St. Martin of Tours, St. Cuthbert, St. Augustine of Canterbury, St. Bernard of Clairvaux, St. Francis of Assisi, St. Catherine of Siena, St. Stanislaus, St. Vincent Ferrer, St. Francis Paola, St. John Bosco,

---

24. Hilary of Poitiers, Tract on the Psalms, 64.15.

25. Theodore of Mopsueste, as quoted in Cyrus W. Harris, *Understanding God's Divine Healing: How You May Be Healed* (Nashville: Thomas Nelson, 2011), 39.

26. Augustine, *De Spiritu et littera*, 24, 41, as quoted in Elizabeth Livingstone, ed., *Studia Patristica*, vol. 22 (Leuven: Peter's Press, 1989), 198.

27. Augustine, *City of God*, bk. 22, chap. 8.

28. Gregory the Great, quoted in Giuseppe Bentivegna, SJ, *St. Gregory the Great on Charismata*.

St. Seraphim of Sarov, St. John of Kronstadt, St. Pope Kyrillos VI, and St. Pio of Pietrelcina, to name a few.

Great theologians confirm that charismatic activity has been an important part of the Church's life in many ways. St. Thomas Aquinas (1225–1274) devoted an amazing thirty-two thousand words to an examination of the charismatic gifts mentioned by St. Paul, especially those of 1 Corinthians 12:8-10, which we focus on in this book.[29] Pope Benedict XIV (1675–1758), considered one of the most learned men to ever exercise the papal ministry, produced an enormous study on the charisms listed in that passage. What is interesting about these two great works is that Thomas tended to focus on the charismatic gifts in the service of the Church's call to evangelize, whereas Benedict emphasized the role of charismatic gifts in light of the call to holiness.

Although these spiritual gifts did not die out completely, over time they did seem to seem get lost from the mainstream life of the Church, no longer the regular experience of most ordinary believers within their local communities. Spiritual gifts such as healing, prophecy, supernatural knowledge, and the power to drive out demons and perform miracles tended to be manifested at times of revival and in the lives of the saints and their disciples. To aspire to exercise such gifts was often considered presumptuous. Most common people sought miraculous interventions by visiting shrines, using relics, and asking the intercession of the saints. While these have played an important part in the supernatural life of the Church, they are not of the category of charisms that we deal with here.

While in general the people of God lost the expectation of spiritual gifts in their lives, these gifts were still experienced in a quiet way in ordinary Christian communities. I know of a woman who was born into a devout Catholic family in Ireland in the early twentieth century. She was an ordinary girl but was considered from childhood by those in her large village to have "the gift." If a person in the village was sick, she was often sent to sit in the same room; the person would regularly feel better or even recover. She became a nurse, and unusual experiences of healing continued to take place. Later she was baptized in the Holy Spirit and developed an effective healing and deliverance ministry. Other stories of prophetic gifts, deliverance from demons, and miracles among the faithful are also found throughout the centuries.

---

29. See Collins, 56.

Despite such stories, and there are many like them, it could be argued that by the early 1800s, the manifestation of the spiritual gifts in the wider body of the Church was perhaps at an all-time low. This was a long way from the promises of Jesus, the experience of the early Church, and the exhortation of the word of God in St. Paul for all to earnestly desire the spiritual gifts.

However, in the second half of the 1800s, things began to change. What had always been upheld, at least theoretically by orthodox theology, received a dramatic boost

Spiritual Revival

In 1868 the First Vatican Council sought to authoritatively reaffirm the Church's doctrine concerning several aspects of faith and the reality of supernatural gifts in Christianity. This was especially in response to new challenges from secular philosophy, certain political movements, and theological liberalism, which claimed that either miracles were a thing of the past or they had never been real. St. Augustine (354–430) had encountered such opinions in his own time. He writes, "It is sometimes objected that the miracles which Christians claim, no longer happen. . . . However the malice of the objection is in the insinuation that not even the earlier miracles ought to be believed."[30]

In its chapter on faith, the council declared,

> In order that the obedience of our faith might be in harmony with reason, God willed that, to the interior help of the Holy Spirit, there should be joined exterior proofs of His revelation; to wit, divine facts, and especially miracles and prophecies, which, as they manifestly display the omnipotence and infinite knowledge of God, are most certain proofs of His Divine Revelation, adapted to the intelligence of all men. Wherefore, both Moses and the Prophets, and most especially, Christ our Lord Himself, showed forth many and most evident miracles and prophecies; and about the Apostles we read: "But they, going forth, preached everywhere, with the Lord

---

30. St. Augustine, as quoted in Fr. Albert J. Hebert, SM, *Saints Who Raised the Dead* (Rockford, IL:TAN, 2012), 42–43.

cooperating and confirming the word with signs that followed" (Mark 16:20).[31]

Several solemn dogmatic canons were also promulgated, including:

3. If anyone says that divine revelation cannot be made credible by external signs, and that therefore men and women ought to be moved to faith solely by each one's internal experience or private inspiration: let him be anathema.

4. If anyone says that all miracles are impossible, and that therefore all reports of them, even those contained in sacred scripture, are to be set aside as fables or myths; or that miracles can never be known with certainty, nor can the divine origin of the Christian religion be proved from them: let him be anathema.[32]

Such statements from a council of the Catholic Church were critically important, as they carried for Catholics the power of the authoritative interpretation of Scripture.

Many Protestant churches had never been able to embrace the spiritual gifts because of the dispensationalist theologies of some of the major reformers, especially John Calvin. However, around the time of Vatican I, something very significant was happening in the Protestant churches that was to prepare the way for a worldwide revolution in the exercise of spiritual gifts. The theme of divine healing had been developing among the Holiness churches through leaders like Dr. Charles Cullis and A. B. Simpson with his Fourfold Gospel—of Jesus as Savior, Sanctifier, Healer, and coming King. A widening interest in divine healing was evidenced by events such as the International Conference on Divine Healing and True Holiness, held in London in June 1885. Through the establishment of healing homes and newsletters, interest grew at the grassroots level, with the message of divine healing embraced by those from other streams, including Anglicans.

Many of us Catholics have been uncomfortable at times with some of what we have seen in other churches (although the same could be said about parts of the Catholic Church at times). But it is clear that in spite of this,

---

31. Vatican I, Dogmatic Constitution on the Catholic Faith, chap. 3, catholicplanet. org/councils/20-Dei-Filius.htm.

32. Vatican I, Canons on Faith, 3, 4, papalencyclicals.net/Councils/ecum20.htm.

God has been profoundly at work in many wonderful ways among our Christian brothers and sisters. There have been breakthroughs in ecumenical relations in recent decades, and the Church and the popes have encouraged us to be open to what the Lord is doing in this area, so there can be, as Pope St. John Paul II expressed it, an "exchange of gifts."[33] An exchange is not a one-way relationship but a two-way one. As the Second Vatican Council tells us, "Whatever is wrought by the grace of the Holy Spirit in the hearts of our separated brethren can contribute to our own edification."[34]

In the mid to late 1800s, amazingly gifted individuals arose in Catholic, Orthodox, and Protestant churches, including St. John Bosco in Italy, St. John of Kronstadt in Russia, and John Alexander Dowie in America. But it was among Protestants that there began a revival of healing and prophetic gifts that involved ordinary people. In some individuals, these gifts operated in what one can only describe as biblical proportions. Through these people, a healing and prophetic revival was ignited in America that in some ways prepared the way for the birth of Pentecostalism, which in turn impacted the historic churches, including the Catholic Church through the Charismatic Renewal.

A historic breakthrough

At the end of the nineteenth century, an Italian nun, Blessed Elena Guerra, proposed to Pope Leo XIII that the twentieth century be consecrated to the Holy Spirit. Pope Leo agreed, and he implemented this on the first day of 1901 with the solemn singing of the *Veni Creator Spiritus*. What is remarkable is that on that very same day in Topeka, Kansas, Agnes Ozman, a Methodist, requested prayer for the baptism in the Holy Spirit from her minister, Charles Parham. She was powerfully and dramatically filled with the Holy Spirit and received the gift of tongues. This prompted an explosion of prayer for the baptism in the Holy Spirit, resulting in a Pentecostal spiritual movement that spread steadily across America.

In 1906 the movement experienced a watershed moment through the ministry of a deeply prayerful and humble man, William Seymour, at a small mission building on Azusa Street in Los Angeles. Here an outpouring

---

33. Pope St. John Paul II, *Ut Unum Sint*, Encyclical on Commitment to Ecumenism, 28, May 25, 1995, citing *Lumen Gentium,* 13.
34. Vatican II, *Unitatis Redintegratio,* Decree on Ecumenism, 4, November 21, 1964.

of manifestations of the Holy Spirit and spiritual gifts—including healings, prophecy, speaking in tongues, and a "glory cloud" (see chapter 11, on miracles)—took place and continued daily for three years. People traveled from all over the world to attend the meetings. The result was an international explosion of Pentecostalism, reaching in the following decades hundreds of millions of people across the world. While Catholics wouldn't agree with all of the theology, the great truth that Pentecostalism grasped was that each person could experience a "personal Pentecost" and that the spiritual gifts are available to everyone.

Pope St. John XXIII and the Second Vatican Council

Then in 1958, Pope St. John XXIII was elected and, to everyone's amazement, called the Second Vatican Council, which ran from 1962 to 1965. As we have noted, this pope authored a prayer for the council that the whole Church was encouraged to pray. It began, "Lord, renew your wonders in our time, as though for a new Pentecost."[35]

Pope John asked all the cardinals across the whole Church to prepare for their attendance at the Second Vatican Council by reading the Acts of the Apostles. Clearly, Pope St. John had a vision for a renewal of New Testament Pentecostal life in the Catholic Church.

At Vatican II, there was a debate among the cardinals about the place and role of charisms in the Church. The two opposing positions were articulated by Cardinal Ernesto Ruffini and Cardinal Leo Joseph Suenens. Cardinal Ruffini proposed that while charisms were widespread in the early Church, these had ceased after the first few centuries. From that time forth, such gifts, he believed, were exceptional and normally only granted to persons of great holiness. Cardinal Suenens responded by proposing a very different position. He asserted that the charisms were at work in many graced activities of members of the Church and were not restricted to the early Church or those of exceptional holiness. He also argued that the charisms should be encouraged and welcomed as a normal part of Christianity, as available to any member of Christ's Church.

The Council Fathers rejected Ruffini's view and endorsed Suenens'. In case one might be uncertain about Suenens' defense of the spiritual gifts of 1 Corinthians 12:7-10, let us quote from what has been described as his testament: "[T]he charisms of the early Church are not things of the past. . . .

---

35. *Humanae Salutis*, 23.

[T]he Lord's desire is to accomplish marvels of grace in us and through us, by the power of his Spirit."[36] As a result, the following texts were inserted into the Council documents, "canonizing" the role of charisms, including what have been called extraordinary ones, as normal in the life of the Church:

> The Lord . . . distributes special graces among the faithful of every rank. By these gifts [charisms] he makes them fit and ready to undertake various tasks and offices for the renewal and building up of the Church, as it is written, "the manifestation of the Spirit is given to everyone for profit" (1 Corinthians 12:7). Whether these charisms be very remarkable or more simple and widely diffused, they are to be received with thanksgiving and consolation since they are fitting and useful for the needs of the Church. . . . Those who have charge over the Church should judge the genuineness and proper use of these gifts, . . . not indeed to extinguish the Spirit, but to test all things and hold fast to what is good (cf. 1 Thessalonians 5:12 and 19-21).[37]

Significantly, the council also speaks of charisms in the document on the laity:

> However, for the exercise of the apostolate he gives the faithful special gifts besides (cf. 1 Corinthians 12:7), "allotting them to each one as he wills" (1 Corinthians 12:11), so that each and all, putting at the service of others the grace received, may be "as good stewards of God's varied gifts" (1 Peter 4:10), for the building up of the whole body in charity (cf. Ephesians 4:16). From the reception of these charisms, even the most ordinary ones, there arises for each of the faithful the right and duty of exercising them in the Church and in the world for the good of men and the development of the Church, of exercising them in the freedom of the Holy Spirit who "breathes where He wills" (John 3:8).[38]

---

36. L. J. Cardinal Suenens, *The Christian at the Dawn of a New Era* (Fiat, 1999), 77–78.

37. *Lumen Gentium*, 12, in Flannery, 363–64.

38. Second Vatican Council, *Apostolicam Actuositatem*, Decree on the Apostolate of the Laity, 3, in Flannery, 769.

Recent popes on the charisms

Since the Second Vatican Council, the popes have been outspoken in affirming that the Church should welcome and cultivate the supernatural spiritual gifts. Blessed Pope Paul VI, speaking at the Synod of Bishops in 1974, said:

> We cannot but desire that these gifts come—and may God grant it—with abundance. Besides grace, let God's church be able to obtain and possess the charisms. . . .
>
> . . . God grant that the Lord would still increase this rain of charisms to make the church fruitful, beautiful, marvelous and capable of inspiring respect, even the attention and amazement of the profane world, the secular world.[39]

Pope St. John Paul II, at the Pentecost vigil in St. Peter's Square in 1998, gave this heartfelt plea: "Today, I would like to cry out to all of you gathered here in St. Peter's Square and to all Christians: Open yourselves docilely to the gifts of the Spirit! Accept gratefully and obediently the charisms which the Spirit never ceases to bestow on us!"[40]

In his document on the laity, *Christifideles Laici,* the pope wrote, "The Holy Spirit, while bestowing diverse ministries in Church communion, enriches it still further with particular gifts or promptings of grace, called *charisms.* . . . Even in our own times there is no lack of a fruitful manifestation of various charisms among the faithful, women and men."[41]

Pope Benedict XVI, who as a young theologian had worked with Cardinal Suenens on the Malines Documents,[42] also in his papacy spoke powerfully about the need for a new Pentecost and a fresh outpouring of the Pentecostal gifts of the Spirit upon the Church:

> Let us pray to God the Father, therefore, through our Lord Jesus Christ, in the grace of the Holy Spirit, so that the celebration of the Solemnity of Pentecost may be like an ardent flame and a blustering wind for Christian life and for the mission of the whole Church. . . .

---

39. Pope Paul VI, quoted in McDonnell, 8.
40. Pope St. John Paul II, Speech to Ecclesial Movements and New Communities, 5, May 10, 1998, Vatican.va.
41. Pope St. John Paul II, *Christifideles Laici,* Apostolic Exhortation on the Vocation and the Mission of the Lay Faithful in the Church and in the World, 24, December 30, 1988, Vatican.va.
42. These were theological and pastoral texts on the Charismatic Renewal.

Upon all of you I invoke an outpouring of the gifts of the Spirit, so that in our time too, we may have the experience of a renewed Pentecost. Amen![43]

Pope Francis has had a very personal Pentecostal experience and has seen the fruitfulness of spiritual gifts in Argentina across the churches there. He has given tremendous support to this stream of grace in the Catholic Church, promoting among all believers the New Pentecost as well as the exercise of charisms. In the Olympic Stadium in Rome in 2014, he addressed members of the Catholic Charismatic Renewal, the movement that, more than any other, has encouraged and promoted the spiritual gifts of 1 Corinthians 12:7-10 in the Catholic Church. Expressing his gratitude and sincere desire that every Catholic experience the baptism in the Holy Spirit, he said, "I expect you to share with everyone in the Church the grace of baptism in the Holy Spirit (a phrase we find in the Acts of the Apostles)."[44] Later in 2014, Pope Francis taught,

A charism is much more than a personal quality, a predisposition that one can be endowed with: a charism is *a grace, a gift bestowed by God the Father, through the action of the Holy Spirit*. And it is a gift which is given to someone not because he is better than others or because he deserves it: it is a gift that God gives him, because with his freely given love he can place him *in service to the entire community*, for the good of all.[45]

Highly significant is the document *Iuvenescit Ecclesia*, already cited, which was released under Pope Francis' pontificate by the Congregation for the Doctrine of the Faith and addressed to all the bishops of the Catholic Church. This document addresses the relationship between hierarchical and charismatic gifts in the life and the mission of the Church and stresses

---

43. Pope Benedict XVI, Homily at Pentecost Vigil with Ecclesial Movements and New Communities, June 3, 2006, vatican.va/content/benedict-xvi/en/homilies/2006/documents/hf_ben-xvi_hom_20060603_veglia-pentecoste.html.

44. Pope Francis, Address to Participants in the 37th National Convocation of the Renewal in the Holy Spirit, June 1, 2014, vatican.va/content/francesco/en/speeches/2014/june/documents/papa-francesco_20140601_rinnovamento-spirito-santo.html.

45. Pope Francis, General Audience, October 1, 2014, ewtn.com/library/PAPALDOC/f1genaud61.htm.

unequivocally the essential place of the charisms in every age: "The authentic charisms, therefore, come to be considered as gifts of indispensable importance for the life and mission of the Church."[46]

Moving from Theory to Encounter

As we have seen, the word of God exhorts us to have a strong desire for spiritual gifts, and the Church emphatically affirms this. Why is this so important? Because spiritual gifts manifest the loving, transforming presence and power of a living Jesus in the power of the Holy Spirit. They are a point of encounter, an in-breaking of the kingdom. As Cardinal Ratzinger wrote, "A dogmatic faith unsupported by personal experience remains empty."[47] Through the exercise of these gifts, God's love and truth are transformed from doctrines and theory into an experience that makes God real to untold millions. When Scripture speaks of "knowing" God, it means knowing him by experience. Spiritual gifts often prompt the conversion of the unbeliever and lead believers to deeper conversion and a more radical response to the gospel.

Paul explains that his proclamation of the gospel was not in word alone: "Our gospel came to you not only in word, but also in power and in the Holy Spirit" (1 Thessalonians 1:5). And his preaching in Corinth was "not in plausible words of wisdom, but in demonstration of the Spirit and of power" (1 Corinthians 2:4).

In our world today, people generally do not accept "authorities" in the same way they did in past times. Rather, people's opinions about spirituality are formed by their personal experiences. Sadly, their perception of the Church is often of an organization set on taking all the fun out of life and exchanging that fun for a narrow existence centered on boring church services that seem irrelevant. This was not people's perception of Jesus, the early Church, and those who ministered effectively in the spiritual gifts down through the ages, because spiritual gifts touch people at a point of need.

---

46. Congregation for the Doctrine of the Faith, *Iuvenescit Ecclesia*, 9.
47. Cardinal Joseph Ratzinger, Foreword to *Renewal and the Powers of Darkness* by Cardinal Leon Joseph Suenens (Ann Arbor, MI: Servant, 1983), https://www.ewtn.com/expert/answers/charismatic_renewal.htm.

Love or spiritual gifts, which is more important?

In the Christian life, we seek to make love our aim (1 Corinthians 14:1). In the Old Testament, the law was portrayed as something to aim at. Sin means to "miss the mark" or to miss the target. In the New Testament, Jesus sums up the whole law in two commandments of love: "You shall love the Lord your God with all your heart, and with all your soul and with all your mind. . . . You shall love your neighbor as yourself" (Matthew 22:37, 39).

In aiming for love, the Bible tells us we should earnestly desire the spiritual gifts as expressions of that love. Spiritual gifts are channels and mediators of God's love; they offer encounters with Christ that help people grow in their love of God and others. When spiritual gifts are discussed, some people assert that love is the greatest charism and that this should be our only focus, not spiritual gifts. But in fact, love is not, strictly speaking, a charism, because charisms are "distributed gifts" that the Lord gives to whom he wishes. Love, on the other hand, is a virtue for all. In any case, this is to set up a conflict between love and the spiritual gifts that does not exist in the Scriptures.

Love is supreme, of course, but Paul, rather than diminishing spiritual gifts in comparison to love, yokes them together: "Make love your aim, and earnestly desire spiritual gifts" (1 Corinthians 14:1). It is not a matter of one or the other but both. Having strongly exhorted the Church to desire and cultivate the spiritual gifts, he promotes love as the most excellent "way" in which they should be ministered (1 Corinthians 12:31). Spiritual gifts are *tools of love*. Love must be the motivation for desiring to exercise them so that we can share the love of Christ more effectively with others and extend his kingdom.

One gift each?

One of the misconceptions many people hold about charisms is that God may only grant us one of them and that aspiring for more is not appropriate. It is clear from the New Testament that God is generous and often equips believers with the gifts they will need for the variety of situations in which they find themselves. Clearly, if we are faithful, we will tend to develop certain gifts and ministries, but this does not mean that it is impossible for us to be used through other charisms, should the need arise. Cardinal Suenens explains, "The Spirit who gives me strength today for a particular mission, can tomorrow confide to me another. He is able also to manifest himself in me, not only in one gift, but in many, either successively or all at once."[48]

Only for "the mature and holy"?

Despite what Vatican II has taught, some people think that acquiring the spiritual gifts is a long and arduous journey. Of course, coming into a mature charismatic ministry does take time. But our experience is that very real and powerful spiritual gifts can be received by anyone the Lord chooses who is open. "All these are inspired by one and the same Spirit, who apportions to each one individually as he wills" (1 Corinthians 12:11).

The misconception that spiritual gifts are only granted to mature Christians has two effects. First, it makes ordinary people think they are naturally disqualified because they are not holy enough. Second, people disregard the possibility that others can use spiritual gifts, because they regard them as not holy enough either!

Often people have not been helped when someone they know or some high-profile minister has misused spiritual gifts through exaggerations, abuses, or flamboyant presentations. Such experiences can leave observers thinking that the ministry's claims are false—perhaps motivated by love of money or fame—which in turn can lead to the conclusion that the exercise of spiritual gifts is risky and therefore better avoided. Paul's response is different. Recognizing that not all that was claimed to be prophecy in Corinth was actually so, he encouraged discernment rather than an outright ban: "Let two or three prophets speak, and let the others weigh what is said. . . . For you can all prophesy one by one" (1 Corinthians 14:29, 31). And again, "Do not quench the Spirit, do not despise prophesying, but test everything; hold fast what is good" (1 Thessalonians 5:19-21).

Of course, all are called to holiness of life. Among those who exercise spiritual gifts, I repeat, the ones who pursue holiness yield more fruit for the kingdom than those who do not. But clearly God gives his gifts as he pleases. Spiritual gifts are not necessarily proofs of a person's holiness but rather proofs of God's grace and generosity.

---

48. Léon Joseph Cardinal Suenens, *A New Pentecost?* (Glasgow, Scotland: William Collins, 1977), 82–83.

Giving people time and space to grow

With the best wills in the world, sincere people sometimes just get it wrong. The reason this scandalizes some observers is because they have a preconceived idea that spiritual gifts arrive fully mature. Our experience is that normally, spiritual gifts begin in small ways, and if the person exercising them is faithful with little, God often grants a greater anointing and increase of power. On this journey, mistakes are made, and the sincere and humble disciple learns from his or her mistakes.

For this maturing process to take place, we need an encouraging, healthy context in which to grow, among those more experienced than ourselves. This context should allow us room to step out and take risks but minimize the possibility of doing harm. Leaders need to be well formed and free from envy and insecurity, delighting to see people grow in the spiritual gifts and not threatened by God's anointing upon others. Disciples need to be teachable and submissive, taking correction humbly and free to take risks because of the love they have for those to whom they minister, within the boundaries set by those overseeing them. It is this humility, faith, and love on the part of both leaders and disciples that foster growth, maturity, and multiplication of the spiritual gifts in the Church.

In the Charism School (our training school in spiritual gifts), tens of thousands around the world, with little or no experience, have had amazing experiences of exercising spiritual gifts. We are quite clear in our teaching that these gifts cannot be switched on and off at will; they depend on the action of the Holy Spirit, as we have already said. Yet whenever we lead a workshop helping people open up to this action of the Holy Spirit, we are astonished by the abundance of gifts that are released.

In our prophetic word of knowledge workshop, for example, after we have given the teaching, we put participants in pairs with people they do not know. Before the workshop, usually about 15 to 25 percent have received an accurate and meaningful prophetic word of knowledge for someone else. We lead everyone through a process of listening to the Holy Spirit and opening up to revelational prophecy (prophecy that includes knowledge they could not have humanly known). Then we ask each participant to pray and listen about which area of life the Lord wishes to address in the partner, to encourage, exhort, or comfort.

After the workshop, I separate each person from his or her partner, asking people to return to their own seats. This gives people the freedom to answer honestly when I ask, "Now, who has received an accurate and meaningful prophecy from his or her partner?" Usually about 90 percent raise their hands.

Participants are invariably shocked and thrilled. Our testimony forms are filled with wonderful feedback:

- "Astonished how the words given me were so accurate—when my faith struggled with the idea that the Holy Spirit would actually give such words to me."

- "I received a very powerful prophecy, which was spot-on. I was extremely blessed and encouraged by it."

- "Jesus made his presence in my life extremely clear to me. He did this through absolutely accurate prophecy given to me."

A similar thing happens in our physical healing workshops. Participants are put into groups of five or six and pray for one another. Many have never before even seen a physical healing, let alone performed one. They are amazed when they witness people being instantly healed though their simple prayers. People are healed of all degrees of sickness, from sore knees to tumors, blindness, deafness, lameness, and even incurable and congenital conditions. Here is a witness from one participant, who went on to join our community:

In 2002 I went to a Charism School run by Damian and the Community in Lublin. I was running a prayer group for eighty young people. We had been running lots of evangelization events and had seen God working powerfully among us. However, I had never seen or witnessed any physical healing in my life. We began the physical healing workshop time, where we were supposed to pray for physical healing. There was a girl who had a deformed spine from birth that caused her shoulder blades to protrude so much that she couldn't sleep on her back. I put my hands on her, starting the prayer with not much expectation. As I prayed, I could feel my hands moving and saw how her spine was being straightened. She started to jump and say, "Thank you, God," as she was completely healed, and at the same time she experienced God's love.

Since that experience, during the following years, I have been see-ing more and more miracles, including the blind seeing, the deaf hearing, and tumors disappearing. All glory to God!

It has become clear to us that God wants to pour out these gifts in abun-dance and at a level that almost everyone in the Church has simply not anticipated. We have run the Charism School for tens of thousands on five continents. The results are always the same—an extraordinary outpour-ing of spiritual gifts upon ordinary Christians trying to follow Jesus. Paul's exhortation to seek after spiritual gifts for the service of the Church and her mission is directed not to particular individuals but to the whole Church. It is obvious but needs to be stressed that if God's word calls us to "earnestly desire the spiritual gifts" (1 Corinthians 14:1), it must be *because God ear-nestly desires to grant them!*[49]

---

49. Some people are confused on this issue because of some of the teaching of St. John of the Cross on not desiring visions and locutions. An important distinction needs to be made here. John was fighting a heretical sect called the Alambrados, who thought that the more visions, prophecies, and ecstasies a person had, the holier he or she was. Of course, we know this is not necessarily the case. What Paul is speaking of here is not personal experiences for oneself, which we seek as trophies, but gifts sought in love and offered for the upbuilding of the Church and the fruitfulness of her mission.

Part I
The Prophetic Gifts

CHAPTER 2

THE THEOLOGY OF PROPHECY
AND A SHORT HISTORY

It shall come to pass afterward,
that I will pour out my spirit on all flesh;
your sons and daughters shall prophesy,
your old men shall dream dreams,
and your young men shall see visions.
—Joel 2:28

Prophecy has many forms, but I define it essentially as an inspired message that carries within it the creative, transforming power of the kingdom of God. It can be addressed to individuals or groups, within the Church or in the world. It is delivered through inspired evangelistic proclamation, words of knowledge, the sharing of God's heart, words of wisdom, inspired teaching and preaching, or any inspired actions that express God's message. The word *inspired* as I use it here refers to an action of the Holy Spirit in us, not simply something that appears brilliant or very well executed. As we shall see in this chapter, prophecy was central in the New Testament and is described as one of the main signs of the presence of the Holy Spirit in the lives of Christians.

About a year ago, I felt that the Lord wanted me to attend a day for leaders of mostly black Pentecostal churches in London. Even though I was one of the only white participants and the only Catholic, I was very warmly welcomed. After some worship and teaching, we were invited to gather in small groups and pray with each other.

I prayed with a pastor's wife for another pastor, and as we prayed, I sensed the Lord showing me something. In my mind's eye, I saw this pastor at a funeral. During the funeral, he stood up and preached. Then he led an altar call, in which he invited the people present to come forward and commit their lives to Jesus, and many did so. Even though I knew that Pentecostals don't normally have an altar call at a funeral, I shared the image I had received with him.

The pastor then told me that his mother had just died, and he was going back to Africa in the next few days to bury her. I prayed with him, that he would have the courage to lead an altar call at the funeral and that God would lead many souls to Christ. A couple of weeks later, he contacted me and related his experience in Africa.

At the funeral, when all the family and friends had arrived, they gathered together around his mother's coffin, and he stood up and preached. Following his preaching, he held an altar call, inviting people to come to the front and give their lives to the Lord. Now, many of his large extended family, which included brothers, sisters, cousins, and all their children, plus numerous other relations, were not churchgoers, and some were very resistant to the gospel. However, at that altar call, *every single member* of his extended family came forward and gave their lives to Jesus.

The pastor simply couldn't believe his eyes. It was a miraculous moment and one that made a profound impact on him. After the funeral, those who had been converted could be seen leading members of the staff hired to serve at the reception to Christ. What marvelous fruit from one simple prophecy! Who could have imagined such a thing happening at a funeral? All glory to God! Prophecy has the power to truly change lives and advance the kingdom of God.

Jesus as Prophet

If we are to get a good understanding and foundation for the prophetic gifts, we have to begin by looking at Jesus. It is common for Christians to refer to Jesus as king or high priest, and our concept of him in these roles is fairly familiar. However, it remains rare in Christian circles to refer to Jesus as prophet. Perhaps this is because of the fear that in doing so, we might undermine his divine status and give the impression that he is only one prophet among many. If we are to understand what prophecy is, we must come to understand how Jesus, although uniquely the divine Son of God, is also a prophet and what importance prophecy had in his life and mission.

The Second Vatican Council was specific in its use of the title "prophet" when speaking of Jesus: "Christ, the great Prophet, who proclaimed the kingdom of His Father by the testimony of His life and the power of His words, continually fulfills His prophetic office until His full glory is revealed" (*Lumen Gentium*, 35).[1]

---

1. *Lumen Gentium*, 35, in Walter Abbott, *Documents of Vatican II* (Washington, D.C.: America, 1966), 61.

The baptism of Jesus in the Jordan has enormous prophetic significance. Apart from John, who received the Holy Spirit on encountering Jesus in his mother's womb, there had been no true prophet in Israel for four hundred years. Even though we read of such figures as Simeon and Anna in the Temple who prophesied, there were none who had the true status of prophet as did prophets before them. So when the Scriptures say that "the heavens were opened, . . . and behold, a voice from heaven, saying, 'This is my beloved Son, with whom I am well pleased'" (Matthew 3:16-17), this was not simply a symbol of favor but a dramatic sign asserting that the prophetic drought that had beset Israel for four hundred years had ended. Heaven, in which God's word had been "shut up," was irreversibly rent open, and the clear voice of God was heard like thunder, initiating the ultimate prophetic era through the ministry of Jesus and his Church.

The Book of Revelation proclaims, "For the testimony of Jesus is the spirit of prophecy" (19:10), which means that "'the witness of Jesus' is the word of God to which Jesus testifies and which is implanted in every Christian . . . and which inspires the prophets."[2] Jesus refers to himself as prophet several times (including in Matthew 13:57 and Luke 13:33).

Jesus as *the* prophet

Jesus clearly understands himself as superior to all his predecessors. In Matthew 12:42, he declares himself "greater than Solomon"—greater than the kingly tradition. In Matthew 12:6, he announces himself "greater than the temple"—greater than the priestly tradition. In Matthew 12: 41, he proclaims that he is "greater than Jonah"—greater than the prophetic tradition. Jesus is uniquely the King, the High Priest, and the Prophet.

When Jesus is described by the Gospel writers as "the prophet" (John 7:40), this openly refers to the fulfillment of Moses' words in Deuteronomy 18:15: "The Lord your God will raise up for you a prophet like me from among you, from your brethren—him you shall heed." Jesus is *the* Prophet in the same sense that he is *the* Martyr, *the* Son of God. Our sonship is a share in his sonship. Christian martyrdom is a share in his martyrdom. Christian prophecy, likewise, is a share in his prophetic identity and ministry. Theologian Karl Rahner has written, "Jesus Christ is *the* Prophet, the

---

2. *The New Jerusalem Bible* (London: Darton, Longman & Todd, 1985), note on Revelation 19:10.

divine self-communication and its expression in person."[3] Jesus is not only one who communicates the Word; he *is* the Word, the origin of all authentic prophecy, past, present, and future.

Jesus is also the fulfillment of prophecy (Matthew 4:14-16; 8:17; 21:4-5; John 12:38; 13:18; 15:25). "Do not think that I have come to abolish the law and the prophets; I have come not to abolish them but to fulfill them" (Matthew 5:17). In one sense, all of Jesus' actions were prophetic, but some seemed to be especially so, such as the cursing of the barren fig tree (Matthew 21:19), the expelling of the traders from the temple (Mark 11:15-18), his turning water into wine (John 2:1-11), the multiplication of the fish and loaves (Matthew 14:13-21; 15:32-38; Mark 6:30-44; 8:1-9; John 6:1-14), and his many healings and deliverances. Like some of the Old Testament prophets, Jesus' anointing as prophet was confirmed through his interactions with the heavenly realm. Jesus' baptism is one example; others include the Transfiguration (Mark 9:2-8) and angelic visitations (Luke 22:43).

Jesus' use of prophetic knowledge and the reading of hearts

Many of us are aware of Jesus' prophecies regarding the future, such as his predictions of his passion and glorification (Mark 8:31-32; 9:30-31; 10:32-34). But we often overlook the extent of other kinds of prophetic activity in his ministry. One of these is his prophetic, supernatural knowledge of things he could not have humanly known.

He used his prophetic knowledge in evangelistic situations, such as his encounter with the woman at the well. When Jesus revealed to her that he knew that she had five husbands, her heart was opened, and this became the catalyst for her conversion and incredibly that of many in her town (John 4).

We witness in the Gospels Jesus' foreknowledge of miraculous events. In Luke, he commanded the disciples, "'Put out into the deep water and let down your nets for a catch.' . . . They caught so many fish that their nets were breaking" (Luke 5:4, 6, NRSV). And at Cana, Jesus knew exactly what was to take place when he instructed the servants to "fill the jars with water" and "draw some out, and take it to the steward of the feast" (John 2:7, 8).

Jesus also prophesied to individuals their future ministries. After having witnessed the miraculous catch of fish, Peter fell on his knees, crying, "Depart from me, for I am a sinful man, O Lord." Jesus responded by

---

3. Karl Rahner, ed., *Concise Theological Dictionary* (New York: Herder, 1965), 384.

prophesying Peter's calling: "Do not be afraid; henceforth you will be catching men" (Luke 5:8, 10). What is most interesting in this particular episode is that while the miracle astonished Peter and revealed to him both his unworthiness and Jesus as Lord, it was the personal prophecy of his future that gave him the confidence to leave everything and follow Jesus.

Jesus also engaged in the prophetic renaming of people, as God had done in the Old Testament: "And I tell you, you are Peter, and on this rock I will build my Church" (Matthew 16:18). We see Jesus calling many people by name in the Gospels, and we have to ask ourselves why the simple calling of a person by name would have the power to cause such radical responses. There are numerous examples of the saints receiving, by prophetic knowledge, the personal names of individuals before ever being introduced to them. When this takes place, the impact on the person is profound, and he or she is struck with awe. I think it is highly likely that the same was taking place in the ministry of Jesus.

The prophetic gifts also played a great part in Jesus' ministry of healing. He demonstrated prophetic insight about who would be healed: "Go; your son will live" (John 4:50), and "Stretch out your hand" (Matthew 12:13). He knew that Lazarus would rise from the dead (John 11:23). He also knew the condition of souls—for example, the treachery of Judas (John 13:21) and the salvation of the good thief: "Truly, I say to you, today you will be with me in Paradise" (Luke 23:43).

Jesus' prophetic knowledge included not only human events but divine ones as well. Perhaps one of his greatest prophecies was his knowledge of the plan of the Father to pour out the Holy Spirit at Pentecost: "And behold, I send the promise of my Father upon you; but stay in the city, until you are clothed with power from on high" (Luke 24:49).

Prophecy in the New Testament Church

Of course, there are amazing examples of prophecy and prophetic ministry in the Old Testament, from Balaam's ass (Numbers 22:21-35) to the astonishing figures of Moses and Elijah, who as we know had prophetic knowledge of acts of God in nature, plagues, and fire falling from heaven. The prophetic, supernatural knowledge of hidden events and conversations is stunningly demonstrated in an incident in the life of Elisha, when the Lord revealed to him the strategies of the king of Syria to such a detailed degree that the king assumed he had a traitor among his generals who was relaying precise information to the Israelites. However, it was made known to the king that the reason for this incredible knowledge was not betrayal but rather, as one of his officers declared, "Elisha, the prophet who is in Israel, tells the king of Israel the words that you speak in your bedchamber" (2 Kings 6:12).

Significantly, Peter declares that Joel's prophecy about the great outpouring of the Spirit of prophecy is fulfilled on the day of Pentecost (Acts 2:17-18). It seems, then, that the outpouring of the Holy Spirit upon the Church is synonymous with this outpouring of the spirit of prophecy. The birth of the Church inaugurates an entirely new dispensation among the people of God in the manifestation of prophetic gifts. This does not mean all will have the ministry of a prophet, but at least all have the potential to prophesy. "When compared with the Old Testament, New Testament prophecy exhibits undeniably new features. The most obvious of all is the great difference in the extent of the phenomenon. Whereas for Joel the universal event of prophecy remains a wish (Joel 2:28-32), here in contrast, all believers, at least potentially, are in the condition of being able to prophesy."[4]

Following Pentecost, there are numerous references to prophets and prophecy in the New Testament Church. In the Book of Acts, Ananias receives very accurate words of knowledge: "Rise and go to the street called Straight, and inquire in the house of Judas for a man of Tarsus named Saul: for behold, he is praying, and he has seen a man named Ananias come in and lay his hands on him so that he may regain his sight" (Acts 9:11-12).

At prayer for the outpouring of the Holy Spirit, converts prophesied when hands were laid upon them (Acts 19:6). The mention of prophecy as one of the gifts bestowed upon the Church is frequent (Romans 12:6; 1 Corinthians 12:10, 28, 29; Ephesians 4:11-12).

Finally, we read in Ephesians that the Church is "built upon the foundation of the apostles and prophets" (2:20). "Prophets" here does not mean those of the Old Testament but those of the New: "That Paul has Christian prophets in mind is confirmed by two other passages of the same letter, where he speaks of 'apostles and prophets' as those to whom the mystery of the calling of the Gentiles has been revealed (Ephesians 3:5)."[5] The full reve-

---

4. René Latourelle and Rino Fisichella, eds., *Dictionary of Fundamental Theology* (New York: Crossroad, 2000), 795. See 1 Corinthians 12:28-30 and Ephesians 4:11.
5. Sullivan, 94.

lation of salvation was given not only to the apostles but to New Testament prophets as well.

We are told to value prophecy (1 Thessalonians 5:20) and to desire and seek it more earnestly than the other charisms (1 Corinthians 14:1). St. Paul, reminding the church of Corinth what the authentic practice of prophecy is like, writes, "But if all prophesy, and an unbeliever or outsider enters, he is convicted by all, he is called to account by all, the secrets of his heart are disclosed; and so, falling on his face, he will worship God and declare that God is really among you" (1 Corinthians 14:24-25).

The phrase "the secrets of his heart are disclosed" can legitimately be interpreted in two ways. First, this can refer to the kind of exhortation that uncovers the condition of our hearts and calls forth a heart response. Something similar happened at Pentecost in response to Peter's preaching, when the crowd experienced being "cut to the heart" (Acts 2:37). The second valid understanding is what has been known as prophetic knowledge, the reading of hearts or what is referred to in Pentecostal and charismatic circles as "words of knowledge." These words of knowledge, which we will expand upon later, give extraordinary dynamism and impact to prophetic utterance.

Examples of Prophecy from Church History

The Church makes a clear distinction between public revelation—the Bible and dogmatic Church teaching, for example, on the Holy Trinity and the natures of Christ, which are for all Christians—and private revelation, which can be helpful for some but which we are not bound to believe. Examples of private revelations include certain apparitions of Jesus (the Sacred Heart, Divine Mercy) and of Mary (Lourdes, Fatima, Guadalupe). Even if these are recognized by the Church as "worthy of belief," we are not obliged to believe in them. They may be very helpful, incredibly accurate, and at times irrefutable, but they should not be confused with the status of the Scriptures and the official dogmas of the Church (see CCC 67).

Included in private revelation are innumerable examples of the gift of prophecy down through the history of Christianity, and many of the early saints and Fathers of the Church give us insight into just how prevalent, dynamic, and influential this gift was.

- Eusebius, the third-century historian, records that just prior to the destruction of Jerusalem by the Roman general Titus in AD 70: "The whole body, however, of the church at Jerusalem, having been commanded by a divine revelation, given to men of approved piety there before the war, removed from the city, and dwelt at a certain town beyond the Jordan, called Pella."[6] Thus the entire community was preserved.

- The Didache, otherwise known as the "Teaching of the Twelve," is a Church manual from the early second century and makes several references to prophets. "Every true prophet who settles among you deserves his food. . . . With a jug of wine or of oil, take the 'first fruits' and give to the prophets. . . . And so with money and clothing and every possession."[7] Interestingly, the Didache also speaks of the importance of the role of local prophetically gifted people within the liturgy, in particular in the moment after Communion: "But permit the prophets to make Thanksgiving as much as they desire."[8]

- Justin, the second-century Christian apologist, speaks of prophecy in his famous Dialogue with Trypho (a Jewish rabbi), saying, "Even to this day the gifts of prophecy exist among us Christians."[9]

- St. Irenaeus of Lyons, writing in the late second century, said, "We . . . hear many brothers in the Church who possess prophetic gifts, and bring to light for the general benefit the hidden things of men."[10]

---

6. *Eusebius' Ecclesiastical History* (Grand Rapids, MI: Baker Book House, 1981), 86.

7. *Didache*, chap. 13, see newadvent.org/fathers/0714.htm.

8. *Didache*, chap. 10.

9. Justin Martyr, *Dialogue with Trypho*, chap. 82, in *Ante-Nicene Fathers*, vol.1, 240.

10. St. Irenaeus, *Against Heresies*, in *Ante-Nicene Fathers*, vol. 1 (New York: Christian Literature Col, 1890), 532, as quoted in Bruce Yocum, *Prophecy: Exercising the Prophetic Gifts of the Spirit in the Church* (Ann Arbor, MI: Servant, 1976), 21.

- St. Augustine, in the early fifth century, wrote, "So long as our knowledge is imperfect, the eternal light of the evident truth is made known to us through the many and diverse forms of prophecy."[11] Augustine also left a list of pastoral instructions regarding the practice of prophecy in the Church.[12]

Many examples of extraordinary prophetic activity continued through the ages among the saints, including St. Bernard of Clairvaux (d. 1153); St. Anthony of Padua (d. 1231); Blessed Margaret of Castello (d. 1320); St. Frances of Rome (d. 1440); St. Francis of Paola (d. 1507); St. Mary Magdalene de Pazzi (d. 1607); and St. Martin de Porres (d. 1639), to name just a few.[13]

In the modern era, we still see extraordinary degrees of prophetic gifts among the saints. Three examples are St. Anthony Mary Claret, St. John Bosco, and St. Padre Pio of Pietrelcina.

St. Anthony Mary Claret (1807–1870) exercised a remarkable gift of prophecy. He scheduled a mission during harvest time, and many of the farmers did not want to attend because they feared losing their crops. The saint assured them that if they attended, God would bless their wheat fields, but if they didn't, their crops would be destroyed. Two days later, an unexpected and fierce hailstorm destroyed the crops of the farmers who had stayed home, while the crops of those who had attended not only were spared but produced a greater than expected yield.[14]

St. John Bosco predicted public events and prophesied recovery of the critically ill. He also forecast the imminent deaths of prominent people. He knew supernaturally when certain boys at his schools were committing particular sins, and he would send an assistant to apprehend them in the acts. He once said, "Place in front of me any boy; one whom I have never seen before, if you like, and just by looking at him, I will be able to tell

---

11. Augustine, *De Spiritu et littera* 24, 41, as quoted in Livingstone, 198.

12. See Fr. Joseph Bentivegna, SJ, paper, "The Witness of St. Augustine on the Action of the Holy Spirit in the Church and the Praxis of Charismata in His Time," 30–31, in Elizabeth Livingstone, ed., *Papers Presented to the 10th International Conference on Patristic Studies*, vol. 22, 199.

13. See more at "Prophecies in the Lives of the Saints," miraclesofthesaints.com/search?q=prophecies.

14. Ibid.

you every sin he has ever committed."[15] Yet another time, he said, "I can see nothing, but whenever the welfare of souls desires it, the phenomenon always occurs."[16] The precision of his "knowledge" was extraordinary in its detail. For example: "In such a year, at such a time, in such a place, you did this and this. . . ."[17]

St. Pio of Pietrelcina

St. Padre Pio's gifts of prophecy were astounding even among the saints. He regularly prophesied future events with astonishing accuracy.

> One of his spiritual sons asked, "Padre, will they bomb Genoa?"
> With a nod of his head he affirmed that they would bomb Genoa.
> "I am afraid," said his penitent. "Your fear will avail nothing, Genoa will be bombed." All at once Pio grew pale, and looking afar his eyes glistened with tears.
> "Oh, how they will bomb the poor city. So many homes, buildings and churches will crumble." Then he turned and cheerily consoled him saying, "Be calm, your house will not be touched."
> That prediction did not remain a secret. When the bombs rained down pitilessly on the great city, among the mass of ruins the only house that remained standing was the one whose preservation had been predicted.[18]

Like St. John Bosco and many other saints, St. Pio could read the conditions of people's hearts and know precise details regarding their sins as well as personal details concerning people and events in the past, present, and future. His prophetic knowledge was so extensive and detailed that at times, according to some who knew him, it seemed that there was nothing he did not know. He prophesied the date of his death fifty years before it happened. He could read the thoughts of persons, including whom they were thinking about, what they were thinking about them, and whether or

---

15. Anderson SDB, *Don Bosco* (Bombay Salesian Society, 1984), 387.
16. Ibid.
17. Ibid.
18. Rev. Charles Mortimer Carty, *Padre Pio: The Stigmatist* (Rockford, IL: TAN, 1989), 24.

not it was true. He often knew in detail the actions of a person, as though he had been present when they occurred.

Another amazing story of Padre Pio's prophetic gifts is told by a man named Joe Greco. In a dream, Joe met Padre Pio—who was still living at that time—and asked him to save his father, who was very ill and about to undergo a dangerous operation. The father recovered. Joe then decided to go to San Giovanni Rotundo in Italy, where Padre Pio lived, to thank him in person for his prayers.

Joe managed to get to confession after a four-day wait. When Padre Pio saw him in the confessional, he said immediately, "Well, your father's all right then." This shocked Joe, because he'd never been to San Giovanni Rotundo before, had never met or spoken to Padre Pio, and knew no one in the surrounding area. He then posed in his mind this question: "Was it you? Was it you?" Padre Pio replied, "In the dream. In the dream." To which an utterly astonished Joe responded, "Yes, Father, in the dream, Father."

Joe then confessed his sins, and before granting absolution, Padre Pio said, "Now then, there is something else you know." Joe replied that he couldn't remember anything else. Padre Pio then described an incident with a girl in a park when Joe was first in the army. All the details of the incident, which Joe had never confessed, came flooding back to him. Padre Pio concluded by telling Joe that the event had taken place in 1941 in Blackburn, England.[19]

Padre Pio knew when people would die. He also could foresee accidents, after which he would be the channel through which the injured person would be healed. He could even tell the number of days a person had prayed for the Lord's help through his intercession. According to my research, he was quite possibly the most prophetically gifted person of the twentieth century. He has continued to act prophetically even after his death, through his interventions in the lives of thousands of people all over the world—bringing healing, comfort, and encouragement to their Christian lives.

Prophetic gifts in the Orthodox and Coptic churches

Remarkable prophetic gifts are not only experienced in the Catholic Church. There are also extraordinary examples of these gifts at work in the Orthodox, Coptic, and Pentecostal Churches.

---

19. "Joe Greco Tells a Miraculous Story of St. Padre Pio," youtube.com/watch?v=cncpvYav3eE.

The Orthodox Church has a wonderful treasury of holy people with extraordinary gifts of prophetic knowledge. Among the most famous is St. Seraphim of Sarov, who famously shone like the sun and, as a matter of course, knew people's names and their problems without being told.

A modern example of a man who had similar gifts is Elder Paisios of the Holy Mountain, who died in 1994. When asked about his prophetic gifts, he answered, "I know who is coming, what problems they have, and what I need to tell them. I know all this before they arrive."[20] The following testimony reveals the level of his gift:

> Father Paisios emerged from his enclave, inspected all of us, and called us by our own names. . . . He did not know me, but he said, "You there," calling four of us by name. "You and you!" He proceeded to take the four of us inside, and without our even mentioning our individual problems, he began to analyze the situation of each individual. To the first man he said, "You, my child, have a problem with your arm. This has happened to you because you once went out for a drink, and someone put something in it. From that moment on, you started having this problem." He said to the second man, "You have started to take drugs. Soon you will end up in the grave if you don't stop. You have to stop immediately." To another present, who had foolishly consulted a wizard and had been experiencing strange and frightening things in his home, he correctly again, with no human information, uncovered the cause. "You, my child, are facing serious problems. Someone has performed witchcraft on you. When you leave from here and get home, look for a square stone near the steps in front of your house. Lift that stone, and you will find a small bag underneath. That is the source of the witchcraft performed on you. You will take this bag and throw it into the fire."[21]

As not many Westerners know much about our Coptic brothers and sisters, let me introduce Pope St. Kyrillos (1902–1971). He was without doubt one of the most supernaturally gifted Christians of the twentieth century, and his life mirrors the many miraculous deeds of the great Desert

---

20. *Saint Paisios Athonite*, Russian film with English subtitles, youtube.com/watch?v=htluet5iKvA.
21. Ibid.

Fathers. He was a hermit chosen to be the Coptic pope when he wasn't even ordained a bishop. He had the same gifts as Padre Pio, in similar measure. Here is one man's testimony of the pope's prophetic gifts:

> I insisted on talking to him about a personal matter of great importance to me. As I kissed his hand, he started talking to me as if he read my exact thoughts. Astonished, I kept staring at him after he finished, I had nothing to say. He had completely covered all my concerns. This was repeated many times. I realized that it was God's spirit.[22]

In another example, a man who was not Christian was annoyed by the reception the pope had received when visiting his city. The next morning, the man woke up terrified because Pope Kyrillos had appeared to him in a dream and told him not to be upset. The man later went to ask for the pope's forgiveness, and Pope Kyrillos said the same words to him as he had said to him in the dream: "Are you upset, Hassan, because they cheered a little for the Christian leader? Don't be upset, Hassan." He then prayed for the man and blessed him.

A biographer wrote this:

> Indeed, Pope Kyrillos did open his heart to the people. His door (his heart before his door) was always open to everyone. He empathized with each individual in his congregation and shared in their happy and sad moments, with tears, tenderness and mercy. He had a visionary gift from God that enabled him to know the spiritual, physical and mental condition of those in his presence, thereby addressing their concerns before they even declared them.[23]

---

22. Protopriest Arsanious Zaki, Masr Newspaper, May 10, 1960, quoted in Hanna Youssef Ata and Rafael Ava Mena, *The Life of the Saint Pope Kyrillos the Sixth* (Maryut, Egypt: St. Menas Monastery Press, 2002), 27.
23. *The Fruits of Love: The Saint Pope Kyrillos VI*, 2–3, zeitun-eg.org/stcyril6/popekyrillos_fruits_of_love.pdf.

Prophetic gifts in the Pentecostal and Evangelical Charismatic tradition

A large number of Pentecostals have possessed tremendous prophetic gifts, among them Maria Woodworth-Etter, John G. Lake, and Smith Wigglesworth. But perhaps the most famous of the twentieth century was William Branham (1909–1965).

Branham was a very humble, prayerful, and holy Pentecostal who led what became known as the Voice of Healing, a movement of many Christian healing ministries that impacted vast numbers around the world but especially in the United States in the 1940s and 50s. Although Branham's theology became rather unorthodox toward the end of his life, he remained always a deeply godly man with no trace of scandal. He always accredited everything to Jesus, scrupulously giving him all the glory. Here is an example of his prophetic gift to a woman brought to him on the platform for healing.

> "Of course, you're sick, and you're suffering with a condition. . . . It's a form of cancer, and the cancer is located on the breast, . . . and you've got a rupture condition, and the rupture is in the bowel, and you have stomach trouble also. A severe heart trouble that caused you fainting. . . . Are those things the truth?" "Yes, all true." . . . "I see you, your name is Eva, and your last name is York, and you live in this city." "Yes, Sir, I do." "And your house number is 613 Sixth Street. . . . You're going home to be well in the name of Jesus Christ."[24]

I want to conclude with a very recent story of prophecy in the evangelical charismatic tradition. Two years after the election of Pope Benedict, in 2007, Cardinal Jorge Bergoglio of Argentina attended an ecumenical event in Buenos Aires. An American evangelical charismatic woman named Stacey Campbell was in attendance. Cardinal Bergoglio chose to speak on the text of chapter two of Philippians. Stacey had never met the cardinal before, but as she listened, she was granted a very powerful spiritual experience, in which she saw the whole auditorium filled with the glory of God in heavenly light. She then heard the audible voice of God

---

24. "William Branham Giving a Word of Knowledge," https://www.youtube.com/watch?v=Xe-vlOd7EB4.

saying, "These are not just words on a page to this man; this is his whole life," and she began to weep.

When the cardinal had finished, Stacey turned to Matteo Calisi, one of the organizers, and asked him to ask the cardinal to pray over her for an increase of humility. In those days, Matteo was not that fluent in English, and knowing that Stacey had prophetic gifts, he misunderstood her request, thinking she was offering to deliver a prophecy to Cardinal Bergoglio. So moments later, Stacey stood before the cardinal with her hands open, ready to receive his prayer, and to her shock, Matteo announced that instead, she was going to minister to the cardinal!

Stacey didn't know what to do, so she simply laid her hand on his shoulder, and the Spirit of God came upon her. She began trembling and then said first what God had shown her earlier: that those were not just words on a page to the cardinal, but that was his whole life. Then the rest of Philippians 2 came to her mind: "'Therefore, God has highly exalted him and given him the name which is above every name.' And because you have humbled yourself, I am going to highly exalt you, and I am going to give you the highest name in the Catholic Church, and you will be the next pope."[25] As we all know now, on March 13, 2013, Cardinal Bergoglio was elected pope and took the name Francis.

25. "Stacey Campbell—Unity, Pope Francis & Prophecy," youtube.com/watch?v=UmtmWraqn1w.

CHAPTER 3

THE PRACTICE

OF

PROPHECY TODAY

Whoever speaks must do so as one speaking the very words of God.
—1 Peter 4:11 (NRSV)

Truly anointed Christian speech is powerful. The New Testament Greek word that constantly characterizes the word of God is the adjective *energes*, "efficacious," that which works, which always produces a result.

> St. Paul, for instance, writes to the Thessalonians that they, on receiving the divine word of the Apostle's teaching, have heard it not as human words but as it really is, as "the word of God, which is at work [*energeitai*] in those who believe" (1 Thessalonians 2:13). The difference between the Word of God and human words is here presented, implicitly, as the difference between the Word that works and the word that does not work, between the efficacious Word and the inefficacious, empty word. So, too, in the Epistle to the Hebrews we find this concept of the efficacy of the divine Word: "The Word of God is living and effective [*energes*]" (Hebrews 4:12).[1]

When St. Jerome was translating the Greek Bible into Latin, he decided that the most precise way of expressing the original and dynamic meaning of the passage of John's Gospel, chapter one, verse one, "In the beginning was the word," was "In the beginning was the *verb*." In other words, in the beginning was a word that does things. A word of God is an act of God!

And this word can be on our lips through the action of the Holy Spirit. Prophecy is not vague platitudes. A true word from the Lord does what it says. If it is a word of comfort, it actually brings comfort. If a word of conviction, it actually convicts. The Spirit invites us to proclaim words that

---

1. Fr. Raniero Cantalamessa, *The Mystery of God's Word* (Collegeville, MN: Liturgical Press, 1994), 45.

have creative power, not only to people but to the material world as well. All things are waiting for the liberation that comes through the proclamation of the word of God and the action of the Holy Spirit.

"In the beginning was the Word, and the Word was with God, and the Word was God. He was in the beginning with God; all things were made through him, and without him was not anything made that was made" (John 1:1-3). The synod of bishops meeting in May 2008 asserted, "The Word of God is a *living, effective* reality (Hebrews 4:12); it is *eternal* (cf. Isaiah 40:8), *'all-powerful'* (Wisdom 18:15), *a creative force* (cf. Genesis 1:3ff) and originator of history."[2]

Everything that has been created has been so through the Word and the Holy Spirit at the will of the Father, and everything that will be created will be done so in the same way. The Word and the Spirit have aptly been called the "two hands of the Father." Prophetic charisms empower us to proclaim God's word to people, situations, injustice, sickness, demonic forces, and all of creation.

Many Christian acts are possible with the aid of "ordinary" grace, but prophecy, like all true charisms, requires something more:

> The essential difference, then, between prophecy and any other kind of speaking by which the community can be built up is the element of inspiration that is proper to prophetic speech. In other words, the preacher or teacher has a habitual gift, which he can use at will; the prophet can only prophesy when he is inspired to do so.[3]

Prophecy is for "upbuilding and encouragement and consolation" (1 Corinthians 14:3) and to convince (14:24), instruct (14:31), direct (Acts 13:2), or predict (27:10). It comes in many forms and at various levels. But it is possible to distinguish two main kinds of prophecy, which have been described as inspirational and revelational.

---

2. Synod of Bishops, XII Ordinary General Assembly, The Word of God in the Life and Mission of the Church, 15, May 11, 2008, Vatican.va.
3. Sullivan, 101.

Inspirational prophecy

This is the kind of prophecy that is often heard in charismatic prayer meetings. It is usually simple and expresses something that is already known but endeavors to do so under the prompting and anointing of the Lord. For example, "I believe the Lord is saying, 'I love you, my children,'" or, "I feel the Lord is saying, 'I am with you.'" These truths are already known to us through Christian revelation, and consequently, some dismiss this kind of prophecy as humanly inspired, "regurgitating doctrine in a holy voice." I would not agree with this assessment.

Certainly at times such words have been of human origin, but I have been in meetings when prophecies of this kind were shared and they changed the atmosphere in the room. Somehow, as the words were spoken, people experienced the reality. "I am with you" became a revelation by experience of the presence of the Lord in that moment. Or "I love you, my children" caused this theoretically accepted doctrine to somehow drop from our brains into our hearts.

Such a word can also be experienced in spiritual direction, confession, general prayer ministry, and even in conversation. While by itself the word might seem unimpressive, it can have a genuine impact. For example, at a time when I was beginning to feel overwhelmed by all the miracles we were seeing, I had a chat with a holy nun named Teresa Clements. She simply said to me, "It's all God's work." From that moment, the burden lifted, and if ever those feelings returned, I simply repeated this phrase, and the burden was driven away.

This form of prophecy can therefore have great value. People need help to know how to discern what to share, when to share it, and how to share it, but prophecy of this nature can bear great fruits.

Revelational prophecy

Most people's experience of prophecy plateaus at the inspirational level. But as we have seen from our glance at prophecy in the history of the Church, there is another level. This we call "revelational prophecy," and it includes words of knowledge.

For example, the Lord gave me a word of prophecy for a friend who was an executive in a multinational company. As I prayed, the Lord showed me my friend's office and much of its layout, including a description of a distinct piece of furniture. I saw my friend praying in his office and sprinkling holy water around. The Lord was telling me to let my friend know that he was with him in this situation and pleased with these activities. My friend responded that just the previous day, he had blessed his office for the first time with holy water.

The Lord also showed me a young woman with fair hair. She was distressed, and the Lord told me why. He revealed that her name was Susan, and I saw her in a blue tailored jacket. I felt that the Lord wanted my friend, who was her boss, to speak to her about what the Lord told me she was feeling about a particular situation in her life. Having shared this with him, he informed me that there were two women with that name in his office, and both had fair hair. Neither had ever worn a blue tailored jacket to work. What was he to do?

The next morning, when I got back from morning Mass, I found a message on my voice mail. One of the "Susans" had arrived at work that day wearing a blue tailored jacket for the first time! My friend took her into his office and asked about the situation that the Lord had shown me as well as her feelings. In tears, she shared that the situation and her feelings were as the Lord had described, and my friend gave her the Lord's encouragement and reassurance. She left the conversation built up and consoled. May God be praised!

Sharing God's Knowledge, Heart, and Wisdom

When we train people how to be open to God's gift of revelational prophecy, we encourage them to remember that, at this level, we desire three things. These are the sharing of God's knowledge, his heart, and his wisdom. Here is a made-up prophecy showing very simply these three components:

First, the words of knowledge: "I received the name Tom and saw that you are an accountant. I felt that you have been struggling with feeling unvalued at work, and this has caused you to feel quite depressed."

Second, God's heart: "As I prayed, I sensed God's great love for you and that he has seen how conscientious you have been at work. I felt he wants to affirm you and encourage you, that even if others don't recognize your worth in this situation, your heavenly Father does. He cares deeply about you and will reward you for your hard work. So be encouraged: you are not alone in this situation; the Lord is with you."

Third, God's wisdom: "I sensed that the issue has its roots in your relationship with your boss. I think the Lord is inviting you to pray for him regularly, and you will see a change."

Sharing God's knowledge

The *Oxford English Dictionary* defines *knowledge* as "familiarity with facts." The supernatural revelation of facts and details, not learned by the natural mind, that we experience in revelational prophecy is often referred to as "words of knowledge." This term can also describe an inspired utterance given by the Holy Spirit that relates to some mystery of the faith in a preaching or teaching context. Both are legitimate uses of the phrase.

For our purposes, we use the term here in the first sense of factual information communicated to us by the Holy Spirit in the context of prophetic ministry. This gift, in the Catholic tradition, is known by various names: "the reading of hearts," "prophetic knowledge," or in some traditional books about the saints, "clairvoyance"—from the French, literally meaning "clear vision." The word simply means the faculty of "perceiving things or events in the future or beyond normal sensory contact." In a past, predominantly Christian culture, the term *clairvoyance* had little or no association with the occult. Today this word can be highly misleading because it has become almost entirely associated with mediums and the occult, so it is perhaps best avoided when referring to Christian prophecy.

Words of knowledge can be as detailed as a series of facts or as simple as one word. For example, I remember being given a woman's first name when ministering to a man. He was immediately convicted, remembering a sinful sexual encounter that he had never brought to the Lord in repentance.

If used in a humble and loving way, words of knowledge, in the sense of the supernatural knowledge of unknown facts, have two main fruits in Christian prophecy.

First, the person or group to whom the prophecy is directed realizes that what is being said is not from a human source. This gains their attention and increases their faith that God is speaking. And second, this has the effect of expanding the heart so that the next part of the prophecy—in which God communicates what he wants to say in order to build up, encourage, comfort, or guide the person—penetrates in a greater way.

Just last Thursday, a man came to one of our prophetic ministry appointments, and this is what the Lord showed me to share with him: "God told me a man named Stephen (I have changed his name to protect his identity) was coming today for prophetic ministry. You have been hoping for a relationship with a young woman; is her name Sarah or Anne? (Actually, it was Anna, which was close enough.) The Lord wants you to make sure that he is in the central place in your life, so that your other relationships bring you joy. He is also encouraging you to keep up your work with a (named) charity organization."

Imagine someone speaking to you who knows all these things about you: your name and the name of the woman you are interested in, the state of your desire, God's wisdom about the situation, the name of an organization you volunteer for, and the fact that this is pleasing to the Lord and part of his plan for your growth. It would amaze you. Invariably, people are shocked and deeply touched as they realize that the details of their lives matter enough to God that he would reveal them to others for their blessing.

Sharing God's heart

God, having raised faith and opened the heart of the person or group through words of knowledge, then reveals his heart toward them.

In some sense, this is the core of the prophecy. Without this part, which reveals the heart of God, the other parts of the prophecy lose much of their meaning. Here God can infuse into our hearts something from his heart, often deepening profoundly our sense of his love for us.

When I go to my doctor, he can by his knowledge diagnose what is right or wrong with me, and at the end of the appointment, he can give me wisdom about how I should act to improve my health. However, neither his knowledge nor his wisdom means he has a real love for me, only a professional concern. Supernatural knowledge and wisdom can be impressive and practically helpful, and we should pray for them, but without the heart element of prophecy, people can be left feeling that God is relating to them in an impersonal way rather than as his beloved children.

It is in this "heart" part of the prophecy that the depth of the relationship with God of the person prophesying can be revealed. If their relationship is superficial, the prophecy will reveal a certain shallowness or blandness at this point, which can result in a sense of emptiness. Sometimes the person speaking overcompensates for this lack of real depth by misguidedly attempting to supplement this deficiency with an overly emotional delivery, resulting in a sentimental prophecy that fails to penetrate the deep regions of the heart. That is not to say that emotions cannot be part of prophecy; they certainly can if the heart is truly involved.

When a person with a deep relationship with God speaks, the words burn in our hearts and often touch our deepest longings. I remember being at a pro-life rally where St. Mother Teresa was supposed to speak but was unable to attend. Instead, she had sent a recorded message. With a quarter of a million people in the park, a substantial number of police were present. There was a very large policeman standing just a few feet away from me, looking slightly threatening and detached.

As Mother Teresa's gentle voice, filled with God's love, echoed over the huge crowd and spoke about the beauty of the unborn child, I glanced across at the policeman. To my great surprise, I saw him choking up and trying to smother his emotion. Mother Teresa's words had prophetic power for him that day because they came straight from the heart of God, whom she knew and loved deeply. Time and time again, when people sense God's heart in prophecy, they are profoundly moved, very often to tears, joy, or a deep sense of God's presence.

Sharing God's wisdom

Wisdom has been defined as "the possession of experience and knowledge together with the power of applying them."[4] St. Paul includes the "word of wisdom" in his list in 1 Corinthians 12 (verse 8). It is important to distinguish here between ordinary wisdom and this particular gift of wisdom. It would be foolish to give a word of knowledge and then share your "ordinary" wisdom, assuming it to be God's will. This could be a good example of starting in the Spirit and ending in the flesh (Galatians 3:3).

Words of wisdom are not a permanent gift or a kind of abiding wisdom from life that one draws on. The word of wisdom is as supernatural as the word of knowledge. It is inspired by the Holy Spirit. While general wisdom is very helpful, this gift is different. It is the special gift of knowing precisely the right piece of wisdom from God for this person, at this time, for this situation. Not always exercised alongside words of knowledge, this gift can "stand alone."

My wife, Cathy, has a particular gift in this area. I was leading our Catholic Miracle Rally for the first time in another country. We were scheduled to

---

4. Petts, *Body Builders: Gifts to Make God's People Grow* (Mattersey, England: Mattersey Hall, 2002), 225.

have a large Miracle Healing Service as the climax of the event on Sunday, which would considerably swell the crowds. But on Saturday, the grace of healing was poured out in tremendous measure, and hundreds were healed. I phoned Cathy that night and shared this with her.

"What am I to do now? People are expecting many healings tomorrow, and the Lord seems to have healed most of the sickness today. How am I going to follow that?" Without a second's thought, Cathy replied: "You don't follow it; God does, and you follow God." Brilliant! I was freed in an instant, and the next day, God did great things.

The word of wisdom is a tremendous gift, and it completes and complements the word of knowledge and the prophecy of God's heart. Sharing these can be powerful, but without truly inspired wisdom or counsel, they often fail to bring the fruit God intends. God may tell me, for example, what your job is and what his heart is for you in this situation, but if he doesn't then give me a word of wisdom about that situation, you may have no idea of how to move forward.

What distinguishes Christian revelational prophecy is the combination of supernatural knowledge about a person, group, or situation; supernatural revelation of God's heart; and God's inspired wisdom, revealing how to move forward. This is a "complete" prophecy, but as we have said at times, the different parts may be given by different people or come at different times. However, it's good to be open for all three.

God has an objective for every prophecy, and it is important to try to grasp what this is when we prophesy.

How Does Prophecy Come?

There are a variety of ways that the Lord communicates with us. Catholic theology tells us that grace builds on or perfects nature.[5] Often the Lord uses our natural faculties to speak to us; and at other times, he raises the form of communication beyond these faculties, so that knowledge is infused or communicated directly to our spirits and bypasses our natural faculties.

Sometimes God speaks to us through our "seeing" faculty. This can be through everyday things, people, or events (Jeremiah 1:11-14) or through

---

5. St. Thomas Aquinas, *Summa Theologica*, , I, q. 1, art. 8, reply to obj. 2, newadvent.org/summa/1001.htm.

our imaginations. Some might receive a supernatural vision of an angel or one of the saints or the Lord himself. Mary (Luke 1:26-38), Cornelius (Acts 10:3-7), Peter (Acts 10:10-16), and Stephen (Acts 7:55-56) all experienced visions.

A vision might be of people or situations of the past, the present, or the future. Paul had a vision of a man beseeching him to go to Macedonia (Acts 16:9). Visions might happen with our eyes closed or open and might vary in intensity and clarity. Sometimes it's possible to see words or numbers, either in the mind's eye or with eyes open, as if you were reading a street sign. Sometimes we might see a symbolic picture in our minds that communicates something from the Lord.

If we receive a vision, we should seek an interpretation. On some occasions, this might come from another person or the one to whom we are ministering. At other times, the Lord might communicate through our hearing. This can on occasion be an audible voice, but more often it is an inner voice or message. At times the audible voice can sound like someone we know (1 Samuel 3). Often this voice can be as gentle as a whisper (1 King 19:11-13).

The Lord speaks to us through the Scriptures, and at times he can highlight a verse or section of the Bible that has remarkable power and relevance to a particular person, group, or situation. Sometimes people find they are prompted to open the Bible to a passage that confirms something the Lord is saying in other ways. At times the Lord shows me where to open the Bible and exactly where on the page to look before I open it. I then find there a passage of amazing relevance to the thing I am praying about.

Since I have moved to using a Bible on my phone, two new things have started to happen. Either I receive in my mind a chapter and verse, or I "see" written, on the wall or the floor, a verse of the Bible. When I look it up, the same thing happens: it speaks right into the presenting need.

The Bible also speaks of the Lord communicating through a prophecy in tongues. At times this can be in a known language and a translation is required, but usually it is in a "spiritual" language and, as Paul writes, an interpretation is required (1 Corinthians 14:27). Some prophecies come as simple impressions in the mind. Others appear in our dreams. Sometimes we just know something and don't know how we know it. We might receive information through our emotions or through feelings in our physical bodies.

At this level, there is also a kind of word of knowledge that, while less factually detailed, can speak deeply to the needs or aspirations of the individual or group. For a person who is struggling with loneliness, an inspired prayer may be given, such as "May you feel the company of the Lord with you always and know that you are never alone." Or in a time of particular temptation to despair, "May the Lord give you his hope and confidence for the future." Such inspired prayers about situations not known to the one ministering can often be "accidental," in that the person praying doesn't realize how appropriate his or her prayers are.

Three Elements of Prophecy

There are three parts to a prophecy. First, the information. This is what the Lord shows us, and it is important we don't jump to conclusions but make sure we grasp what the Lord is really showing us. Second is the interpretation. Often prophecy loses its power or gets disfigured at this point in the process, because people apply their own agendas or make assumptions rather than being attentive to the Lord's interpretation. Finally, the application. This tells us what we are to do about what God is telling us.

A good example that illustrates this process comes from a prophecy the Lord gave me when I was running the Charism School in Kenya. As usual, before the prophetic time, I had prayed over some of the names of those known to the hosts of the school. This was what I received for one of the men, about whom I knew nothing:

First, I saw him in a small building with a group of people praying and praising. The problem was, the roof of the building kept falling in. I could have stopped here and prophesied just this, but the Lord had taught me to give him time to finish all that he has to show me.

Then I saw a very large building being built, which was to be a center for preaching and teaching, praise and worship, Eucharistic adoration, and miracles. The Lord wanted this man to move from the small building to this new center. It would have been easy at this stage too to simply prophesy such a wonderful future, but God had something more crucial in the next what-to-do stage of the prophecy. He showed me that the man should not try to raise this building on his own but take this word to the leadership of the diocesan Catholic Charismatic Renewal and work with them on establishing the center.

The man's testimony was as follows. He and his team were meeting in a small building to worship, pray, and seek the Lord. It was true, as the prophecy had said, that the roof kept falling in. When he heard this detail, he knew that God was speaking very specifically to him, knowing his situation. He took the word about the new center very much to heart. He went to the diocesan leadership and shared the word with them, so they could work together on the project. They did not have the money or the land, but two weeks later, out of the blue, an elderly woman gave the Catholic Charismatic Renewal the gift of a large piece of land in the capital city. Money became available, and they began to build a center.

When I arrived in their city to lead the Charism School and Miracle Healing Service the following year, I found myself standing in the fulfillment of the Lord's word. Twelve hundred people attended the conference, and we had great times of praise and worship, adoration of the Blessed Sacrament, Holy Mass, and literally hundreds of healings. It was a very moving experience. God is so good!

At times, the three elements of prophecy—information, interpretation, and application—are not all received by the same person. It can be that one receives the information from the Lord in a word or picture or vision but doesn't understand it. Such was Peter's experience after his vision on the roof, in which he was told to "kill and eat" (Acts 10:13) and, "What God has cleansed, you must not call common" (10:15). Afterward he "was inwardly perplexed" (10:17). It required the confirmation of the messengers of Cornelius, arriving at that moment, and the testimony of Cornelius' encounter with the angel to give Peter the interpretation that then gave him the mandate to preach to Cornelius' Gentile household.

Effects of Prophecy

We have already seen some examples of the effects of prophecy, but often people don't realize how diverse the impact of the prophetic gifts can be for the advancement of the kingdom. Here are some examples.

Restore dignity and self-respect

Prophecy can restore people's dignity and self-respect, as it did for the woman at the well (John 4). The following is a true story of how the spirit of prophecy anointed a conversation in the streets of Uganda in a dramatic way.

A Christian man was driving across Uganda and stopped to get something to eat. A prostitute approached him and made him an offer of sex. "How much?" the man asked. "Five shillings," the woman answered. "Only five shillings?" the man replied, shocked. The woman looked at his surprised face and said, "Well, ten shillings, actually." "Only ten shillings?" the man exclaimed. "Thirty shillings then," the woman retorted. "Surely not only thirty," the man said. "Okay then, one hundred shillings." Then the man said, "But when I look at your beauty, I cannot think you are worth only that." "Well, how much do you think I'm worth?" she asked.

He took the woman by the hands and looked into her eyes and said, "Let me tell you how much you are worth. You are worth the life of Jesus, the priceless Son of God, who paid for you with his life on the cross, and you are worth everything to him. Can I pray for you?" The woman agreed, and as he prayed, she wept and gave her life to Jesus. Then she immediately went back to her room, picked up her few belongings, and left with the Christian man. They drove to another town, where he connected her with Christians. Today she works in a ministry saving other women from prostitution.

That man allowed the Spirit to inspire him prophetically, and his words carried the power of the kingdom into the woman's broken life. Those words redefined her; they built a road to freedom for her; they created a new future for her in Jesus. This is the power of the prophetic gift.

Bring correction or warning

We see correction and warning in the ministry of many prophets. Perhaps Jonah is the best known for his warning to Nineveh. But such warnings can be granted to Christians today. Here is a modern example coming from a man with a strong prophetic ministry.

Shawn Bolz was granted a meeting with a dictator in a certain country because a relative of the dictator knew him. During the conversation, Shawn said, "[God] told me that he wouldn't help you with this," and then shared a set of words that he did not understand. As he did so, the leader abruptly told him to stop speaking and made everyone except his closest aides leave the room. He asked how Shawn knew the code words for a military action. Shawn shared that God had told him, and then he began to share another very personal word with the leader, bringing him to tears at the revelation of God's mercy and forgiveness.[6] Needless to say, the proposed military action was cancelled.

Reveal sin

Sometimes the Lord can reveal to us people's sins. This is an area of prophetic ministry that requires tremendous delicacy, compassion, and humility. I strongly recommend that if this particular kind of revelation begins to operate in your life, you should beg God that you would see your own sins more clearly than those of others, that you might "in humility count others better than [yourself]" (Philippians 2:3). Pray too to become skilled in recognizing the virtues of others more easily than their sins. If handled with humility and love, this kind of revelation can be very helpful and even vital for some people, as we saw in the lives of saints like St. Pio and St. John Bosco.

There are people alive today who have this gift in a big way. Our experience is very poor in comparison, but it does happen now and then. When it happens, we keep in mind that we could be mistaken, so we only share with caution, in a way that protects the dignity of the individual. If we have judgment in our hearts, it is possible that we can end up suffering from the same sinful issues we were sent to help resolve. As Jesus warns us, "Judge not, that you be not judged" (Matthew 7:1).

Provide an agenda for prayer

Prophecy can provide an inspired agenda for prayer, especially for intercession or when ministering to others. In our ministry, it is common for us to pray together before an event, and often we receive guidance about what the Lord plans to do. Sometimes he will show us details about the building we will be in and problems to look out for or opportunities to make the most of. Sometimes the Lord can really inspire us in our personal prayer to know what to pray for and how to intercede. Someone might come to mind, and a need might be made known. Or we might be assured of a particular answer to a prayer we are making.

---

6. Shawn Bolz, *Translating God: Hearing God's Voice for Yourself and the World around You* (Glendale, CA: New Type Publications, 2015), 55–57.

A lady living in America wrote to me on Facebook, explaining that she was thirty-eight years old and had been trying to have a baby for years. Sadly, although she had conceived three times, she had never been able to keep the baby beyond a few weeks. I sent her a message encouraging her to make a good confession for any sexual sins she might have committed, and when she had done this, I would pray.

The woman soon contacted me to say she had done what I had asked. So in December 2014, I wrote to her that I had prayed that the Lord would give her a healthy baby by December 2015. Later she and her husband attended our Healing Signs and Wonders Conference in Washington, D.C., with their beautiful baby girl, who had been born in December 2015, just as the Lord had said. In fact, her birthday was December 8, the feast of the Immaculate Conception.

Bring an anointing to preaching

Prophecy also opens up the Scriptures and brings an anointing to teaching and preaching (Ephesians 3:4-5). If preachers and teachers open themselves to the inspiration of the Holy Spirit in the preparation and delivery of their message, then there is the possibility of an inspired prophetic dimension or anointing on those occasions. Thus we sometimes speak of "prophetic teaching" or "prophetic preaching." In our experience, this causes the content of the message to be more dynamic, to have more impact, and to speak more precisely to the hearts and needs of those present.

Alternatively at times, when I am in the middle of preaching or teaching, I find myself saying something quite inspired that I had never thought of before, and I can sense it touching people in a special way. Something changes that brings fervor to the preaching as my heart, and those of my listeners, is illuminated or inflamed by the words. Glory to God!

Evangelize

Prophecy can facilitate evangelistic breakthroughs by helping us know who to approach, what to share, and how to share it.

When I was at college, I had my first experience of this. In prayer one day, the Lord showed me a young student who was trapped in an extremely depraved lifestyle. The Lord instructed me to challenge him lovingly about this and invite him to change his life. I was very nervous, so I told the Lord that I'd only speak to the student if he came and sat right opposite me that day in the large, busy refectory, something he had never done, as we hardly knew each other. I sat a long way from the serving area and kept my head down.

Needless to say, to my dismay the young man walked past all his friends, planted himself in the chair opposite me, and struck up a conversation. After some time, I gathered all my courage and lovingly shared what the Lord had told me. At that moment, change began in his life.

A short while later, I was at Mass, and the Lord told me someone would approach me after Mass, and I was to invite the person to a Life in the Spirit Seminar. After Mass this young man spoke to me, so I invited him. His experience at the seminar totally changed his life. His conversion sent reverberations around the college because he was so well known. For thirty years since, he has continued to serve the Church, on fire with a radical love for Jesus.

Identify gifts and callings

Prophecy can also identify or confirm a particular gift or a calling.

Some years ago, we were in Denmark running a small conference. I had asked for a list of the names of the participants so my team could pray over the names and see if the Lord might give us a prophecy for anyone. At a certain point quite early on in the conference, I invited my team to minister prophetically with what they had received. One of them came forward and asked, "Is Niklas here?"

Niklas duly rose from his seat. The team member proceeded to reveal to him what the Lord had shown her. Her word was simple and undramatic: "I see you feeling like an outsider. The Lord is inviting you to come into the fold." Another person then prophesied, "You have a calling to leadership and leading teams, and God is going to use you in teaching ministry."

None of us knew the young man or anything about him, but we later discovered that he was the only non-Catholic in the group. His wife was Catholic, and they had found their home in the Catholic Charismatic Renewal. But as he has since explained, "For me, 'Come into the fold' could only mean one thing—to join the Catholic Church." This word ended a protracted debate he had been having with himself on the subject, and not long afterward, he became a Catholic.

Within a couple of years, this man and his family left Denmark and joined Cor et Lumen Christi, living full-time for the Lord in one of the community houses. The second part of the prophecy, about the gift of leadership, was also fulfilled, as he was elected leader of the house, a position he held for nine years. He continues to serve on our national team. He also saw the fulfillment of the prophecy about teaching gifts, and he regularly runs teaching conferences.

When Niklas received the prophecy, he was a new Christian with no settled church family and no ministry. Prophecy changed his life and empowered him to step into his calling. Today it is a common occurrence for us to know through the gift of prophecy what a person's ministry is or is going to be in the Church or in the world.

Bring healing, praise, and perseverance in battle

Prophecy can give insight for inner healing and bring healing. It is common when praying for people to receive the revelation of a situation that the Lord desires to heal (Matthew 8:5-13).

Prophecy can motivate repentance or praise in a gathering (1 Corinthians 14:24-25), and it can restore faith, as we see in the ministries of Elijah and John the Baptist.

It can also greatly help us to persevere in the battle. St. Paul exhorts Timothy: "This charge I commit to you, Timothy, my son, in accordance with the prophetic utterances which pointed to you, that inspired by them you may wage the good warfare" (1 Timothy 1:18). Jesus knew the prophecies of the Old Testament that referred to him, and he regularly pointed to these. Do we know the prophetic promises of the Scriptures about ourselves? Every promise of Jesus that is given for "believers" is a prophecy for each of us, and we need to learn how to engage with these statements of Jesus in faith so as to inherit all that he has prepared for us.

I was given a lot of prophecies from well-known and highly gifted people, as well as unknown people, about the gifts of miracles and healings the Lord wanted to release in my life. Every time I am preparing for a Miracle Healing Service or a time of major ministry, I get these out and pray over them, and they greatly strengthen my expectant faith.

Cautions Regarding Prophecy

St. Paul exhorts all to prophesy (1 Corinthians 14:1-5), and he is adamant that prophecy should be integrated into Christian gatherings and liturgy (14:26). He is aware, however, that a prophecy's meaning can at times be unclear and even on occasion false, so the Church is encouraged to "weigh what is said" (14:29).

While there are true prophecies and false ones, there is also another category that I would describe as "pious sharings." These utterances are attempts at prophecy that do not come from a false spirit but are really just the pious thoughts of the individual. Unless these are doctrinally misleading, they are normally harmless in themselves. They are often the result of poor teaching on prophecy, or they come in an initial stage of prophecy, when a person in good faith takes a risk with what he or she thinks might be a prophecy. Such persons should not be crushed for their mistakes. Rather, they should be encouraged to see how to improve and grow. Sometimes it is not the content that needs correcting but the presentation or the timing. Leaders need to discern the difference between people of goodwill and humility who want to learn and those with other motives.

"Pious sharings," as I have said, cause little harm if given by teachable beginners. These cause problems when they become established as a pattern in a person or a group. In such cases, people are not helped to grow past this stage, and they get stuck. This can be because of ignorance or because of a refusal to be corrected.

With groups or individuals for whom this form of sharing has become habitual, real harm can come about, because genuine prophecy is drowned by pious sharings not inspired by God. New people come into the situation and, after a time, seeking to be open to what they think is a form of prophetic utterance, simply imitate the poor example they have seen modeled. Such groups do not progress, as the vague and bland words they share do not challenge, comfort, or build them up.

While there are exceptions, as we see in the lives of some prophets, most people's gifts of prophecy start out fairly immature and develop over time. Key to growing in this gift is to receive good teaching and experience good models from those more mature in prophecy than we are. I have found that with this gift, as with others, there are a few keys to experiencing a breakthrough, some of which are outlined in the section "Preparation for Prophecy" below. I would only add here that St. Paul makes a distinction in the levels of prophesying. He writes, "Let two or three prophets speak, and let the others weigh what is said. If a revelation is made to another sitting by, let the first be silent. For you can all prophesy one by one, so that all may learn and all be encouraged" (1 Corinthians 14:29-31). Perhaps he refers here to general prophetic exhortation in comparison to an intervention of the Spirit in a more dramatic way.

Many people have an idea that Jesus would only say nice things to them and that anything challenging and demanding can't be from God. The problem with this attitude is that it finds no validation anywhere in Scripture. We can't receive the "blessing" prophecies very deeply if we are not willing to receive the "change your life" prophecies. If we foster a culture in which prophecy is just about giving people spiritual sweets, real prophecy will die, and people will fail to grow. If we want God's word to really come with life-giving power and authority, we have to give the Lord freedom to say what he pleases.

In the Old Testament, many so-called prophets simply prophesied words that their kings and masters wanted to hear rather than the word from the Lord. It's helpful to remember that both blessing and challenging prophecies are actually blessing prophecies in their own ways. But without integrity in our groups and ministries in this regard, even the blessing prophecies will fail to bless us.

Self-control in prophecy

Many groups have no protocol to facilitate and discipline the practice of prophecy, and from time to time, we come across people who feel that disciplines in this area are just means to control the prophetic people and quench the freedom of the Spirit. But as anyone who has been ministering in prophecy fruitfully over many years will know, it is a highly disciplined ministry that requires great care in what, how, when, and to whom prophecies are given.

At times we have seen people prophesy at the wrong time in a meeting or other situation. They often justify their actions by telling us that they had some confirming manifestation in their bodies; for instance, their heart was beating rapidly or they began feeling great heat. We regard such manifestations as secondary, and even if at times they are authentic indications (not proof) that the Spirit is wanting to speak through a person, this in no way frees the person from adhering to the disciplines of the group and the authority of the leadership.

Some people say they "had" to prophesy. This is a mistake. St. Paul makes it quite clear that we are perfectly able to control the exercise of prophecy: "The spirits of prophets are subject to prophets" (1 Corinthians 14:32). Those who refuse to follow this discipline should, in my opinion, be kindly but firmly asked to be quiet. If they cannot submit to leaders who are responsible for the direction of the meeting, they should not be exercising the gift in that context (Hebrews 13:17). On the other hand, leaders should not be too heavy-handed but find ways to encourage prophecy, realizing its power to bring life and dynamism. In my experience, unhelpful "prophetic" sharings are usually results of poor formation, not bad will or a spirit of false prophecy.

What if it's strange?

On occasion, what comes to us can seem strange, but let me say right away that "weird" should not be normal. I witnessed some amusing attempts at prophecy in prayer groups in the 1980s, which were possibly more the results of people's indigestion and vivid imaginations than the Holy Spirit. Even so, sometimes real prophecies can seem strange. Especially when we are learning about prophecy, we should proceed with caution.

On one occasion, I was leading a Miracle Healing Service, and I looked to my right, "saw" a man dressed in a Batman outfit, and received the name "George" plus some information and encouragement about his life and work. I pointed at where he was standing in the crowd (although I did not know exactly which man it was), and said, "I see a man dressed in a Batman costume and the name George," and then I delivered a word of encouragement to him about his life and his work situation.

The following day, a man gave a testimony about the word and its impact upon him. Apparently, as the first line of the prophecy was given, his wife nudged him in the ribs and said, "That's you, honey." Batman had been his favorite superhero as a boy, and he continued to be a fan in adulthood. He had an ongoing Batman theme running in his family. For example, if he asked the kids to do a chore or get up in the morning, he did so in a Batman voice for fun.

The name George was not his real name but did have great significance for him. He was born on the birthday of President George Washington, and his family used to call him "Little George." Had I called out his real name, he could have thought I had noticed this on his conference name badge beforehand, but he knew for certain when I began to speak that these details were without a doubt unknown to me naturally. He knew that these words of knowledge could only apply to one person in that congregation, and I was pointing at him.

Youth is no disqualification

The Lord is eager to release his gift of prophecy and knowledge to those who want to be instruments of love in this way, even to those who are very young. So we should be careful not to make youth a disqualification.

My son, who was eighteen years old at the time, had already been used powerfully in prophetic knowledge. At the request of my daughter, who was fourteen, he agreed to help her be open to prophetic words of knowledge. He got her to pray over the names of the people in his small group, whom she did not know. She wrote something down that she felt God had told her about each person. When he shared these with the members of the small group a day or two later, they were deeply touched, as many of the words she had received were very appropriate and accurate, even about events in their lives.

Growing in the Word of Knowledge Gifts

I remember leading our Prophecy School in Africa, and as usual, part of the school involved the team prophesying over particular people whose names the hosts had given us. When I came to prophecy over a particular woman, I gave the small words I had, and then out of the blue, as I was looking at her, I just knew a stream of things about her. I prophesied over her virtually nonstop for almost fifteen minutes, with no need to stop and think.

I have had long prophetic words for people before with lots of knowledge, but this was quite different. It was like no other experience I had had before. The only way I can describe it is that it was as though I was simply describing a person I already knew. In that moment, I understood how saints like Padre Pio could operate continuously at this level of revelation without having to stop for breath or even try to tune in for revelation.

While I was prophesying, a priest standing against the left-hand wall began to weep. Afterward he approached me, and I asked him if he was okay. He answered that he was weeping because he had spent an hour with the woman that afternoon, and she had poured out her life to him. In the prophecy, I had spoken precisely about many of the things she had shared with him. He was overcome by the grace of God for her. I could only thank and praise the Lord.

Because of the power of prophecy with words of knowledge, we have trained people around the world how to be open and respond to this gift. Following my experience when praying over names, we established an appointment system for personal prophetic ministry (free, of course). Our teams are only told the gender of the person coming and nothing more. They pray, and at the appointment, they share what they have received.

People have been amazed and profoundly blessed. They say things like "It was Jesus speaking to me when you spoke" or "You spoke truths right back to my childhood." Often the revelation is amazingly accurate, down to the knowledge of items of clothing the person will be wearing, aspects of their appearance, what their jobs are, details about their families and ministries, and so forth. Here is one testimony of a person who came to such an anonymous appointment with my team:

> On April 10, 2015, I experienced being prophesied over by a group of people from Cor et Lumen Christi who had prayed for me prior to our meeting without knowing anything about me. . . . The first lady described how, as she had prayed, she had seen a big bloke in Texan gear and checkered shirt who was outwardly confident—which described my attire and demeanor very accurately. She then proceeded to speak into my inner life and childhood wounds and tell how the love of God would build me up again, which I was totally open to, considering her previous words! She also spoke into my gifting, particularly how the Lord was building me up in the prophetic and in areas of evangelization, which happened to be my full-time work.
>
> Finally, she shared a word in regard to the Lord blessing my resources, which made no sense at the time, as I was in no particular need. However, six months later, I found myself moving out of the community I was a part of, getting married, and taking on a new evangelization role, where I was blessed abundantly in regard to resources—far more than I could have asked or imagined.
>
> The next man proceeded to share how he had seen me working with young people, and that the Lord was giving me a new

creativity to reach them. As I worked in schools and led a youth ministry, this was pretty accurate!

The final prophecy spoke of me as a teacher but not in a school, which again described my full-time work. He then described a vision of Christmas lights being draped around the land and me plugging them in. The lights represented people or small groups, and he started to see a growth in the light as well as new sockets, representing centers of evangelization starting to evolve around the land. This was deeply encouraging, as it very much aligned with a vision that was developing on my heart as well as in reality, in which young people were being discipled all over the nation through specific hubs. From those hubs, they would then be sent into their localities and therefore light up the nation.

Receiving names

In the last couple of weeks, while I've been writing this book, we have tried to be open to the Lord showing us people's names in prophecy more frequently. This is not so we can show off. Jesus knew the names of people he encountered, as did many of the saints. When this happens, it has an amazing impact on the person, allowing the power of the prophecy to immediately reach the person's heart.

An interesting thing happened just the other day. My wife and I were on our way to have dinner with some friends when a name dropped into my head, then an image of a young blonde woman in her mid-twenties, and finally some information that would encourage her. After the meal, I asked my friends, "Do you know anyone named Mary?"

They said they knew two people with that name. "This one has blonde hair," I said. The husband then got out his phone and showed me a photo of a young woman. I recognized her as the woman I had seen in my mind's eye and shared the word about her I'd received.

After chatting about this, suddenly another name dropped into my mind: Charlotte. I saw a woman with brown hair who had musical gifts and led worship. I then received some information about prayer and worship in her life, and the prophecy concluded with this: "Married life can be a life of worship through love. Saw your family home, a place thick with God's presence, because of the prayer and worship that happened there."

These friends knew a young woman named Charlotte with brown hair who had musical gifts and led worship. Amazingly, she had gotten married only the day before!

Immediately afterward, I received yet another name—Mark—with a lot of accompanying information. Many of the facts about him our hosts could confirm as correct; others they didn't know. This was all a bit strange for me, as it was an experience I had never had before.

I was then prompted to run an optional gathering for some of our community, to share my experience and to see if the Lord might do the same for some of my brothers and sisters. After a bit of sharing, we had a workshop to listen for names and facts about people we did not know in the lives of the prayer partner we had been paired with. People listened to the Lord for five minutes and wrote down what came to them. Of the twenty-two people present, thirteen received a person's name and accurate factual information about the person as well as a word of encouragement, edification, or consolation. For all but two participating, this was a totally new experience.

That morning I was astonished that, in five minutes, I received thirteen words of knowledge, including two people's names and details about them. One of these names was Sajin, a name I had never heard of, and the Lord also showed me the man's face. For the second person, the Lord showed me his first and second name and his profession. These prophecies will now be recorded as short films and sent to the people they were about, to encourage them.

How exactly this gift will develop, I can only guess. But its impact on people has been tremendous. To have the experience of God revealing one's name as well as details about one's life to a total stranger, who then brings a word of love and encouragement from God, is an awesome thing. Even though I have been using the word of knowledge for many years, to suddenly experience such a leap into a new level is rather shocking and wonderful, for which I can only praise God.

Preparation for Prophecy

The Church needs people who can powerfully share God's prophetic word with others. We can prepare ourselves in many ways to grow in the gift of prophecy. Here is what I have found most helpful in assisting others to develop this gift.

Ongoing exposure to prophetically gifted people

Nothing seems to ignite the desire for this gift more than experiencing its operation in mature prophetic people as they minister either to others or to ourselves. I remember the first time I witnessed a mature gift of prophecy being exercised with revelational knowledge; it left me astonished because of its incredible impact on people. Getting alongside such people is always the best way to learn.

Prayer

We need to love God for himself in prayer more than for his gifts. Without this principle in place, none of our motivations have a safe foundation, and the ministry, however gifted, will in time go astray. It is possible for people to have tremendous gifts yet show near to nothing of the face or character of God. People are hungry for the heart of God, and we can only speak out of the heart of God if we ourselves have spent time in his heart in prayer.

Meditation on God's truth

We need to spend time meditating on God's truth and his ways so that our prophesying is rooted in the word of God and the teachings of the Church. Meditation helps us to put on the mind of Christ (Philippians 2:5). If we don't learn to live in the truth of revelation, we will be in danger of having our prophecy infected with error. The prophets, rather than simply studying truth, had a personal relationship with him who is Truth. For this to become a reality in our lives, we need to learn how to engage with the Scriptures as a prayerful dialogue with the living Persons of the Trinity, Father, Son, and Holy Spirit.

Praying in tongues

Experience tells us that praying in tongues can greatly assist in "tuning in" to God's prophetic word and liberating our spirits. This can happen in a fairly short time, even a few seconds. At times, however, I have been prompted to pray in tongues for extended times, once for three hours. Whenever this has happened, it has been the prelude to a special release of prophetic knowledge.

Praise

Some find that praise, even simple repetition of phrases of praise, can help to attune our spirits to what God wants to say. We have found that praise and worship of God often release prophetic gifts. Free praise is something many have not experienced, but it was an intrinsic experience of the early Church (Ephesians 5:19). For nine hundred years, times were allotted to it in the Mass in the Western Church.[7]

Desire to prophesy

One might think it unnecessary to state that we need to desire to prophesy. Even so, it has been the experience of many in this ministry that we often simply forget to open up to prophecy, and opportunities pass us by. People lose their desire to prophesy for two reasons: either they have had a bad experience and felt rejected or misunderstood, or they have forgotten the critical and life-giving place God desires prophecy to have in the life of the Church and what incredible fruits can result.

For many years, I did not care that much about prophesying because the manifestations of prophecy I had witnessed were not very powerful and their fruits were limited. But once I saw truly inspirational and revelational prophecy, my desire to prophesy completely changed. I then prayed and sought it earnestly.

Expectation

Our expectation of prophecy depends a great deal on our theology in this area. If our theology informs us that God doesn't often speak prophetically today, we are not likely to expect much prophetic activity in ourselves. If, however, we have the theology of the New Testament, our expectations for the regular manifestation of the prophetic gifts, like St. Paul's, will be high.

It is our experience that this gift can be stirred up by clear teaching and the creation of a faith environment. This is not to say that we can switch the gift on and off with certainty. Rather, very often when we open up to it and actively seek its manifestation, God is there, pressing in with his word

7. Eddie Ensley goes into great detail on the history of this gift in *Sounds of Wonder: A Popular History of Speaking in Tongues in the Catholic Tradition* (New York: Paulist, 1977).

of light and love. Therefore we can step out with strong expectations and confidence.

Thanksgiving

We need to thank the Lord for his grace in prophecy in the past and give him praise. This protects our humility, which in turn guards the anointing. It is very easy to become forgetful about thanksgiving, but if this becomes a habit, forgetfulness in thanksgiving can lead to presumption, and presumption to pride.

Rejoicing over others' successes

Be aware of envy; we all have it in some measure. Envy is sorrow at another's blessing. Sometimes we experience envy of another's gift. A good solution is to pray for genuine joy at the blessing and gifting of others.

Often what we envy is the recognition and praise that people receive for their gifts. Many of our motives are not as pure as we'd like, and it is important to acknowledge this. It has been my experience that as I seek to mobilize others in the gifts, God trusts me with more anointing.

Honesty

Do not exaggerate. A person called to prophecy is a minister of God's truth. Exaggeration is a distortion of the truth; it is a lie. God will trust us to minister in prophecy only if we are careful in our handling of the truth.

Motivation

Test your motivation. What is driving you to prophesy? Is it a desire to be seen or heard or to impose your opinion, or a desire to serve? Personal agendas need to be set aside ruthlessly if we wish to do good and not harm. Ensure you are motivated by love (1 Corinthians 14:1).

Reflection

It is very helpful to reflect on past experiences of prophecy that have been accurate and anointed, fruitful and life giving, and prophecy that perhaps has not. It is critical to admit when we have made mistakes and not sweep them under the carpet; we must learn from them. Sometimes as we reflect, a pattern emerges, and we can weed out things that cause problems for us. If we do not take the time to reflect on our practice and its results, we will not mature, and our effective prophesying will remain occasional at most.

Purity

It seems that personal purity plays a big part in this ministry. "Happy are the pure in heart, for they shall see God" (cf. Matthew 5:8). This is broader than sexual purity, but sexual purity does seem to be especially important in the deepening of this gift. If we want the Lord to trust us with revelational prophecy that brings God's knowledge, heart, and wisdom into people's lives, we need to pursue purity in a serious way and cut off opportunities for the devil to make inroads into our lives in this area.

Repentance

It is important to try to keep our hearts clean if we are going to prophesy. Known unrepented sin can be a real block and cause confusion. We need to repent of the ways we have ignored God's voice in our own lives and or casually disregarded it on many occasions. We need to face up to those times when we knew in our hearts that God was speaking to us and we turned away.

It is also important that we regularly examine how we have handled the word of God in our relations and ministries. What are the sins of our day-to-day speech—things that should not come from the same mouth that prophesies? These are all questions I have to regularly ask myself and by which I am often convicted.

A Model for Ministering

When seeking to prophesy to individuals, keep these steps in mind:

- Pray.

- Be open to God's knowledge.

- Be open to God's heart.

- Be open to God's wisdom.

- Offer the message you have received in humble love with faith.

- Pray for the person, group, or situation if possible or appropriate.

- Praise and thank God.

Delivery

I only want to say a few things about the delivery of prophecy. First, in general, offer what you receive rather than imposing it, because you could be wrong. Second, try to ensure that you get the timing right, because some prophecies are not to be shared immediately.

Third, do your best to get the right person. Amusingly, Ananias seemed to assume that God couldn't possibly be referring to Saul when he told him to go and restore his sight (Act 9:13, 14). And in looking for God's anointed, Samuel, upon seeing Jesse's son Eliab, assumed, "Surely the Lord's anointed is before him." One after the other, the Lord rejected Jesse's sons. Only on seeing David did the Lord say, "This is he" (1 Samuel 16:6-13).

Now, you may ask, how does one achieve these three goals? All I can say is, through prayer and not jumping to conclusions. Take time to ask the Lord questions about what you receive, and with humble perseverance and a teachable heart, by God's grace, you will improve. If you get a challenging word, for example, check that it's not for yourself first before assuming it's for some other poor sinner!

It is also generally advisable to avoid introducing your prophecies with phrases like, "Thus says the Lord," especially when you are learning. Much better to say, "This is what I sense," or, "I think the Lord might be saying such and such." If your prophecy has the Lord's anointing, it won't need any hype.

Also try to avoid the "pious voice." Speak the word in the spirit of the content. In other words, if it is about peace, speak in peace. If it is about strength, speak with strength. If it is about joy, speak with joy. Allow God's heart to fill your heart for the person. If the prophecy is given with sensitivity to the Holy Spirit, it will carry the presence of Jesus.

We should avoid being negative or judgmental or using prophecy to control people or impose our own agendas. We should ruthlessly weed out any attitudes of manipulation. Even—and perhaps especially—if we have a difficult word to bring (which should normally be rare), people should feel loved, as far as it is in our power to help them feel so.

How to respond to prophecy

Our basic response to prophecy in the Church should be one of openness but not naiveté. God wants to speak, and we should expect prophecy to be normal in God's Church. Scripture gives us excellent advice: "Do not despise prophesying, but test everything; hold fast what is good" (1 Thessalonians 5:20-21). If we feel that something is from the Lord, then we must do as Mary did and ponder "all these things" in our hearts (Luke 2:19, 51).

An Extraordinary Story of Prophetic Guidance

Many years ago, I was in my brother's bedroom with a few members of our small prayer group, when all of a sudden, my brother felt that the Lord wanted to give our little group the pope's blessing. It seemed utterly ridiculous, but we tried to believe, telling ourselves that anything is possible. As time passed, this idea receded, and we got on with other things.

Then, two or three years later, when praying I began to feel that it was time for me to go to Rome and receive Pope John Paul II's personal blessing for the two young people's prayer groups. As I sat in the chapel and prayed about this feeling, I sensed the Lord prompting me to turn over the book in front of me. When I turned it over, I saw that the text was about Rome. "Probably a coincidence," I thought. After a few more minutes, I felt the Lord prompting me to get up and read an open Bible that was sitting on one of the pews at the front of the chapel. I was surprised to see that the only heading on the page was "Paul travels to Rome."

Later, as I was leaving the chapel, a deacon friend of mine entered and said, "Damian, I woke up this morning and felt that I had to tell you to go to Rome." (I had not told anyone what I was thinking or what the Lord had been showing me.) We decided to go for a walk and talk it over. As we were strolling across the park, the Lord drew my attention to a small piece of crumpled-up paper on the grass, which I picked up. Opening it, I saw that it had text upon it that was all about Rome. The combination of these signs was enough to persuade me to go.

I informed my friends that I was going to Rome to meet the pope and receive his personal blessing. I had already bought a European rail pass to travel to a shrine. From there I would go and attempt to see the pope. I had no appointment but was trusting God to find a way.

Once I had packed, I realized that I had no money to get into London to catch my train to the coast, where I would catch a boat to France. (Suburban trains weren't covered on my European rail pass.) I searched through every square inch of my possessions and clothes, including the pockets of the denim jacket I was wearing. I could not withdraw money from the bank because I had no overdraft facility on my account. How was I to get to London?

I stopped and prayed. Then I put my hand again in the small left chest pocket of my jacket and discovered three one-pound coins. I was absolutely stunned, since I had just checked that pocket. But in a few moments, I came to my senses, grabbed my bag, and hurried to the station.

When I arrived in London, I went straight to the platform for my train, which was leaving in just a few minutes. As I got on the train, I was shocked to discover that all the rail-pass seats had been taken, and the only seats left required a reservation. I was told I had to go to the ticket office and pay £1.80 to purchase a reserve seat! I didn't have £1.80. I ran to the ticket office.

When I arrived at the counter, I said to the ticket seller, "They tell me I have to reserve a seat on my train that's leaving in two minutes, but I don't have any money. Listen, I'm going to a shrine where miraculous things are happening, and then I'm going to Rome to meet the pope, but I have no money." (Remember, this is England, where 93 percent of the people don't go to church.) The guy looked back at me and said, "Okay, here's your ticket, no charge." I ran back to the train, making it by seconds.

After ten days at the shrine, I traveled to Rome, where I stayed with a new community. At the end of my stay, nothing had materialized regarding the pope, so I just assumed that I had been mistaken. The head of the community house reserved seats for my trains back to the French coast, where I would catch the boat to England. I arrived at the Rome terminal that afternoon, only to discover that my train had been triple booked! I spent the next hour or so trying to reserve seats on the five trains needed to get me across Europe.

In the end, I sat down on the floor of the terminal feeling very frustrated and prayed. Out of the blue I heard—I can't say how—"Sleep in St. Peter's Piazza tonight." Really? The word went deep in me, but I felt I needed some confirmation. So I prayed that the Lord would confirm it through the Scriptures. After praying, I opened my Bible at random. When I looked down, to my amazement I saw the heading "Paul remains in Rome." I closed my Bible and prayed for further confirmation. I opened again and looked down, and my eyes fell on "Go up to the holy city." So I obeyed.

As I walked into St. Peter's Square, it was already dark. Everything was silent except for a group of young people sitting on the ground, quietly singing worship songs. I approached them and stood nearby. When they finished, a young man from the group stood up and greeted me. We chatted a little, and I told him my story about coming to Rome hoping to meet the pope for his blessing. He then casually said to me, as one might tell someone the time, "Oh, we have a spare ticket to see the pope tomorrow. Would you like it?" At these words, it felt like something shifted in the universe. Awe fell on me, and looking to heaven, I threw up my arms and began shouting God's praises at the top of my voice. Everyone in the group stared at me in surprise.

In an instant, I saw all those funny little signs in their true light—they had truly been from almighty God. My reaction may seem strange to you, but you have to remember that, while these signs did give a growing sense that God wanted to do something, I still had to walk in faith, and it was possible that I had misunderstood them. Now, however, I grasped how radically I had been walking in the precise will of God. That night I prayed and slept in my sleeping bag on the cobbles of St. Peter's Piazza, as the Lord had instructed me.

I had assumed that I would attend an intimate meeting of about thirty or so people with the pope. But when the following morning we waited in a long queue and then entered the Paul VI Audience Hall next to St. Peter's Basilica, I realized that I was going to be one of six thousand, all desperate to meet the pope. The young people told me their seats were three rows from the front on the right, but I felt a prompting to go to another part of the seating area, toward the back and next to the middle aisle. I went there and sat down on the floor in the foot space of someone else's seat. I promptly fell asleep.

Finally, after a long wait, the pope came onto the stage, a small white figure who seemed miles away. After preaching, he descended the stairs and walked right in the direction of the young people. Seeing my empty seat next to them, I started to severely reprimand myself: "You fool! Don't you think God knows how to give you the right seat to fulfill his plans? Who do you think you are? Why did you think you knew better than God?"

But suddenly the pope changed direction, turning away from the area where my empty seat was before reaching it. He slowly made his way to the middle aisle. He was coming. "Oh, no!" I thought. "Now he's crossing over to the other side." Then he crossed back again. He gradually made progress, crisscrossing up the aisle while I had my heart in my mouth. Would he come all the way? Was he going to cross back to my side? If not, should I leap over the barrier?

I was praying desperately any way I knew how. There was a sudden clambering of bodies around me, and a mass of Italian and Spanish ladies piled up behind me. Before my conversion, I had had a similar experience of being crushed in the front row at an AC/DC rock concert, but I hadn't really expected something similar for the pope.

Finally, he was back on my side and only yards away. "Stay on this side, stay on this side," I prayed. And then, all of a sudden, Pope St. John Paul II was standing in front of me. I wasn't going to miss my chance now, so without a thought, I grabbed him by both his arms (he didn't even flinch) and cried, "John Paul, John Paul, will you give me your blessing for our young people's prayer groups?"

He looked at me, then lifted his hand and laid it on my head, stood still in silent prayer, and took his time. With all the noise and cheering, there was a moment of silence between us. He must have prayed for almost a minute, which in that context seemed a long time. Then he made the Sign of the Cross on my forehead and said in English, with his Polish accent, "God bless you," and he slowly moved on.

I was left in a kind of bubble for a few seconds, and then something quite unexpected happened. A kind of power started bolting through my body. It did not feel like electricity or anything like that, but the effect was that I was bounced up and down very quickly with tremendous force, so my feet were coming off the ground, more than a foot in the air. I was quite unable to stop this. I had never experienced anything like it before, and I desperately grasped the barrier to try to control what was happening. It must have been the power of God. After a short while, it was over, and I stood in a kind of daze, trying to take in all that had taken place. That evening I made my way back to England rejoicing.

From that moment, our little young people's prayer group thought of itself completely differently. We knew that God had something special in store for us, and this blessing sustained us in the foundational years and still encourages us today. That prayer group eventually became the Cor et Lumen Christi Community. We know that God chose to give us, sinners that we are, a great sign of his blessing on our life and ministry, so that against all odds and every opposition, we would persevere, knowing that his heavenly blessing was upon us. Glory to God!

My reason for relating this story is that there are many lessons in it. In hindsight, there can be no question that the prophetic word I received from the Lord to go and meet the pope and receive his blessing was true because of the miraculous way it was fulfilled. This is important, because often we are tempted to think of some of the ways in which God spoke to me as rather insignificant and unimpressive: a faint sense in my mind that I should go to Rome to meet the pope for his blessing; a prompting to turn over a book and read an open Bible; a sense from a friend that I should go; a prompting to pick up a crumpled piece of paper in a park; the appearance of money in my pocket (now, that was a shock!); opening the Bible to allow God to speak to me; a phrase, like an inner whisper, telling me to sleep in St. Peter's Piazza. How easy it would have been to miss it all!

I have often asked myself since then, "If this was so important to God, why didn't he just send me an angel rather than relying on so many fragile and precarious signs?" But he knows what is best for each of us. I now take much more seriously such means of communication from the Lord, especially when they are confirmed. What matters, after all, is not the way God speaks to us but that we receive what he's saying and respond.

Part II
The Healing Gifts

CHAPTER 4
THE THEOLOGY OF HEALING AND
A SHORT HISTORY

And Jesus went about all the cities and villages, teaching in their syn-
agogues and preaching the gospel of the kingdom, and healing every
disease and every infirmity.
—Mathew 9:35

A young nurse was working in the hospital when a man who was intox-
icated came in and attacked her. He broke her spine and severely
damaged her spinal column. As a result, she underwent a total of
forty medical interventions, during which several metal plates and bolts were
inserted into her spine, but none of the treatments helped. The damage to
her spine was so severe that for six years, she could not even get out of bed.
Standing was completely impossible. Although she was on very high doses of
morphine, the doctors were unable to properly manage the pain. She could
not even sit herself up in her bed. Her speech had been affected, and she did
not have complete use of her arms. Because of the damage to the spinal column, she could not cope with light, so she had to always be in the dark or
wear sunglasses. For six long years, she lay bedridden in pain in a dark room.

In desperation her mother brought her in her wheelchair to a healing
service. I preached, and then we heard a joint testimony of healing from
a woman and her physician husband. At one of our previous services in
France a year before, this woman had been healed of an incurable degener-
ative condition that had kept her bound to a wheelchair.

As I led the time for healing, I asked the Christians in the auditorium to
place their hands on the sick near them and pray. As God prompted me, I
commanded conditions to be healed in Jesus' name. I concluded, "Be freed
from your crutches, be freed from your sticks, be freed from your paralysis, be freed from your wheelchairs, in Jesus' holy name." Then I told the
people, "Now in Jesus' name, do what you couldn't do before." All over
the room, hundreds demonstrated their healings.

Suddenly we heard a big cheer from the center of the crowd. I jumped
off the stage and approached the area where the excitement was. There was

the young woman standing next to her wheelchair, hugging her mother. I asked what had happened, and they explained that she had just stood up with no pain. All the strength had returned to her legs. I could see that she was completely stunned.

I walked her to the stage. With her empty wheelchair next to her, she gave a brief explanation of her incredible healing. She walked up and down the platform freely and then jogged back and forth, shaking her head in wonder and wiping tears from her eyes. The people were cheering and shouting the praises of God. A year later, she was still completely healed.

It was reported to me afterward that some male members of the security staff for the facility in which we were meeting were moved to tears. Through witnessing such a beautiful act of God, they were convicted of the lordship of Jesus and then and there asked for his mercy and invited him into their hearts as their Lord and Savior. Glory to God!

The Vatican document *Instruction on Prayers for Healing* states, "'People are called to joy. Nevertheless each day they experience many forms of suffering and pain.' Therefore, the Lord, in his promises of redemption, announces the joy of the heart that comes from liberation from sufferings (cf. Isaiah 30:29; 35:10; Baruch 4:29). Indeed, he is the one 'who delivers from every evil' (Wisdom 16:8)."[1]

The prophet Isaiah announced a future time in which sickness and infirmity will be overthrown and there will be a great outpouring of healing grace:

> Then the eyes of the blind shall be opened,
>   and the ears of the deaf unstopped;
> then shall the lame man leap like a hart,
>   and the tongue of the dumb sing for joy.
>   (Isaiah 35:5-6; see also 65:19-20)

This is a prophecy of the messianic era. Jesus' ministry was the fulfillment of Isaiah's prophecy, and the Church is the continuance of the ministry of

---

1. Congregation for the Doctrine of the Faith, *Instruction on Prayers for Healing*, 1, September 14, 2000, quoting Pope St. John Paul II, Apostolic Exhortation *Christifideles Laici*, 53.

Jesus in the world through the power of the Holy Spirit. One aspect of that ministry is the ministry of healing, which is inseparably linked to the proclamation of the Christian gospel.

Jesus' Ministry of Healing

The amount of time that Jesus gave to healing the sick was considerable. He clearly understood this ministry as having a central role in his mission. It was a demonstration of the in-breaking of the kingdom, not only the confirmation of his message. At times this ministry is described as an expression of his compassion; at other times, as an attack against the influence of the evil one; and at still others, as a sign of the glory of God. Looking at the Gospels, it is inconceivable to imagine Jesus without healing miracles, because they were so prevalent. This is from the Vatican's *Instruction on Prayers for Healing*:

> In the public activity of Jesus, his encounters with the sick are not isolated, but continual. He healed many through miracles, so that miraculous healings characterized his activity: "Jesus went around to all the towns and villages, teaching in their synagogues, proclaiming the Gospel of the kingdom, and curing every disease and illness" (Matthew 9:35; cf. 4:23). These healings are signs of his messianic mission (cf. Luke 7:20-23). They manifest the victory of the kingdom of God over every kind of evil, and become the symbol of the restoration to health of the whole human person, body and soul.[2]

Jesus' ministry is summed up by Peter: "God anointed Jesus of Nazareth with the Holy Spirit and with power; . . . he went about doing good and healing all that were oppressed by the devil, for God was with him" (Acts 10:38).

When Jesus commissioned the Twelve, he "gave them authority over unclean spirits, to cast them out, and to heal every disease and every infirmity" (Matthew 10:1). He said to them, "Heal the sick, raise the dead, cleanse lepers, cast out demons" (10:8; see Luke 9:1). This makes it clear that the Church potentially has within its power the grace to heal every disease and sickness, even to the raising of the dead (cf. Matthew 10:8). This commission was not restricted to the apostles. The seventy-two were also commissioned, when they were sent out to "heal the sick" (Luke 10:9).

---

2. *Instruction on Prayers for Healing*, 1.

In the conclusion to the Gospel of Mark, as well as in the Letter to the Galatians, the expectation that healings are to be normal in the ministry of ordinary believers and the local church is clear. It is highly significant that there is no commissioning of Jesus' disciples to proclaim the gospel that is not accompanied by the command to heal the sick. In the four Gospels, more than one-third, or 38.5 percent, of the narrative text refers to the healing of the sick in one form or another.

The New Testament Church:

A Model of Proclamation with Healing Power

The conclusion of Mark's Gospel, speaking of the disciples, declares, "And they went forth and preached everywhere, while the Lord worked with them and confirmed the message by the signs that attended it" (16:20).

The first preaching of the gospel described in the Acts of the Apostles was accompanied by numerous miraculous healings, which demonstrated and confirmed the power of the gospel proclamation. The Vatican's *Instruction on Prayers for Healing* notes, "This had been the promise of the Risen Jesus, and the first Christian communities witnessed its realization in their midst: 'These signs will accompany those who believe: . . . they will lay hands on the sick, and they will recover' (Mark 16:17-18)."[3]

Such an emphasis on healing and miracles as natural accompaniments of the proclamation of the word of God is clearly expressed in the prayer of the early Church. In a moment of persecution, when caution might have seemed the prudent response, the community of disciples prayed, "And now, Lord, look upon their threats, and grant to your servants to speak your word with all boldness, while you stretch out your hand to heal, and signs and wonders are performed through the name of your holy servant Jesus" (Acts 4:29-30).

Following Pentecost, multitudes were healed through Peter and the apostles. But only after this second outpouring of the Holy Spirit, when power for healing was specifically requested, is Peter recorded as being used to heal them all (Acts 5:16).

The healing gifts are widely distributed among believers in the Acts of the Apostles and the letters of the New Testament. The Vatican document

---

3. Ibid.

on prayers for healing states, "The wondrous healings are not limited to the activity of the Apostles and certain of the central figures in the first preaching of the Gospel."[4] The preaching of Philip in Samaria was also accompanied by miraculous healings: "multitudes with one accord gave heed to what was said by Philip, when they heard him and saw the signs which he did. For unclean spirits came out of many who were possessed, crying with a loud voice; and many who were paralyzed or lame were healed" (Acts 8:5-7).

St. Paul describes his own proclamation of the gospel as being characterized by signs and wonders worked by the power of the Holy Spirit. He writes, "For I will not venture to speak of anything except what Christ has wrought through me to win obedience from the Gentiles, by word and deed, by the power of signs and wonders, by the power of the Holy Spirit" (Romans 15:18-19; see also 1 Thessalonians 1:5 and 1 Corinthians 2:4-5). It is clear from the accounts of Paul's ministry that miraculous healings were among these signs and wonders to which he referred. Such wonders were also occurring among the faithful in the local church: "Does he who supplies the Spirit to you and works miracles among you do so by works of the law, or by hearing with faith?" (Galatians 3:5).

Healing in the History of the Church

Of course, the Church has been committed to healing through the medical profession and the establishment of hospitals through the ages. This developed alongside the activity of charisms of healing, as we see in the lives of St. Cosmas and St. Damian (c. AD 287), both medical doctors who also exercised gifts of healing.

As with prophecy, the expectation of healing miracles continued in a dramatic way in the early centuries of the Church. In the second century, St. Irenaeus (AD 130–202) wrote, "By praying to the Lord who made all things, only by calling upon the name of Our Lord Jesus Christ, [does the Church] even now cure thoroughly and effectively all who everywhere believe in Christ."[5] Likewise, Origen (c. 185–c. 254) testifies about healings in his age: "We too have seen many set free from severe complaints, and loss of mind, and madness and numberless other such evils, which neither men nor dev-

---

4. *Instruction on Prayers for Healing*, 3.
5. Irenaeus, *Against Heresies*, bk. 2, chap. 32, 5.

ils had cured."[6] And Hilary of Poitiers, a Church Father and Doctor of the Church (c. 315–c. 367), writes, "We become steadfast in hope and receive abundant gifts in healing."[7]

Later, in the fifth century, St. Augustine of Hippo says "with regard to the goods of life, health, and physical integrity, . . . 'We need to pray that these are retained, when we have them, and that they are increased, when we do not have them.'"[8]

Many of the testimonies of these Fathers are vigorously upheld by Blessed John Henry Newman in his great *Essays on Miracles*.[9]

Dr. Ramsay MacMullen, professor of history and classics at Yale University, in his book *Christianizing the Roman Empire AD 100–400*, asserts that healing and deliverance from demons—and not only social advancement, as some secular critics have claimed—were major factors in turning the pagans of the empire to Christianity. The reason was that these miracles clearly demonstrated that the Christian God was greater than all the gods of Rome.[10]

The number of reports of healing miracles in the ministries of saints down through the ages would be impossible to count. One example of a saint with healing gifts was St. Patrick (385–461):

> For the blind and the lame, the deaf and the dumb, the palsied, the lunatic, the leprous, the epileptic, all who labored under any disease, did he in the Name of the Holy Trinity restore unto the power of their limbs and unto entire health; and in these good deeds was he daily practiced.[11]

After the fourth century, there seems to have been a decline in expectant faith for healing as a ministry exercised by ordinary Christians. However, there continued to be amazing stories of miracles in the revivals led by many saints, including St. Augustine of Canterbury, St. Cuthbert of Lindisfarne, St.

---

6. Origen, *Contra Celsus*, bk. 3, chap. 24.
7. Hilary of Poitier, *Tract on the Psalms*, 64:15.
8. St. Augustine, Epistle 130, VI, 13, as quoted in *Instruction on Prayers for Healing*, 4.
9. John Henry Newman, *Essays on Miracles*, newmanreader.org/works/miracles/.
10. See Ramsay MacMullen, *Christianizing the Roman Empire AD 100–400* (New Haven, CT: Yale University, 1984), chap. 4.
11. Edmund L. Swift, *The Life and Acts of St. Patrick*, quoted in Hebert, 193.

Bernard, St. Francis, St. Dominic, St. Collette, St. Vincent Ferrer, St. Francis of Paola, St. Anthony of Padua, St. Paul of the Cross, and others. From apostolic times, healings have been present in the Church in what French theologian René Laurentin calls "a constant tradition,"[12] and it would be hard to find a period when they were entirely absent from the Church.

Yet the records we have tend to be, for the most part, demonstrations of healing in the ministries of the saints, holy men and women, and at shrines, or through relics. The point I want to make here is not that healing miracles were not a part of Catholic culture and belief; they certainly were. However, the expectation of them as regular components in the life of Christian communities, through the prayers and actions of ordinary good Christians, in the first four centuries had faded.

"During the first eight centuries of the Church's history, the anointing of the sick was regarded as a rite of healing for all kinds of illness," writes Fr. Laurentin. After the ninth century, spiritual healing became more emphasized, although physical healing was accepted as a real possibility. "Only by a distortion that began in the nineteenth century did it become the 'sacrament of the dying.'"[13]

Healing in the Orthodox and Coptic traditions

Healings continued in the Orthodox Church in a similar way. Some Orthodox saints were remarkable in their healing gifts. Especially well known are St. Seraphim of Sarov, who was a contemporary of the Curé of Ars, and St. John of Kronstadt, who died in the early twentieth century. St. John's life is sometimes referred to as "a sea of miracles."

Here is just one story from St. Seraphim:

> The sick nephew of Princess Shahaeva was carried into St. Seraphim's cell. The saint told him to lie facing away from him, but the man in time turned to look at the saint and saw him levitating in the air in prayer. The young man was healed but admonished to never tell what he had seen until after the saint's death.[14]

---

12. René Laurentin, *Catholic Pentecostalism* (New York: Doubleday, 1977), 112.
13. Ibid.
14. "The St. Seraphim of Sarov," orthodoxinsight.com/icons/deticon4.html.

In 1903 St. John of Kronstadt appeared in his gold vestments to a man who was dying of typhoid, and as he blessed him, he held the man's hand. This was no ordinary vision. St. John was mysteriously physically present in that room, although he was known to be present simultaneously in another place many miles away. He assured the man that he would recover and then stepped away and disappeared into a white haze. The man quickly recovered. When he told his father about the priest who visited him, his father explained that he had sent a telegram to Fr. John in Kronstadt asking him for his prayers.[15]

The Coptic saint Pope Kyrillos VI (1902–1971) was the instrument of thousands of healings, recorded in eighteen volumes. In one healing, he gave a cup of water that he blessed to a woman who had been diagnosed with an undeveloped uterus, which made having children quite impossible. Eight months later, she was experiencing pain and enlargement of her abdomen, and she consulted a new doctor who did not know of her medical history. To her astonishment, he told her she was eight months pregnant. The woman's husband showed the doctor her previous medical reports, and the doctor was amazed that the woman had been able to get pregnant and carry the baby to nearly full term. "Can it be that we are still in an era where clergy pray on water and miracles are performed? God created a new womb for her," he said. This same physician attended the delivery.[16]

Healing in the Pentecostal and Evangelical charismatic tradition

Maria Woodworth-Etter's healing services and revivals attracted people from all over the United States in the early twentieth century. Dying people would be brought in cots and find themselves instantly raised up. The blind, deaf, and lame were regularly healed, and often in large numbers. Even the dead were raised. One of the miracles that took place in her ministry that was witnessed by a medical surgeon, John H. Bowen, was the total healing of a child with several chronic conditions.

> There was a boy seven years old, who had never walked; he was born insane, blind, deaf and dumb; he was always pounding his

---

15. "A Sea of Miracles" (Orthodox Photos.com, 2003), orthodoxphotos.com/readings/portrait/miracles.shtml.
16. Fr. Rafael Avva Mena, quoted in Ata and Mena, 27–28.

head and beating himself like the maniac among the tombs. They tried everything, including the best medical help, but the doctors could not locate the cause, and they said he would never have any sense. . . .

[But after the prayer he] can hear and see perfectly. God has given him a bright, intelligent mind; he laughs and plays and walks around in front of the pulpit every day in view of all the congregation; before he was healed, he had spasms, as many as twenty a day, but now he is well and happy.[17]

Hundreds of thousands, perhaps even millions, of healings were experienced through ministries such as these in the first part of the twentieth century. These were followed by the healing revival of the 1940s and 50s, which swept across North America. Meetings took place in tents that could hold up to eighteen thousand people. In the sixties and seventies, Kathryn Kuhlman became renowned for her extraordinary healing ministry. Such large numbers of healing miracles took place in her ministry that she was sometimes referred to by Catholics as a "Walking Lourdes." Kuhlman was very happy to have met with Blessed Pope Paul VI, who gave her his blessing and assured her of his prayers.

As we have stated, the "canonizing" of the enduring place of charismatic gifts among the people of God in the texts of the Second Vatican Council opened the way for a renewal of charisms of healing being exercised among "ordinary" Catholics. The Sacrament of the Sick was restored to its original intention as a sacrament of healing, and the language of healing can now be found in many of the liturgical texts of the Church. In 2000 the Vatican also published a document encouraging the charism of healing in the Catholic Church.

Healing Ministry Today

In today's culture, it is common to hear the term *healers* used of both Christian and non-Christian practitioners of healing. However, such a title is inappropriate when referring to Christians exercising healing gifts. Like

---

17. Maria Woodworth-Etter, *Signs and Wonders* (New Kensington, PA: Whitaker House, 1997), 130–131.

other spiritual gifts, healing is not something we receive one day and possess for the rest of our lives, as though we carry it in our pockets and bring it out whenever a need presents itself. Every time we seek God's intervention for healing, we depend on his free gift.

While this total dependence on the Lord's action never changes, there are those who, if faithful, can be used in this way very regularly and often with increasing power as their faith grows. In such cases, we refer to "a ministry of healing." Professor Francis Sullivan explains:

> Paul never speaks of a "gift of healing," nor does he speak of any individuals as "healers." Paul mentions healing three times in 1 Corinthians 12 (vv. 9, 28, 30), and each time he uses the phrase *charismata iamaton*, which means "charisms of healings." The consistent use of this phrase suggests that Paul saw each healing as a charism, or gift of grace. But his statement, "To another [are given] charisms of healings," . . . suggest[s] that when Paul talks about those who "have charisms of healings," he has in mind not the people who are healed, but people who are in some way involved in the healing of others. Paul's way of speaking of this implies that he does not see this as a habitual "gift of healing"; on the other hand, it does suggest that certain individuals are used with some frequency as channels or instruments of the healings that take place. If this is the case, then it would seem legitimate to speak of such people as having a ministry of gifts of healing for other people.[18]

An exercise of the kingly anointing

When we were baptized, we were made sharers in Christ's priestly, prophetic, and kingly anointing. Often the emphasis on the kingly anointing has been one of conforming the world to the values and purposes of Christ through social action—by influencing work, politics, education, commerce, and the environment, so that God's values reign there. This is quite true, and its importance can hardly be overestimated. It is something in which all of us are called to play a part in one way or another. But this is not the whole story.

In Genesis, Adam had dominion over creation. Before the fall, all creation could be mastered by man: "Fill the earth and subdue it; and have

---

18. Sullivan, 151.

dominion" (1:28). *The New Jerome Biblical Commentary* tells us of the word *subdue*, "The nuance of the verb is 'to master,' 'to bring forcefully under control.'"[19] *Dominion* in Greek is *kratos*, and according to one definition, it means "force," "strength," or "might," and "more especially manifested power." It is derived from the root word *kra*, which means "to perfect, to complete."[20]

Thus, to exercise dominion is to have mastery over and bring to full order and completion God's creation. This exercise of dominion is a kingly authority that Adam and Eve exercised over creation before the fall. According to *The New Jerome Biblical Commentary*, "In the ancient Near East, the king was often called the image of the deity and was vested with God's authority; royal language is here [Genesis 1:28] used for the human."[21] Adam named creatures as Jesus named people. In other words, he creatively defined them. This is not naming as one might name a pet; rather, Adam's words carry the very power of God as God's son in a sinless state. "The giving of names [by Adam] is in itself a creative act."[22]

In the Liturgy of the Hours, we read in one of the intercessions in Lent: "May we gain through the second Adam what was lost by the first."[23] Supernatural ministry such as physical healing demonstrates the kingship of Christ in a particular way. Jesus says to his disciples, "All authority in heaven and on earth has been given to me. Go therefore . . . " (Matthew 28:18-19) There is nothing that is not under his authority. The kingly authority of the risen Jesus is not only over the spiritual realm but also over the physical realm, and it is possible to exercise this kingly authority even now, imperfect as we are.

When I am standing before a crowd, many of whom are physically sick, I stand with the authority of Christ exercising my kingly anointing

19. Raymond E. Brown, Joseph A. Fitzmyer, Roland E. Murphy, eds., *The New Jerome Biblical Commentary*, 11.

20. *Vine's Expository Dictionary of New Testament Words* (Peabody, MA: Hendrickson), 334. The word *kratos* "also signifies dominion, and is so rendered frequently in doxologies, 1 Peter 4:11; 5:11; Jude 25; Revelation 1:6; 5:13 (RV); in 1 Timothy 6:16, and Hebrews 2:14 it is translated 'power.'"

21. *New Jerome Biblical Commentary*, 11.

22. Bishop Kallistos Ware, *The Orthodox Way* (Crestwood, NY: St. Vladimir's Seminary Press), 54.

23. Divine Office, Lent weeks 1 and 3, Thursday morning intercession.

in him. As I speak to the various conditions—"Ears, hear; eyes, see; legs, be strong; cancers, be gone," and so forth—I do not simply speak with hope. I speak with faith and authority, knowing that if I am acting in the Holy Spirit, people's bodies will resonate to the creative word of Christ on my lips—not to my voice but to the words of Jesus from me.

Now of course, unbelief can present an obstacle, as we see even in Jesus' own ministry in his hometown: "And he did not do many mighty works there, because of their unbelief" (Matthew 13:58). But I believe that God has woven into his created material world a programming that recognizes the voice of its Creator. The Sea of Galilee had no ears, but it "heard" the voice of its Lord in Jesus' command to be still (see Mark 4:39). The fig tree had no ears but "heard" the voice of its creator in Christ and withered (Matthew 21:19).

When we speak in authority, in faith, in a faith environment, our words have tremendous creative power through the power of the Holy Spirit. Now, unless I have specific revelation about a particular sickness to be healed, I cannot be absolutely certain I will see healing in all the areas I've mentioned, but I have a general faith expectation that is not wishful thinking. At every service we run, we normally see deafness, levels of blindness, and lameness healed, and sometimes in large numbers. It's common to see incurable and terminal conditions, as well as many smaller conditions, instantly healed.

When we command healing, we do so as people exercising the King's authority over what he has made. This is why cancerous tumors, even large ones, often shrink and even vanish. When the Scripture says, "For the creation waits with eager longing for the revealing of the sons of God" (Romans 8:19), this is because the children of God hold the material world's healing in their hands. As coheirs with Christ, we are the kings and queens over God's creation; we are called to exercise his dominion in love, turning back the effects of the fall and establishing the kingdom.

CHAPTER 5
PHYSICAL HEALING

"Stretch out your hand to heal."
—Act 4:30

Sometimes I hear people question why physical healing is important. They say that what really matters is spiritual healing, and physical healing is of only secondary importance. Such a statement denies the value Jesus himself put on the ministry or gift of physical healing. In the New Testament, we see the great emphasis Jesus placed on the healing of the body alongside the preaching of the kingdom and the casting out of devils. God is interested in the whole person. We are not "souls"; we are people made up of "spirit and soul and body" (1 Thessalonians 5:13; see also Catechism 367). God is concerned with the healing of the entire person.

In Western Christianity, we have been deeply infected by the negative view that the philosopher Plato had of the human body and the material world in general. Plato referred to the human body as "the tomb of the soul."[1] While our secular society has gone to the other extreme in an excess of materialism and a gross oversexualizing of the body, in Christian religious circles, platonic thinking has given rise to the idea that it is only the soul that really matters and that God is not really interested in our bodies. Nothing could be further from authentic Christian teaching. St. Paul says that our bodies are not tombs but temples—temples of the Holy Spirit (1 Corinthians 6:19)!

On the last day, God's children will not be raised as vague spiritual beings, but as the Church teaches, they "will rise again with their own bodies which they now bear about with them."[2] This body will be glorified at this moment of our total healing.

In light of these truths, it is absolutely legitimate for a person to seek physical healing from the Lord through the prayers and actions of other Christians, as Scripture and Tradition make clear. The Vatican *Instruction on Prayers for Healing* confirms this:

---

1. Plato, *Gorgias*, 493a, trans. Leo Strauss, ed. Devin Stauffer, leostrausscenter. uchicago.edu.
2. Fourth Lateran Council, as quoted at New Advent, "General Resurrection," http://www.newadvent.org/cathen/12792a.htm.

[T]he sick person's desire for healing is both good and deeply human, especially when it takes the form of a trusting prayer addressed to God.[3]

The Lord welcomes their requests and the Gospels contain not even a hint of reproach for these prayers. The Lord's only complaint is about their possible lack of faith. "If you can! Everything is possible to the one who has faith" (Mark 9:23; 6:5-6; John 4:48).[4]

Not only is it praiseworthy for individual members of the faithful to ask for healing themselves and for others, but the Church herself asks for the health of the sick in her liturgy.[5]

I do not consider myself to have a healing ministry; rather, I have a call of proclaiming God's word with healing, signs, and wonders. So physical healings alone are not my objective when my team or I minister. While beautiful, unless physical healings move people closer to the Lord, their fruit is limited. I want every healing to prompt a deeper conversion and transformation of life.

Physical healing is also important because it communicates the compassion of the Lord for those who are sick. It reveals a God who intervenes in response to faith. It is very moving to see people weep over the healings they or their loved ones have received.

Recently a mother was testifying on stage at one of our Miracle Healing Services of the healing of her young son. He was born with a twisted spine, and because of this, his shoulders were hunched over. At the beginning of the prayer, she put her hand on his spine and felt clearly the twist in it. Then she removed her hand. From the stage, a word of command was pronounced for healing of spines. The mother then put her hand back on her son's spine, and to her utter amazement, she could feel that his spine was now completely straight and his shoulders were no longer hunched over—for the first time in his life. Her tears of love, gratitude, and joy as she testified moved the whole crowd.

Such physical healings mark a person and a family. When Jesus does these things to someone you love, you are far less likely to turn away from him

---

3. *Instruction on Prayers for Healing*, 2.
4. Ibid.
5. Ibid.

in the future. Such deeds can secure people in their faith for the rest of their lives. And the effect is not just upon them. Unbelievers and lapsed Christians whose friends or family members receive a powerful healing often find themselves warming up to the reality of a relationship with the living Jesus.

A woman flew from another country to attend one of our events in England. She was deaf in one ear. She tried to get her husband to come, but he refused, saying, "I'll only come if your deaf ear is healed." She attended the course and was filled with the Holy Spirit and—you guessed it—her deaf ear was healed. A short while later, her husband flew with her to attend the next event, and he was converted. Praise God! Now many in their family are on fire for Jesus. A person who receives a powerful healing becomes a sign and wonder to all who know him or her.

At our Miracle Healing Services, we always have a time after the healings when we invite people to open their hearts and invite Jesus to be Lord of their lives. The authenticity of the healings people witness simply conquers many doubts and interior arguments with which they may have been struggling for years. We have had the joy of seeing huge numbers of people who did not know God inviting him into their hearts as their Lord. Some of these are unbaptized unbelievers, others lapsed Christians. Some have been staunch atheists.

One man had not been to church since his First Communion fifty years before. He was a committed Communist and would not allow his wife and children to talk about religion in the house. He had been told of healings the day before but came with a cynical attitude. When he saw the wonderful miracles of healing being performed by Jesus, his heart broke, and he began to weep. All his years of hardened atheism fell away from him in that moment. He invited Jesus to come into his heart that day, and the next day he went to confession for his fifty years of rejecting God. From then on, he prayed each day, attended Mass several times a week, and prayed regularly with his wife. Glory to God!

It is very common for people who have been deeply touched by the healings they have witnessed in others to come forward and, after making a commitment to the Lord, go straight to confession, often for the first time in decades. The evangelistic power of physical healing is astonishing.

Why do we often resist praying for physical healing?

One of the fundamental reasons we often resist praying for physical healing is that our theology around it is confused. I hope my previous comments and quotations have provided a clearer basis from which we can form our thinking. Unclear thinking causes us to lose traction in our faith, because we are unsure of God's purposes. We become like the double-minded people James speaks of, who are full of doubts and so can ask for nothing with any confidence (James 1:6-8). Does God want to heal everyone now, or doesn't he? Does he want to heal some people but not others? If he does want to heal, does he intend to use me, or should it be someone else? Such questions can leave us in a state of confusion and doubt with no assurance of how to proceed.

If one looks at the ministry of Jesus and the early Church, where healing was regular and widespread, one is compelled to conclude that God normally desires to heal the sick when they approach him with faith. We can find no occasion in the Gospels when the sick who presented themselves to Jesus for physical healing were refused. Jesus is the same yesterday, today, and forever.

I do not say that we have an obligation to try to heal every sick person alive. Jesus clearly didn't feel that pressure when he walked past the Pool of Bethsaida, a place crowded with sick people, and only healed one man (John 5:2-9). When we pray, Jesus is present in a special way, so we can expect great things if faith is active. This helps me have a firm foundation from which I can orient my prayers.

My expectation is for large numbers of wonderful healings, and by God's amazing grace, this is what we see. However, we can't say that we are in a position to see all healed at our services or in our street ministry just yet! But perhaps this will be possible in the future, and as the number of healings rises, this may not be as fanciful as we once thought.

Although I owe a great debt in this ministry to my Evangelical, charismatic, and Pentecostal friends, I cannot agree with some of them that healing can be claimed from the cross in the same way that forgiveness can, so long as we have enough faith. My response to this is that if it were only a matter of faith, Paul, whose faith was of staggering proportions, would have been able to heal Timothy's minor stomach problem (1 Timothy 5:23). He also left Trophimus sick at Miletus (2 Timothy 3:20). It is unreasonable, to my mind, to assume that Paul, who raised the dead (cf. Acts 20:7-12), didn't have sufficient faith for healing in these cases if all it depended on was the faith to claim it.

The other Scripture passage that suggests that we cannot yet be certain for healing in every case is Revelation 21:2-4, which tells us when death will pass away.

> And I saw the holy city, new Jerusalem, coming down out of heaven from God, prepared as a bride adorned for her husband; and I heard a great voice from the throne saying, "Behold, the dwelling of God is with men. He will dwell with them, and they shall be his people, and God himself will be with them; he will wipe away every tear from their eyes, and death shall be no more, neither shall there be mourning nor crying nor pain any more, for the former things have passed away."

Evidently, we are not living in the era when all "former things have passed away." If death will be utterly and permanently destroyed only at that time, it will only be then that all the causes of death—illnesses and all physical ailments—will also be totally eradicated.

Healings are a taste of heaven, a sign of the kingdom. There is no doubt in my mind that God wants to multiply enormously the number of people who are healed in our day, even to the point of sharing from time to time the experience of Jesus and St. Peter, when "all were healed" (Matthew 8:16; Acts 5:16). However, I have to acknowledge that there are promises about faith that cannot be ignored: "All things are possible to him who believes" (Mark 9:23). Such promises must be faced; Jesus meant what he said, and we need to unpack these promises' deepest meanings and implications. I see healing not as something I can claim from the cross in the same way as forgiveness but rather as a fruit of the cross through the outpouring of the Holy Spirit and his gifts, exercised by "faith working through love" (Galatians 5:6).

Another reason people resist praying for or ministering physical healing is that they have no effective models for it and consider physical healing ministry to be beyond ordinary Christians. At times the fear of failure holds people back. In prayer for physical healing, the issue of success or failure can't be ducked. Inner healing and deliverance are often processes in which confirmation of healing can be gradual, and the results of our prayer need time to prove fruitful. We do not feel humiliated if there is no instant sign or perceivable result, as we know it may show itself in time.

In most cases of prayer for physical healing, everyone can see immediately whether the prayer has been successful or not. This has made prayer for physical healing more threatening to people. "What if nothing happens? I'll look such a fool."

If we are to progress in this area of healing, we have to pray to be freed from the fear of others' opinions. Jesus said, "How can you believe, who receive glory from one another and do not seek the glory that comes from the only God?" (John 5:44). In other words, the exercise of faith becomes impossible if we are worrying about the opinions of others rather than that of God.

We need to come to a point where we care more about the glory of the Lord and the good of our sick neighbor than about our reputation. This demands a growth in love of God and of others in humility and faith.

Is there a place for suffering?

Catholics and some other Christians believe there is a place for "redemptive suffering"—offering our sufferings with the sufferings of Jesus on the cross, for the good of others and ourselves. Some people say that we are called either to redemptive suffering or to healing. This is only partially true, in my view. In one sense, all of us are called to redemptive suffering until we are healed! God's final agenda is without question: our total healing and glorification.

In my experience, most Catholics are open to healing prayer, as are many Christians in other churches today. However, there seems to be some muddled thinking among some about the virtue of offering up our sufferings. If we believe *all* suffering should be offered up, then why do people take painkillers?

I think that the phrase "Offer it up" is often a subtle way of failing to engage our faith for healing. Who in his right mind would say to his child who has cancer, "Offer it up, darling," without begging God for healing or trying every medical avenue for restoration?

Of course, there are times when we come to the end of our human and spiritual resources and, in the mystery of this life, have to accept the hard cross of facing bravely in faith the sufferings before us. Chapter 11 of Hebrews gives us several examples of heroes of faith. We read of those who overcame armies by faith (Hebrews 11:34). They defeated by faith something that was attacking them. Those who are healed fall into this category. But there is also mention of those who by faith "were killed with the sword" (11:37). In other words, these failed to overcome what was attacking them but offered their sufferings in faith; they too are heroes of faith. This category offers hope to those who are not yet healed; their sufferings are not worthless but can be transformed by faith.

I understand that failure in prayer for healing may cause us to conclude that God doesn't really want to heal many people. But with that logic, the poverty of the Church's evangelization in the West means that God doesn't want to save many Westerners! Our theologies should not be shaped by our failures but by the promises of Christ, especially when these promises are confirmed in the writings and experiences of the Fathers and the prayers of the Church.

When I'm praying for someone, I assume an attitude of insistence before the Lord. As Fr. Raniero Cantalamessa writes on healing prayer, "[W]hen it concerns our neighbor, we should dare much and be resolute with God."[6]

Growing in the Gift of Healing

Looking at the Gospels and the Acts of the Apostles, we see that physical healing was very straightforward. Actual prayers for healing are rare; it is far more normal to obtain a healing through a simple touch or word of command, such as "Stand up," "Receive your sight," and so forth. There is almost never a prayer to remove "blockages" beforehand (with the exceptions of the lame man whose sins were forgiven first and the casting out of demons causing the sickness). The vast majority of healings are almost entirely instantaneous.

Gradual healings are the exception rather than the norm. Jesus' promises are unambiguous: believers will perform the same works and miracles that he did (John 14:12), as I explained in the first chapter. God still does this kind of instant physical healing for thousands of people each year who attend our events.

---

6. Raniero Cantalamessa, OFM Cap, *Sober Intoxication of the Spirit: Filled with the Fullness of God*, trans. Marsha Daigle-Williamson (Cincinnati: Servant, 2005), 112–113.

Laying on of hands and other gestures

It is often assumed that Jesus invariably laid his hands upon the sick when he prayed for their physical healing. Because of this, people tend to make the laying on of hands their default approach when praying for healing. But a closer look at the New Testament reveals that many different methods were used. It is important to understand that the effectiveness of this ministry depends not so much on one approach but rather on how well we obey the prompting of the Holy Spirit in each situation and exercise faith.

If we learn this art, which is best learned alongside others more experienced than ourselves, we are much more likely to see the results the Lord intends. The problem with having only one model is that we tend to go into automatic pilot, assuming that we know what to do, and then we fail to listen to the Holy Spirit. It is helpful to have an idea of the variety of approaches that Jesus used so we can be open to the diverse ways the Holy Spirit may lead us.

Even though laying on of hands should not be assumed in every case, Jesus did at times lay his hands upon people for healing (Mark 6:5; Luke 13:13), so we acknowledge this as a very valid and valuable component of some, and perhaps even most, occasions of healing. Our ministry began with prayer through the laying on of hands. Still today the laying on of hands plays an important part in much of the physical healing we see.

Yet Jesus' use of physical gestures in healing varied considerably. On some occasions, he simply touched the sick (Matthew 8:3; Mark 1:41-42; Luke 5:13), taking them by the hand (Matthew 8:15; Mark 1:31) or touching their eyes in cases of blindness (Matthew 9:29; 20:34). When someone brought Jesus a deaf mute, asking him "to lay his hand upon him," Jesus "put his fingers into his ears and he spat and touched his tongue" (Mark 7:32, 33).

On another occasion, some people took a blind man to Jesus "and begged him to touch him." Jesus took the man out of the village, put spit on his eyes, and laid his hands on him. When the man couldn't yet see clearly, Jesus again laid his hands upon his eyes, and the man's eyesight was restored (Mark 8:22-25). Even more surprising a gesture came when Jesus "spat on the ground and made clay of the spittle and anointed the man's eyes with the clay" (John 9:6).

Words of knowledge

In other instances, Jesus issued an order together with a statement show-ing supernatural knowledge about a condition that was being or would be healed. Before visiting Lazarus, he said, "Our friend Lazarus has fallen asleep, but I go to awake him out of sleep" (John 11:11). This too can be part of our experience in ministering healing. Words of knowledge for heal-ing are means by which the Lord communicates to the minister information about what he has done, is doing, or intends to do.

When given by a person ministering from a platform or sanctuary to a congregation, these words commonly come in a form such as this: "There is someone here being healed of deafness in the left ear," or whatever the heal-ing may be. Sometimes people in the congregation know immediately that the word is for them. At other times, people only realize the word refers to them because they experience something unusual happening in their bod-ies—for example, heat or tingling in the part of the body that is unwell. Other people experience nothing while the word of knowledge is given, yet as soon as they check, they find themselves healed.

The other form a word of knowledge can take is a declaration that certain conditions will be healed through the laying on of hands later in the service. (For example, "The Lord wants to heal people with frozen shoulders. Please stand, and we'll pray for you.") For many years, we experienced both of these kinds of words of knowledge at our healing meetings, and good num-bers of healings took place. But I had no idea of the scale that was possible.

During this period, my wife, Cathy, lent me *Ever Increasing Faith*, which is a collection of sermons by Smith Wigglesworth. Wigglesworth was an early Pentecostal of immense personal holiness and power in healing. One chapter tells of a meeting of eight hundred people in South Africa, at which five hundred received physical healing. I had never heard in my life that such rates of healing could even be hoped for. I began to cry out to the Lord, "Lord, let me see this in my lifetime!"

Two months later, I was in Dar es Salaam, in Tanzania, leading the Charism School Physical Healing Workshop. My team and I gave many words of knowledge and encouraged others to do the same. That day more than eight hundred out of the twelve hundred present received physical healing in an hour and a half. This included people who had been blind, deaf, and lame—the latter of whom now walked free of crutches. All glory to God.

However wonderful this was, I had seen in the life of Jesus, the saints, and holy Christian ministers a greater precision in the word of knowledge gift. At times some ministers would know approximately where in the congregation the person was to whom the word of knowledge applied. For example, "God is healing someone in the left section of the balcony of a cancerous tumor." This specifying of the general location greatly increases the expectant faith of the people in that area that God is addressing them.

I began to pray for this greater precision, and in time it manifested itself. Sometimes I had a sense of where and who the actual person was but did not have the courage to point to him or her directly. At other times, I thought I knew and was quite wrong, even though the general area of the venue was correct. So I continued naming the condition and the area only to be on the safe side, and this is how it remained for some time.

After some years and the Holy Spirit's integration into my ministry of the "word of command" (of which I will speak later), I began reading of ministers who, like Jesus, knew exactly who would be healed and had the faith to announce this in front of everyone. That seemed highly risky, but I wanted further help in bringing people to the Lord and in building up people's faith. Jesus had done this, and God had blessed others with this gift, so I began praying and asking again.

In time the Holy Spirit enabled me to have the faith and confidence to go further. As I looked out upon the crowds, I was able to point directly at a spot in the congregation (rather than a general area) and state, for example, "There is a person there [I point to the place] who has paralysis in your right hand. Who is that? Raise your hand, please. The Lord is going to touch you with his healing now," or, "The Lord is healing you now." The person, usually exactly where I was pointing, raised his or her hand, and we prayed.

I find that eight out of ten times, I point directly at the person. Occasionally I am off target, but amazingly, this does not necessarily prove to be a problem. I once pointed at a particular place in a crowd and stated that I believed there was someone there with a problem with hearing. There was no one, but two women six or eight feet on either side raised their hands, and seeing their faith, I said, "Well, if you have faith, God can heal you." And healing resulted.

As I practiced this, I began to notice that particular people in the crowd would stand out to me, and I knew their conditions or the areas of their bodies that God was going to heal. Not feeling absolutely certain, I would say, "That man in the blue shirt or someone near you, you have a problem that runs from your hip down your right leg." And invariably the person or a person standing next to him would have the condition named.

As this gift has grown, the Lord has made it clearer to me who exactly the person is, and I have had the assurance often to say, for example, "That lady with the pink top—you have a lung condition. If that's right, wave your hand. The Lord is going to touch you with his healing power now." Such precision of supernatural knowledge and the healing that follows have a powerful effect on the gathering. This kind of revelation is highly effective in raising faith and validating the authenticity of the word of knowledge and the integrity of what is happening.

I remember when I was first able in London to identify a person precisely who would be healed. I gazed out upon the people, praying for the Lord's guidance, and I saw a woman with a head scarf. I knew she was going to be healed, so I wrote this down with several other words of knowledge. A few minutes later, I announced, "There was a woman standing there [I pointed] who had a head scarf on, who was standing next to you. Someone needs to get her; she's going to have a healing." Someone fetched the woman from the outer hall. When she had found her place, I began to speak as the Lord was showing me:

> Yes, I had a word for you. You've had problems in the lower half of your body and problems in your feet as well. But you've also got problems in the top half of your body; in fact, you need a bit of an overhaul, really. Just open up your hands. Lord, just come and heal her. We just bless this woman with healing right through her body, in Jesus' name. We speak healing to your body in the name of Jesus. In the name of Jesus, be healed from the top of your head to the tips of your fingers, to the soles of your feet; be healed in Jesus' name. Amen!

She fell under the power of God to the ground. Later she stood up to find she was totally healed. She came to the front and testified to her healings and ran up and down the steps and performed freely all the things she had been unable to do before.[7]

At some services now, the Lord in his mercy can grant me eight or nine such words. In our last service, one among many graciously given by the

---

7. See "Miracle Healing Service at Grace and Glory Conference, London 2016," coretlumenchristi.org/videos.php.

Lord was this one: "The lady in the striped top there, you have a problem in your internal organs. If that's right, wave your hand [she waves]. You also have a problem in your head [she waves] and in your circulation [she waves]."

The woman I indicated began weeping. I led a short prayer for healing from the stage as two of my team laid hands on her. Two minutes later, I was handed her testimony, which I read to the congregation. The pain in her head was gone, and a tumor in her stomach area, which had been as big as a fist, had shrunk to the size of a peanut!

The impact on people in such cases is very strong because they have witnessed the whole process, from prophetic knowledge to declaration, command, and testimony of healing. Sometimes in this process, the Lord can also show us a person's name and condition.

To minister fruitfully at this level takes time; one does not just have a go at it. This is something the Lord has to lead us into, and as in my case, one is led into it in stages over some time. Mistakes at this level in public ministry can leave people very hurt and confused, so those aspiring to such gifts should make sure they are under authority and move forward cautiously, step-by-step. While all are called to pray for the sick, not all will be given gifts of this kind for a platform ministry, although the same word of knowledge can be given in one-to-one healing prayer.

This gift can begin in small ways, often simply by knowing what is the appropriate prayer to pray for a person when you do not know the situation. This could happen in church, at a prayer meeting, or in a public situation. However, if one is learning, it is wise not to make promises, such as "God is going to heal you of such and such." Rather, share what you feel may be from the Holy Spirit by asking questions, such as "Do you have a problem in your knee? You do. Would you like me to pray for you?"

If you believe you have such revelation through a word of knowledge about a healing you believe God intends, especially something that identifies an individual personally, you must handle it with great care. Those exercising these gifts can get it wrong or partly wrong. Even those with great track records can be mistaken on occasion.

Therefore, such words that announce a result to a particular individual can only be given if there is a great sense of assurance on the side of the minister. The minister should have a proven track record that what they have received comes from God, and they have come to recognize through trial and error in less public settings that they are usually correct in such a claim.

If one is unsure, perhaps it might be good to say something like "I believe the Lord wants to heal you tonight" or "I believe the Lord is going to touch you tonight." It is perfectly legitimate for people in training to offer words of knowledge in a more general way. In time, people grow in maturity in discerning the authenticity of such words. Once there is a pattern of good fruit, more public ministry opportunities can be offered under the oversight of others.

Explicit orders or words of command

Sometimes Jesus gave an explicit order, as when he said to a leper, "Be clean!" (Matthew 8:3). This command to be well or a command to the sick part of the body to be healed is common in the ministry of Jesus. We hear something similar from St. Paul when he healed a man lame from birth: "Paul, looking intently at him and seeing that he had faith to be made well, said in a loud voice, 'Stand upright on your feet.' And he sprang up and walked" (Acts 14:9-10). The same occurred when Peter ordered the man at the beautiful gate, "In the name of Jesus Christ of Nazareth, rise and walk" (Acts 3:6).

This approach to healing ministry might seem extraordinary to our eyes, and the suggestion that it might be available to ordinary Christians, arrogant in the extreme. Yet I continue to be amazed. Jesus shares with the disciples and all believers the potential of exercising his authority. So when Jesus speaks, things change. When the disciples speak in his name, in the power of the Holy Spirit, things change. The same is available to us.

A year after my first visit, I returned to Tanzania, and we had to minister healing to a crowd of seven thousand people in thirty minutes, because the police had insisted that the crowd disperse by dark. In those days, we would have normally prayed for words of knowledge, announced them, and then had a time of laying hands on the sick for healing. This was not going to be possible in the time available.

As I stood on the platform in Dar es Salaam, asking the Lord to show me what he wanted me to do, once again an experience of Smith Wigglesworth came to mind. I had read in the book *Ever Increasing Faith* how, after some persecution in Sweden, Wigglesworth was forbidden by the authorities from laying hands on the sick for healing. Faced with a crowd of twenty thousand, he sought the Lord. The Lord led him to pray words of command over the crowd for various conditions, and the result was mass healings. I felt the Lord leading me to do the same.

I asked all those with problems with their limbs, eyes, or ears and those with tumors to raise their hands. Then I asked the Christians next to them to put their hands on them. I asked the Holy Spirit to come. Then I prayed and waited. When I sensed the authority from the Lord to do so, I calmly but firmly commanded the arms, hands, shoulders, legs, and other body parts to be healed in Jesus' name. Large numbers of people began waving and lifting their arms, moving their crippled fingers freely, and walking and running amid cheers and clapping. There was a small boy in rags who ran joyfully across the field in front of the stage, with his little homemade crutch held high above his head. Many testified from the platform the next day to the wonderful healings they had received. I was shocked.

Over the three nights we were there, I used this approach and saw incredible miracles: literally thousands proclaimed themselves instantly healed. This was accompanied by hundreds coming forward each night to invite Jesus to be Lord of their lives. These people had never done so before; among them were pagans and non-Christians. It was very moving to see them filled with the Spirit and then praying in tongues.

We had never seen such things before in anyone's ministry. It wasn't that we didn't believe many were being healed. But thousands from a few commands spoken over the crowd and a short prayer? I remember thinking to myself, "They must have misunderstood the question," and, "Maybe they put their hands up to 'claim' their healing by faith, hoping if they did so, God would then heal them." I couldn't help doubting.

The next day, we were to lead a small healing service in a tent, for around three hundred people. I decided to use this opportunity to get to the bottom of things. We led the event as we had done at the large evening sessions, and around two hundred claimed to be healed. I then stationed my team members at the four corners and the entrance of the tent: one for those healed in their hands and arms and legs, one for eyes and ears, one for tumors, and so forth. I instructed the people who claimed healings to go to the appropriate station and explain what their condition had been before the prayer and what was the change, demonstrating that change to my team.

After a long time interviewing all two hundred people, our team gathered and shared what we had heard. Every single person who had claimed to be healed had a genuine testimony of healing and could show how he or she was better. We looked at each other, amazed. My friend Nik and I, who had traveled from England together, went to the car and repented for doubting what the Lord had done on the previous nights. Our vision for what God could do was utterly transformed that day.

Since then, our wonderful God has faithfully reproduced extravagant outpourings of healing at our Miracle Healing Services. I recently returned from Uganda, where I was leading the Charism School and a Miracle Healing Service. In the healing workshop, of the 350 present, an incredible 296 received physical healing through the prayers of the participants after the training. That is better than 80 percent of the attendees. On the following Sunday, eight hundred were healed as a result of a total of thirteen minutes of the word of command and short prayers.

We are seeing the same things happening in the West—though not yet in the same percentages. It is normal in a gathering of a thousand people to see 120 to 200 people physically healed by God's grace, and at times up to 250 or 280. Recently, in an ordinary Catholic parish in London, almost one-third of the people who attended received an instant physical healing. When such proportions are being healed in the Western world, you know God is on the move!

Acting in faith

In several cases, Jesus ordered the sick person to take action himself. For example, he commanded the paralytic, "Rise, take up your bed and go home" (Matthew 9:6). This involved the man taking a step of faith.

When we pray for healing, it is normal for me, after the word of command, to invite people, "In the name of Jesus, do what you couldn't do!" This is a crucial moment of decision, and most people respond by attempting something that was previously impossible without risking harm to themselves. Praise God; in this way tens of thousands have discovered that they are instantly healed!

There are occasions when I look out after the word of command, and I can see that people either are too afraid to try or don't believe anything is going to happen, so they remain timidly in their seats. At this point in one service, I noticed a lady who had remained sitting with two crutches next to her. I approached her and gently encouraged her to try to stand and walk. She was very nervous and had almost no expectation of healing. I took her hand, and to her surprise, she stood up quite easily and then walked briskly back and forth without her crutches.

I was in India leading a Miracle Healing Service, with the archbishop present. At a certain moment, the vicar general asked me to pray for a Hindu man. This man had suffered from at least two strokes and was unable to stand unaided, walk, or raise his left arm. He had been carried into the meeting by two of his sons.

I jumped off the stage with a sense of confidence that God was going to act, laid my hands upon the man, and was joined by several others. After a short prayer, I invited the man to stand. In faith he did so. I said, "In Jesus' name, walk!" and he began walking freely and waving his previously paralyzed arm, to the wonder of all present.

After the service, this Hindu man walked home with no aid from anyone, and on the way, he told everyone in the streets what Jesus had done for him. Some months later, the Indian priest who had originally invited me spoke to the archbishop who had been present at the service. The archbishop told the priest that because the man healed was a political figure, this one healing had a huge impact in the predominantly Hindu town. The name of Jesus had been glorified.

Other Ways Healings Can Happen

Healings at a distance

Distance was no obstacle to Jesus as he ministered healing. When the royal official asked him to heal his dying son, Jesus said, "Go [home]," adding, "your son will live" (John 4:50).

Many have testified to receiving healing at a distance. Once in London, we were concluding a Miracle Healing Service with a prayer for the absent sick loved ones of the people there. As usual, I asked people to hold up their hands and imagine the names of these people before the gaze of God. I then simply prayed for each main part of the body, from the head down to the feet—"Brain conditions, be healed; arms, be healed," and so on.

A young Indian woman held up the name of her father, who had been in a coma in India for two weeks. The following day, she spoke to her mother in India and discovered that her father had woken from his coma at the exact time we had prayed in England. Jesus is alive!

In Rimini, Italy, at the Renewal in the Spirit annual gathering, a parish priest held up the name of his assistant priest, a man in his thirties or early forties who had already had cancer and had recovered after a period of treatment. Now the cancer had returned as a tumor on his brain, which had been confirmed through a biopsy. He was booked to undergo a cancer scan to assess the precise size of the tumor on that Tuesday. However, on his arrival at the hospital, he was told that the machine was broken. He was asked to return in two days.

It was on that Tuesday that his fellow priest held up his name as I prayed for absent sick friends and relatives. Two days later, when the assistant priest went for his cancer scan, the tumor had completely vanished. More than a year later, this priest attended another large gathering in Italy, where I led a Miracle Healing Service. He came to the stage, introduced himself, and told me the entire story, and we praised Jesus.

When I was in central Tanzania leading our Prophecy School, a priest spoke to me about his father, who was partially deaf. Because the older man lived on the other side of the country, he was unable to attend the Miracle Healing Service. I told the priest to call his father and have him listen the best he could on the phone to the service, and the Lord might well heal him.

However, the priest's sister, who lived in the village with their father, decided to gather ten sick people from the village in her home. These included her father, two women so lame they had to be carried to the house, plus others with various ailments. They all listened to the Miracle Healing Service, with the phone on speaker mode. By the time the service ended, seven of the ten had been healed. The priest's father had received his hearing back, and both lame women ran home. God is great!

Healings after the event

Jesus ordered the ten lepers, "Go and show yourselves to the priests" (Luke 17:14). The lepers had not yet been healed at that point, but Jesus ordered them to act as if the healing had already taken place. This was an act of faith that he demanded of them.

We have found that there are often cases of people receiving prayer of one kind or another at our services and there appears to be no change, but the next day or soon after, the healing is experienced. This was the case with the first cancer healing I saw. I have seen it also with people suffering from many other conditions, including people in wheelchairs. Praise God.

Some healings are delayed in their manifestation. It seems that the prayer kills or drives out something at the root of the sickness or sows the seed of the healing. The fruit of this process flowers over the following hours or days.

An organizer of one of our events in the United States related to me the testimony of a blind woman who had come to one of our Miracle Services. At the service, she received only the ability to see light, so we did not allow her to give a testimony from the stage. However, three months later, she returned to the organization that had hosted our service to tell them that over the three-week period following the service, she received all her sight. If people don't have any evidence that they are healed at the time, we encourage them to remain open to God's action over the next few hours and days.

The use of material things in healing

The Twelve "anointed with oil many that were sick and healed them" (Mark 6:13). The Church has taken up this practice in the Sacrament of the Sick. This book is not focusing on the sacraments, beautiful as they are, but only on spiritual gifts, spiritual charisms.

In the history of God's people, material things were often used as channels of God's power. Moses used his staff to split the Red Sea; Elisha inherited the cloak of Elijah, along with a double share of his spirit, and used salt to purify poisonous waters (Exodus 14:16; 2 Kings 2:9-14, 21). Holy water is commonly used for healing in various places and in some healing ministries. People have used cloths that have been prayed over by the person with a healing charism. In the Book of Acts, "God did extraordinary miracles by the hands of Paul, so that handkerchiefs or aprons were carried away from his body to the sick, and diseases left them and the evil spirits came out of them" (Acts 19:11-12).

Often the power of such things is seen in the ministry of deliverance, where the reaction of the evil spirits can be dramatic. But even when dealing with physical sickness, the results can be extraordinary.

I remember the first time I was asked to pray over a hanky for a sick person not present. A nun made this request, and that night she took the hanky and laid it upon a fourteen-year-old girl who was cared for by the sisters in their hostel. The girl was so lame that she was not even able to drag herself across the floor to the shower. The morning following the prayer, the girl woke up and found that she could stand and walk!

On another occasion, a woman asked me to pray over a cloth for her husband. The man had been chronically ill for years, unable to walk unaided or take care of himself. Every morning the wife would get him out of bed, set him up for the day, and prop him in his chair, where he would remain until she returned from work in the evening. On the morning after our meeting, she gently laid the cloth upon him while he still slept, and she then left for work. On her return, she was stunned to find him out in the garden mowing the lawn!

The final example I'll share is of an autistic child, about four years old, who had never been able to talk, show affection, or look into the eyes of anyone; he also had chronic behavior problems. His grandmother requested that I pray over a hanky, which she then laid upon the child with prayer for healing. She left the hanky under his pillow, as I had instructed. Two weeks later, when she returned to the house, she experienced something that took her breath away.

As the woman came through the front door, her grandson came running toward her, looked up into her eyes with his arms outstretched, and called, "Nana, Nana, I've been watching Sponge Bob!" The change was incredible. Not only did he speak and express affection, but his behavioral problems disappeared as well.

When I heard this testimony, I was completely shocked. I had not had the faith for such a result. Even though I had seen many huge miracles, I had never expected to see this. God is great!

Healing through hearing a testimony

One time I was leading a conference in a venue that had a wall of windows all along one side. To encourage faith and teach the dynamic of faith, I told the story of the first person in a wheelchair that the Lord had used me to heal. Suddenly there was a loud cry from the right of the auditorium. Looking over, I saw a very stout woman lying on the floor, groaning loudly. I asked the team to help her outside, but she was unable to walk because the power of God was so strongly upon her. She had to be carried.

This woman had been able to walk only in pigeon steps and with great effort. Her husband had been forced to build a wooden sidecar on his bike to get her around.

Once the woman was outside, I carried on with my talk. Suddenly there were cries and cheers from those sitting on the window side of the hall. We all stared in amazement as the woman outside sprinted up and down the length of the hall, with her arms in the air, praising and shouting.

The woman told us afterward that it was simply hearing the story of the healing of the lady in the wheelchair that ignited in her the faith that she too could be healed. Then God's power had come upon her, and that was that. God had done it with no intervention from anyone.

Prayer for those unable to cooperate

In the Gospel story of Jesus raising Jairus' daughter (Mark 5:35-42), Jesus is told on his arrival at the scene that the little girl is dead. But he replies, "The child is not dead but sleeping" (5:39).

I was in Poland leading a training conference, and one of the hosts approached me rather concerned. He explained that a woman who had been attending the conference was asking if I could go and pray for her seventeen-year-old son, who was in the hospital. He had a serious drug problem and had been taking and selling all kinds of drugs even though he was living at home. The mother had arrived home to discover her son in a comatose state. As was confirmed later, he had consumed all his stock of illegal drugs.

The woman's husband was not around, so she dragged her son into the car and rushed him to the nearest hospital. Blood tests revealed that there was such a huge amount of poison in the young man's system that recovery was absolutely impossible. Even if for some reason he were to awake, the doctors told the mother, he would die within days because of the inevitable damage to his vital organs.

I walked into the intensive care unit with someone from my team, along with a translator and the mother. Two other team members remained outside and interceded. It was a tragic sight. The young man was lying almost lifeless, more like a dead body breathing than a person asleep. We gathered around him and began to pray.

I had witnessed the day before, for the first time, a cancerous tumor disappearing overnight after prayer and a word of command. As I stood there, I felt that if Jesus could cause cancer to disappear, he could do the same with poison. My teammate and I laid hands on the man as his mother stood quietly weeping at the foot of the bed. I invited the Holy Spirit to come in power and commanded the poison to leave his body. We commanded various spirits to leave him and prayed that he would know he was profoundly loved. We also prayed that he be filled with the Holy Spirit.

As I was praying, I had an interior image of the man sitting up and happy. At the end of the prayer, I turned to his mother and told her what I had seen. But I was careful to make her no promises.

A few days later, I received an e-mail telling me what had happened since the prayer. Over the first twenty-four hours, there was no change, and then suddenly, the young man came out of the coma. His first words were "I'm hungry." The doctors reminded the mother that this was only temporary and to prepare for his demise. However, to their utter surprise, the young man remained perfectly well. After twenty-four hours of observation, he was permitted to walk around the ward.

The doctors did a new test and found, to their astonishment, that there was absolutely no trace of poison in his body. Thinking the test results must be a mistake, they did more. Each showed the same result. The young man was totally well in every respect. After forty-eight hours, he was sent home, and the doctor told his mother there was no explanation; this was a miracle.

Such miracles show us that even when there appears to be absolutely no hope and no medical solution, God can intervene in dramatic ways.

Healing in the streets and public places

Jesus' ministry of healing was not restricted to holy places such as the local synagogues or the temple. He also healed people in the streets and in the countryside, as well as in their homes.

The first time I experienced such a healing was in the lane next to our community house not far from London. On the way out with my daughter, Miryam, we passed two construction workers (a tough couple of characters) about to dig up the road with pickaxes so as to put in stronger grills for the drains. It was a very cold day.

As we returned from our errand, we saw one of the workers crouched on the floor, holding his back in agony and groaning. I asked what had happened, and the uninjured one told me, "He's torn a muscle in his back." I replied that we could pray for that, and the worker in agony offered no resistance as I placed my hand on his back and we prayed a short prayer.

Within thirty seconds, the man looked up, startled, and burst out in his London accent, "It's 'ealin'! It's 'ealin'! It's 'ealin'!" I got him to stand up and move around, and he discovered that he was completely restored to health. He immediately became a witness, telling all the other workers and his boss about the healing he had received.

Today we have a weekly ministry on the streets. We were greatly helped in getting started by a young evangelical Christian who has devoted his life to this ministry. Our experience since has been wonderful. On the last day that I accompanied the team, of about twenty people prayed for, most were healed, and three of them were freed from their canes. Several people gave their lives to Jesus for the very first time, including a lovely Hindu couple who were both healed.

On another occasion, two of our guys approached two Muslim young men and offered prayer. As our team prayed, the power of God fell upon the young man they were praying for, and he fell back against the wall behind him three times, under the power of the Spirit. The other was also deeply touched. These young men asked, "What's happening here?" They were really astonished, and my team explained that this was the power of the Spirit of God. At the end, the team led them in a prayer to put themselves under the protection and guidance of Jesus.

Today as I'm writing, I have just received one team's report for today's street ministry. Here are just three examples of what they sent me:

> The first person was a guy in a wheelchair; he had pains in his legs and weakness. After praying for his legs and for deliverance, he got out of his chair, left it behind, and walked around with us for the rest of the day, praying with people!
>
> Next was a Muslim who had a damaged ligament. After a short prayer, he looked up and said, "What did you do?!" And he kept asking if it was black magic. Of course, we said, "No. It was Jesus the healer!"
>
> We prayed for a guy who had arthritis in his hip and knee; his pain went from ten to zero. He then gave his life to Jesus and spoke in tongues.

How wonderful! The fact that the man in the wheelchair who had been healed had only been in a church twice in his life and was unbaptized makes it all the more amazing.

People being healed without expecting it

Although there don't seem to be clear examples of this in the Gospels, people who are not even thinking about being healed sometimes receive healing.

At a Miracle Healing Service for twenty-two thousand people in Europe, I was commanding various conditions to be healed, and the Lord was healing vast numbers. But among the many healings of biblical proportion that occurred that day, one especially sticks in my mind.

There was a humble man who was not attending the conference but working as the janitor. He had been totally blind in one eye for more than twenty years. Suddenly the conference staff saw this man beside himself with excitement and confused astonishment. In a moment, totally and unexpectedly, without receiving prayer, he had recovered his sight in that eye. With much emotion, he demonstrated this by reading small print perfectly.

In another case, a woman with a liver defective from birth attended our Grace and Glory Conference but received no prayer. Two days later, she had a routine scan and discovered that she had a brand-new liver.

So let's not be surprised when the glory of the Lord is being manifest if bystanders get caught up in the power of the kingdom.

Healing through visions and visitations

When I was in India, I had the privilege of leading the Charism School for three hundred leaders and their teams, including about eighty priests, many nuns, and many lay leaders. We also were privileged to lead a Miracle Healing Service for twenty-five thousand, in which we saw incredible miracles. The school went very well, and the Lord poured out his gifts.

After the healing workshop, during which we trained participants how to effectively pray for physical healing, we had a large number of testimonies. When the testimonies were almost over, a nun came up and shared how she had been suffering from an almost completely paralyzed arm, which was now healed. At the end of her testimony, she shared something a bit unusual. As she was healed, she had the impression that her mother, who was suffering from a cancerous tumor in her throat, was being healed at the same time. I rather doubtfully encouraged her to contact her mother and let us know the next day what had happened. The following morning, we found out.

At the very moment of the nun's healing, her mother was sitting at home alone, when suddenly she had an apparition of Jesus standing before her. As she looked up at him, he smiled at her and spoke to her very briefly. Then he leaned forward and touched her. Instantly the tumor in her throat vanished. Then he disappeared.

How does one react to such an amazing event? I was stunned and speechless. I had never heard of such a thing. Here was the Son of God manifesting his presence in such a special way and healing a woman in response to what was happening in our workshop! We glorified God. It was a lesson to me that whatever one thinks the parameters are in Christian ministry, the Lord can do just as he pleases and is perfectly happy to work way beyond our expectations.

Healings from watching a film or TV

We have had reports of people being healed while they were watching one of our short films about healing miracles. But what is more common, at least in our experience, is people being healed while watching live a healing service, either online or on television. We have had many instances of this.

Perhaps the most dramatic was in Brazil. When I commanded the lame to walk in Jesus' name, many in the service were healed, including a woman in a wheelchair and some people on crutches. Even more amazingly, a woman sitting at home in her wheelchair, watching the Miracle Healing Service live on her television, was also instantly healed. She got up and walked.

Healings and medicine working together

In Croatia a young married man was carried in on the arms of two friends. He was very weak with cancer, which had invaded his abdomen and genitals. His doctors had told him that even if they managed to defeat the cancer, he would never have children.

We cursed the cancer and commanded it to die. When he was next examined, the doctors discovered that every one of the cancer cells in his body was dead. In surgery, they cut out all the dead cells, and now he is well and has two lovely children! Alleluia!

No physical change, but everything works anyway

There is a famous cure of a woman who was born with no pupils. She came to confession to Padre Pio, and afterward she could see. But she still had no pupils!

I prayed with a crippled woman many years ago. She was in an electric wheelchair and was on a huge dose of morphine and a cocktail of other drugs because of the pain from three crumbling discs in her spine. She was quite unable to stand unaided. After prayer, she ran around the auditorium. Her x-rays showed that her spine was just the same, yet she was still walking years later! What a mystery!

Repeated prayers

At a service in Minnesota, I commanded eyes to see, and many people had healing in their eyes. One woman came forward and shared how she had been totally blind in one eye, and now she could see shapes but no details. So I prayed over her again, commanding her eyes to see perfectly in Jesus' name. She fell to the ground under the power of the Lord, and I left her with two in my community, who prayed with her as I interviewed someone else who had been healed.

Two minutes later, the woman opened her eyes and, getting up, started calling out, "I can see! I can see!" She could count my teeth and describe details. People stared with their mouths open. She wrote on her testimony form that she now had perfect 20/20 eyesight!

A miracle for a friend

Sometimes people think miracles only happen in large miracle services. In Jesus' own ministry, people were healed when there were crowds but also one-on-one.

A friend of mine had an accident with a saw, which had cut his thumb down to the bone and, his doctor said, right through his tendons. It was very painful, as one can imagine, and it bled profusely. When I saw him, he had a huge bandage over it. He was booked for surgery the next day. We were chatting on his garden bench, so I offered to pray. I said a short prayer for healing and then left.

The following day, I received a text: "Surgeon says he sees no evidence of tendon damage. No operation—on my way home." His tendons, which had been cut in half, had been healed overnight, and he could move his thumb normally. Isn't God great!

You don't have to wait for a Miracle Service to receive a healing. If you dare to believe, God can really surprise you.

Children being used in healing

Children can have great faith for healing. On one occasion, I was about to fly to Ireland but was really suffering from a terribly inflamed eardrum. The doctor said it was so bad that my eardrum was unrecognizable. He warned that if I were to fly, the eardrum would almost certainly burst, and the scarring that would result would cause me to lose some of my hearing.

I was in a lot of pain. If I coughed or sneezed, the pain was like a red-hot poker thrust into my ear. I could not open my mouth more than a centimeter.

I asked my son, John, who was only eight years old at the time, to pray for me. As he did so, I felt something happening, so I encouraged him to command my ear to be healed in Jesus' name. He did so as though he were zapping it like a superhero. I was instantly and totally healed. All pain vanished, and I could move my jaw, which previously had caused me agony. The next day, I flew to Ireland with perfect hearing and not a trace of pain.

It is important to grasp what happened here. All the swelling and inflammation were healed in an instant, and my ear was made perfect.

I have heard many reports of God using children in healing. When his mother was pregnant with St. Vincent Ferrer, a blind woman placed her head on his mother's womb to hear the heartbeat and was instantly cured of her blindness.[8]

Following a terrible flood in Africa, some boys discovered the dead body of their friend. Having seen adults raise the dead, they addressed the Lord in prayer for their friend, who was then restored to life. A member of our community has since met that resurrected boy. Thank you, Jesus.

Healing through forgiveness

It is not always necessary for the sick to forgive before receiving healing, but it does seem to be important in some cases. I remember a lady at a service in the United States who arrived with an avocado-sized benign tumor on her leg. She had had it for years. She had come with a list of intentions of people in need of healing, with no idea of asking for healing for herself. However, as I invited the crowd to join me in praying a short prayer of forgiveness for any person the Lord indicated they needed to forgive, she decided to join in. Within ten minutes, the tumor was the size of a pea.

---

8. St. Vincent Ferrer Foundation of Texas, "Life of Saint Vincent Ferrer," http://svfonline.org/life-of-saint-vincent/.

Another time a lady arrived in her wheelchair at one of our events in London. As I led the prayer for forgiveness, she received the grace to forgive her sister, with whom she had had a falling out forty years before. As she did so, she was filled with light. Five minutes later, she was freed from her wheelchair.

This woman had not spoken to her sister for those forty years, apart from one blunt sentence at a family wedding. Now she was determined to go and be reconciled. She traveled to the north of England, only to discover that her sister had moved from that house several years before. Fortunately, the new owner had kept the sister's new address. The woman took it and set off with some trepidation for her sister's new house.

The woman rang the doorbell, and her sister opened the door. Not recognizing her sister but thinking her to be from social services, she immediately turned and began walking back down the hallway, calling back, "Mind you, don't trip over the dog," who was lying across the hall. My new friend, waiting on the doorstep, called her sister by name. Recognizing the voice, the sister turned back with tears of love and forgiveness. Forty years of bitterness were healed as they fell into each other's arms. The lady who had been healed later went on a solo trip to China and India!

Healing of animals

In our services, we have a time near the end when we pray for absent sick loved ones. We ask people to imagine that the names of their loved ones are written on their hands, and then they hold their hands up to the Lord.

Once in Atlanta, there was a lady whose neighbors were worried because their cow had been very sick for some time. Knowing how they relied on that cow, the woman decided to hold up the name of the cow. Looking out at hundreds of raised hands, I prayed for the healing of all those represented in the way I usually do, unaware that I was also praying for the healing of a cow! The following day, the lady spoke to her neighbors about their cow, and they told her that the cow had completely recovered overnight! We thanked God but couldn't help laughing.

This is not unheard of in Church history, as many of the saints healed animals. St. Macarius, one of the Fathers of the Desert, saw such miracles:

This same Macarius had a hyena's den near his cell. One day the beast brought her blind cubs to him and laid them at his feet. When he realized that the animal was beseeching him concerning the cubs' blindness, he asked the Lord to grant them sight. They received it and followed their mother back to the den. Shortly afterward she emerged with the cubs, carrying in her mouth a great bunch of woolly sheepskins; she brought them to the elder as though they were a gift in return for the favor received, left them on his doorstep, and departed. [9]

Developing Compassion

I remember being in Africa many years ago and being disappointed and actually a bit annoyed that only two blind people had been healed. I had been there the previous year, and five people had been healed of blindness.

It's perfectly fine to want to see an increase of healing year by year, but my feelings were not coming from right motives. I had slipped, at least in part, into relating to people as statistics. If people become statistics to us, we soon lose all joy in the ministry. It is love that makes this ministry a joy. If I love the people, I will rejoice with them when they are healed, and that joy will sustain me.

When I first began leading Miracle Healing Services, I included a lot of minor complaints in my words of command for healing. After a time, as more began happening, I edited out one or two categories because they seemed rather small and wouldn't produce great testimonies for the Lord's glory. If you have deaf, blind, and lame people, why give time in a busy service to lesser ailments? So to save a bit of time, I dropped praying for people's necks to be healed.

A few weeks later, I developed a serious problem with my neck. It became so bad that the pain was waking me up several times each night. I was praying for healing and relief when I realized, with a little shame, that many people might be needlessly suffering in this way because I had ignored their need. Necks were immediately reinstated in my list of conditions to pray for.

Some people think that because all are not healed at our services, we should not offer healing prayer. Their thought is that the unhealed will leave

---

9. *The Church History of Rufinus of Aquileia*, Books 10 and 11, trans. Philip R. Amidon, SJ (New York: Oxford University Press, 1997), 65.

upset. Based on that logic, the medical profession should not offer chemotherapy, because not everyone's treatment for cancer is successful.

A man in his thirties approached me after a Miracle Healing Service at which there had been many healings and said to me, "Don't you think it's cruel to get people's hopes up when some of them aren't going to be healed?" I answered him with a question: "If your mother had cancer and she was the only one healed tonight, would you be asking me the same question?" He graciously conceded the point.

It is not our practice to make promises of healing to people (unless we receive an exceptional revelation). We only want to give testimony to the promises of Jesus and what we have seen him do, encouraging people to be open to his power and love. Even if people are not healed themselves, it is important that they try to exercise a generous compassion and joy for those who are. We want everyone at our services to experience the compassion of Jesus, whether they are healed or not.

I was careful while my children were growing up to not go on an international trip more than once a month. But even with that, I remember one occasion when my little daughter particularly didn't want me to go away. Everything was booked, and there was no way it would have been right to cancel. (In fact, once I have discerned with my wife that I should go somewhere, I never cancel.) So I sat my daughter down, and we had a cuddle and a chat.

I explained, "Darling, if you were living in Africa instead of England, and you were born deaf and mute, and there was a man with a gift of healing who could heal you, would you want his family to sacrifice him for a few days so that your life could be changed?" She completely understood, and all was then fine. After that she always put her hands on me, giving me a blessing, as I left for each trip.

When I'm tired and the last thing I want to do is pray for the sick, I remember how I'd feel if my son or daughter was suffering from the disease or condition I see before me. I try to love the people how I would want my child to be loved, and God has helped me.

Our Basic Model for Prayer for Physical Healing

Jesus did not simply establish a wonderful healing ministry for himself but trained others. It is clear to us that God wants to use lots of "ordinary people" in this ministry.

The people on my own team, who have been trained, have seen wonderful miracles, including healings of deafness, lameness, blindness, lifelong skin conditions, and tumors that shrunk or disappeared. On one occasion, a woman's inability to conceive, which was the result of an operation, was supernaturally reversed. I once sent one of my team in my place with another team member. He led a Healing Service at which, to his amazement, more than 50 percent of the people declared themselves instantly healed.

The first principle in our model for physical healing is to learn how to follow God's guidance. Even Jesus himself highlights the need of this when he says, "The Son can do nothing of his own accord, but only what he sees the Father doing" (John 5:19). Healing models can help because they give a basic framework from which to start, but they must always yield to the guidance of the Spirit.

Before seeking physical healing at an event or in other situations, we often begin by building up people's faith in the power of the Lord to heal through preaching, speaking about God's promises, or sharing testimonies of healings we have seen. Then we use the following steps.

1. **We engage with the person and assess what the problem is.** We listen to the person briefly, and at the same time, we listen to the Lord. We do not want too many details from the person and certainly not a medical history, just something like "I can't lift up my right arm" or "I can't hear anything at all out of my right ear."

2. **Then we invite the Holy Spirit,** and if we feel led, we lay hands gently on the person. We wait until the person appears to be really engaged with God. The more deeply people engage with God, the more likely they will be to receive his power. We encourage them to close their eyes, open their hands, relax, and yield to God's presence as they can.

3. **We discern what actions to take.** Usually, if we haven't done so already and if we are led to do so, we place our hands on the area in need of

prayer. It is very important that this be done in an appropriate way. If we are not led to lay hands, we follow the Holy Spirit's leading, as there may be some other action that is needed.

4. When we feel ready or led to do so, **we command healing in Jesus' name:** "Eyes, see clearly, right now, in the name of Jesus! And any spiritual cause affecting this eyesight, be gone." This is not the only way to pray, but it is a good way to start, because often God wishes to heal quickly. However, some may feel that praying such a prayer is beyond their faith. If so, then just pray with as much faith as you can from your heart.

5. Then we ask the person to **do in Jesus' name what they could not previously do.** For example, "Count my fingers," if they were blind, or "Lift your arm up," if it was paralyzed, or "Try and walk without your crutches," if they were unable to do so before. Sometimes the power of God causes manifestations in the person's body. If such an encounter takes place, do not interrupt but allow the Lord to finish what he is doing. However, be careful to discern the cause of these. If they are not of God, measures should be taken. If emotional things surface, then appropriate comfort and prayer for inner healing might be needed. If there is demonic influence, then prayer for deliverance is necessary.

    There may be what is called in some circles "soulish" manifestations, manifestations that are the result of emotionalism or attention seeking, or some other inappropriate response not prompted by God or the devil and possibly produced subconsciously. In such cases, the person should be gently but firmly helped to calm down, take control of themselves, and focus on cooperating with the prayer for healing.

    Normally there are no external manifestations, and healing is straightforward. When healing happens, we then praise God.

6. On some occasions, the healing is **not complete, but there is an improvement.** In such instances, we pray again for two or three minutes only and, if necessary, repeat this until we gain no more ground or the healing is complete.

7. **If no healing has taken place,** it is kind to pray a compassionate prayer of intercession, blessing, and encouragement, so the recipient does not

feel like a failure or think that God doesn't care. We don't want anyone to go away "empty-handed."

During this whole process, we are open to words of knowledge, words of wisdom, and discernment of spirits, in case there are contributing factors that need to be dealt with before the person can receive the physical healing he or she needs.

Again, make sure that when healing does occur, you give glory and thanks to God. Often people who are used by God in this ministry try to be humble by playing down God's interventions, for fear of pride. Personally, I think that it is better to do as Mary did and praise God for his wonderful deeds (Luke 1:46-55), while reminding ourselves often of our utter unworthiness to be his instrument

CHAPTER 6
LIBERATION FROM EVIL SPIRITS

" In my name they will cast out demons." —Mark 16:17

I was leading a conference in England and had just invited the Holy Spirit upon the congregation. Looking around the room, I noticed a woman near the back. I could see in her eyes, which were clouded with darkness, the presence of an evil spirit.

As the ministry to others proceeded, I approached the woman and began to pray. Sure enough, what was in her was unable to hide in the presence of the Lord and his power. Against her will, she began gasping and making noises and facial contortions, all of which she desperately tried to suppress. I proceeded to calmly command the evil spirits to leave and prayed for inner healing and forgiveness. Certain manifestations took place, but we were able to prevent these from becoming violent. In a few minutes, the woman was completely freed of appalling events from her childhood and a spiritual infestation that had afflicted her most of her life. I left her bathing in the beautiful peace of the Savior.

Later the woman approached me, and her eyes, which had been so dark and cloudy before, were a shiny blue, brilliant with light. No one in the room had such beautiful shining eyes in that moment. She was free. She was full of joy and love for Jesus, and we thanked him together.

Such stories have become relatively common all over the world and especially in the Charismatic Renewal. Although serious, this case was not an especially difficult one, and because much grace was given and received, a great work could be done quickly. Some deliverance prayer is much more dramatic.

Often there is no manifestation when a person is liberated. For example, a priest came to me very distressed because every time he celebrated the holy Mass, he experienced a terrible rage surging through him at the time of the Consecration, as well as a strong hatred for Jesus in the Blessed Sacrament. I had very little time, so I prayed for him for two or three minutes, including a simple prayer very quietly commanding any evil spirit to leave him. He was overjoyed to find at his next Mass that all the rage and hatred for the Lord had vanished completely, and all he experienced was love and devotion for Jesus. This has continued ever since.

Deliverance in the History of the Church

Jesus understood that confrontation with the powers of evil was central to his mission. "And he went throughout all Galilee, preaching in their synagogues and casting out demons" (Mark 1:39). Jesus never shied away from this ministry or called it by another name. He met it head-on and with total authority. He made it clear that liberations from the powers of darkness are signs of the in-breaking of the kingdom. "If it is by the finger of God that I cast out demons, then the kingdom of God has come upon you" (Luke 11:20).

Jesus commissioned his disciples to liberate people from the influence of evil spirits, and he clearly intended the ministry he exercised in this area to be continued in the Church. Every time Jesus sent out his disciples to preach and heal, they exercised authority to cast out demons. In Luke we read, "He called the twelve together and gave them power and authority over all demons and to cure diseases, and he sent them out to preach the kingdom of God and to heal" (Luke 9:1-2; see Matthew 10:5-8; Mark 6:7-13). He sent out the seventy-two, and they returned rejoicing, saying, "Lord, even the demons are subject to us in your name!" (Luke 10:17). In the Gospel of Mark, this commission is extended further still to include all believers: "These signs will accompany those who believe; in my name they will cast out demons" (Mark 16:17).

We see this authority in Peter's ministry: "The people also gathered from the towns around Jerusalem, bringing the sick and those afflicted with unclean spirits, and they were all healed" (Acts 5:16). And the same was true of Paul, who drove from a girl a spirit of divination (Acts 16:16-18).

The Book of Acts also relays occasions when other disciples, not just the apostles, cast out devils. Philip the deacon (not the apostle)

> went down to a city of Samaria, and proclaimed to them the Christ. And the multitudes with one accord gave heed to what was said by Philip, when they heard him and saw the signs which he did. For unclean spirits came out of many who were possessed, crying with a loud voice; and many who were paralyzed or lame were healed. So there was much joy in that city. (Acts 8:5-8)

As with prophecy and healing, this wonderful and important ministry did not cease with the death of the apostles and the first generation of disciples.

Church history has extensive examples revealing its continuance through ordained ministers, catechists, bishops, official exorcists, religious, and lay Christians, both men and women.

The writings of the Fathers

If we wish to gain a better understanding of this ministry so that it might regain its rightful place among the people of God today, it is helpful to look at the writings of some of the Fathers regarding deliverance from demons. It should be remembered that during the era of the Fathers, the power to cast out evil spirits was considered a power granted to all Christians.

Justin Martyr, the famous early Christian apologist born in AD 100, in his Second Apology, chapter 6, addressing the Roman Senate, expressed the conviction that Christians who cast out devils were helping foster belief in Jesus Christ through their work:

> For numberless demoniacs throughout the whole world, and in your city, many of our Christian men exorcising them in the name of Jesus Christ, who was crucified under Pontius Pilate, have healed and do heal, rendering helpless and driving the possessing devils out of the men, though they could not be cured by all the other exorcists, and those who used incantations and drugs.[1]

St. Irenaeus, who was born in AD 130, in the second book of his work *Against Heresies,* confirms Justin's views. He considers the Christian practice of driving out demons a matter of common knowledge.

Later in the second century and early in the third, we find Tertullian agreeing. In chapter 23 of his *Apologetics,* challenging a pagan audience, he asserts that the practice of exorcism is not reserved to any one person or group, lay or clergy. It is a special gift or charism given to *all* Christians.

> Place some possessed person before your tribunals; any Christian shall command that spirit to speak, who shall as surely confess himself to be a devil with truth, as elsewhere he will call himself a god with falsehood. . . . What work can be clearer? . . . [T]here will be no room for suspicion; you would say that it is magic, or some other

---

1. St. Justin Martyr, *The First and Second Apologies,* trans. L. Barnard, *Ancient Christian Writers,* no. 56 (Mahwah, NJ: Paulist, 1997), 76–78.

deceit, if your eyes and ears allowed you, for what is there to urge against that which is proved by its naked sincerity?[2]

Origen of Alexandria, who lived from 185 to 232, in his apology *Against Celsus*, speaks quite extensively about demons and the means of casting them out

> without the use of curious arts of magic, or incantations, but merely by prayer and simple adjurations which the plainest person can use. Because for the most part it is uneducated persons who perform this work, thus making manifest the grace that is in the word of Christ and the despicable weakness of demons, which, in order to be overcome and driven out of the bodies and souls of men, do not require any wisdom of those who are mighty in argument or most learned in matters of faith.[3]

St. Cyprian, who died in 258, drew on Tertullian's conviction that every Christian inherited the power to cast out demons. And for him too, this power was received at baptism.[4] St. Athanasius, in *The Life of Antony*, presents this layman as an exemplary model of Christian virtue and a powerful healer and exorcist: "Through him the Lord healed many of those present who suffered from bodily ailments; others he purged of demons."[5]

The *Catholic Encyclopedia* remains one of the largest collections of Catholic teaching ever assembled in a single work. Of deliverance from evil spirits, it says:

> Besides exorcism in the strictest sense—i.e. for driving out demons from the possessed—Catholic ritual, following early traditions, has retained various other exorcisms, and these also call for notice here. . . .
> We have it on the authority of all early writers who refer to the subject at all that in the first centuries not only the clergy, but lay Christians also were able by the power of Christ to deliver

---

2. Tertullian, quoted in John Henry Newman, *Two Essays on Biblical and on Ecclesiastical Miracles* (London: Longmans, Green, and Co., 1890), 225.
3. Origen, *Against Celsus*, bk. 7, chap. 4. 4.
4. Adolf Rodewyk, *Possessed by Satan: The Church's Teaching on the Devil, Possession, and Exorcism*, trans. M. Ebon (Garden City, NY: Doubleday, 1975), 41.
5. Athanasius, *The Life of Antony* (New York: Harper Collins, 1980), 18.

demoniacs or energumens, and their success was appealed to by the early Apologists as a strong argument for the Divinity of the Christian religion. . . . As is clear from testimonies referred to, no magical or superstitious means were employed, but in those early centuries, as in later times, a simple and authoritative adjuration [command] addressed to the demon in the name of God, and more especially in the name of Christ crucified, was the usual form of exorcism.[6]

Chicago exorcist Fr. Jeffrey Grob, in his doctoral thesis on exorcism, states, "The practice of ordaining the exorcist became normative in the West. However, there is evidence that the earlier practice of allowing any Christian to exorcise continued also in the West. 'The residual assumption remained that all Christians, women included, were able to drive out devils.'"[7]

Moral theologians

The position of the Fathers is confirmed down through the history of the Church, as Fr. Jim McManus states:

In Catholic moral theology, since the Council of Trent, we find very consistent teaching on the role of exorcism in the pastoral ministry. St. Alphonsus Liguori speaks for the tradition when he writes: "Private exorcism [i.e. simple exorcism/deliverance] is permissible to all Christians: solemn exorcism is permissible only to ministers who are appointed to it, and then only with the express permission of the Bishop."[8]

Major moral theologians have upheld this position since then. McHugh and Callen, in their standard text on moral theology, write:

---

6. P. Toner, "Exorcism," *Catholic Encyclopedia* (New York: Robert Appleton, 1909), newadvent.org/cathen/05709a.htm.
7. Jeffrey S. Grob, "A Major Revision of the Discipline on Exorcism: A Comparative Study of the Liturgical Laws in the 1614 and 1998 Rites of Exorcism," dissertation submitted to the Faculty of Canon Law, St. Paul University, Ottawa, 2006, 52-53, quoting Rodewyk, *Possessed by Satan*, 41, heartofthefather. com/wp-content/uploads/2014/11/Grob-Doctoral-Thesis-PDF.pdf.
8. Fr. Jim McManus, *The Ministry of Deliverance in the Catholic Tradition* (London: National Service Committee for Catholic Charismatic Renewal), 14, quoting St. Alphonsus Liguori, *Theologia Moralis*, nos. 111, 112, p. 492.

As to their manner, exorcisms are . . . of two kinds, the solemn and the private. The former are made in the name of the Church in the manner prescribed by the Ritual and their administration is reserved to clerics who have a special and express permission from the Ordinary (Canon 1151). The latter kind may even be made by members of the laity, and we read that certain saints like St. Anthony of the Desert and St. Catherine of Siena, had great power over evil spirits.[9]

Recognized moral theologian H. Noldin writes, "Private exorcism [simple exorcism/deliverance] which truly is not a sacramental can be executed by all the faithful."[10]

C. Marc states, "Private exorcism [simple exorcism/deliverance] is lawful to all, especially priests, nor is there any special permission of the bishop required"[11] D. Prummer agrees, stating, "Nowhere is it forbidden to the laity to use private exorcism [simple exorcism/deliverance]."[12]

It is worth clarifying that "private" does not mean "in private"; rather, it refers to the personal nature of the ministry exercised in faith by a Christian, as opposed to the "public," that is, official ministry exercised by an appointed exorcist of the Church. In addition, *simple* does not mean theologically that the case is necessarily simpler, which suggests that it is easier to deal with. Rather, *simple* means not using the formal ritual and official prayer of the Church. Fr. Gabriel Amorth, the former president of the International Association of Exorcists and chief exorcist of Rome over several decades, said:

A lay person who prays for deliverance from demons offers a private prayer, calling upon the common priesthood of the faithful and the power granted by Christ to all believers. . . .

However, let us be clear on this: *The Lord takes faith into account.* Therefore, the simple prayer of a lay person, even though it is private, could be more efficacious than the prayer of anyone else.[13]

---

9. John McHugh and Charles J. Callan, OP, *Moral Theology*, vol. 2 (New York: Joseph Wagner, 1958), para. 2267(b), p. 365.

10. H. Noldin and A. Schmitt, SJ, *Summa Theologia Moralis* (Innsbruck: Felizian Rauch,1960), ques. 54, vol. 3, p. 43.

11. McManus, 19.

12. Ibid.

13. Fr. Gabriel Amorth, *An Exorcist: More Stories* (San Francisco: Ignatius, 2015), 92.

Gifted saints and lay people

Fr. Amorth upholds the teaching of traditional theology that this ministry is not limited to official exorcists or clergy but that gifted laity can be powerfully used to liberate people from demons:

> And let us not forget who is considered, though never officially, the patron of exorcists, patron of the whole category: Saint Benedict. There's a famous coin, minted long after his time, which depicts him. In exorcisms I always use a crucifix with the St. Benedict coin inlaid. He wasn't a priest either, he wasn't an exorcist, but he cast out demons. And those saints could drive out the devil right away, with a single prayer! We call it exorcism, but it was certainly not the prayer of the Rite. And it must be said that in the end it's not really worth that much, the text of the Rite. . . . It's the faith that counts.[14]

Fr. Amorth cites the example of St. Catherine of Siena, a laywoman: "When an exorcist could not liberate a demoniac, he would send the afflicted person to St. Catherine. Then the saint would pray and obtain liberation."[15]

It must be remembered that while at this time the Church has restricted ministry to those truly possessed to her official exorcists, this is a pastoral decision, not a theological statement, and one that could change. This is because there is no theological basis for excluding others from exercising the power necessary to liberate the possessed should the Lord wish to grant such a charism to any of his children. However, until the Church changes her position, Catholics are bound to submit to her pastoral norms.

Liberating people from evil spirits is often exemplified in the lives of the saints and holy people from many branches of Christianity. Deliverance can affect not only individuals but large groups of people, as in this example from the life of St. Francis of Assisi:

> One of the favorite wiles of Satan is to irritate men against one another, as in the following instance, related by St. Bonaventure: One day the blessed Patriarch Francis went to Arezzo. That city,

---

14. Fr. Gabriel Amorth, *Memoirs of an Exorcist: My Life Fighting Satan* (Milan: Piemme, 2014).
15. Amorth, *An Exorcist: More Stories*, 92–93.

which had long been a prey to civil dissensions, was verging on its ruin. Francis beheld the demons dancing with joy on the walls of the city, and exciting in the hearts of its people the fire of hatred against each other. Calling to him Brother Sylvester, a man of dove-like simplicity, he said, "Go to the gate of the city, and in the name of Almighty God command the devils, in virtue of holy obedience, to depart immediately."

The Brother hastened to fulfill his orders, and cried out in a loud voice, "All you evil spirits who are gathered together in this place, I command you, in the name of Almighty God and of His servant Francis, depart hence." No sooner had he uttered these words than the discordant voices were hushed, the people's angry passions were calmed, the fratricidal feud ceased, and peace was restored to Arezzo.[16]

Deliverance and exorcism in the Coptic and Orthodox traditions

There are stories of deliverance and exorcism in the Orthodox and Coptic traditions as well as the Pentecostal and Charismatic Evangelical traditions. As noted in previous chapters, Pope Kyrillos VI had many spiritual gifts, including power over demons.

When the Pope [Kyrillos VI] was a hermit in Old Cairo, many patients came to him to be healed with the power of God. What astonished many was the power he had over demons. He used to heal as one with authority.

I will mention examples of miracles that took place before my eyes to provide the readers with an idea of the extent of the power of God that accompanied this righteous man throughout his entire life.

Many were waiting for the Pope to come down from his cell. While he was at the top of the stairs, one person screamed, "Keep him away from me! Keep him away from me!" When the Pope inquired about the reason for this screaming, he was told that the

---

16. *Manual of the Third Order of St. Francis: Its History and Short Explanation of Its Rules* (New York: Burns and Oates, 1884), 68.

145

man was demon possessed. As soon as the Pope arrived on the main floor, the man fell to the ground in a state of epilepsy. The Pope helped him up and called him by his name saying, "Arise Abimalik," prayed for him, and ordered him to take communion. The young man arose and repeatedly kissed the Pope's hand. The rest of the attendants were astonished that a touch from this holy man could perform exorcism.[17]

Deliverance and exorcism in the Pentecostal tradition

The legendary Pentecostal Smith Wigglesworth was often used with great power in liberation from evil spirits, as the following story illustrates:

Wigglesworth arrived at the house in London and was taken by the hand to the girl's room by her parents, who wept as they mounted the stairs. They then left Wigglesworth outside the door. Tentatively, he opened the door and was confronted by a shocking sight: before him was a young girl being held down struggling by four men . . . , her clothing torn and disheveled. Wigglesworth entered the room and stared into the girl's eyes, which were rolling around in their sockets. The demon powers that were inhabiting the girl hissed menacingly, "I know who you are. You can't cast us out; we are many."
Wigglesworth takes up the story:

"'Yes,' I said. 'I know you are many, but my Lord Jesus will cast you out.' . . . The power of Satan was so great upon this beautiful girl that in one moment she whirled and broke away from those four strong men. The Spirit of the Lord was wonderfully upon me and I went right up to her and looked into her face. I saw the evil powers there; her very eyes flashed with demon power. 'Though you are many,' I cried, 'I command you to leave at this moment in the name of Jesus!' She instantly began vomiting. During the next hour, she vomited out thirty-seven evil spirits and she named every one of them as they came out. That day she was made perfect and

---

17. Fr. Rafael Avva Mena, quoted in Ata and Mena, 29–30.

whole. The next morning at ten o'clock, I sat at the table with her at a communion service."[18]

Deliverance Today

It is important to remember the distinction between formal, official, or solemn exorcism and private or simple exorcism. The latter has become known in the charismatic and Pentecostal tradition as "deliverance." All Christians are called by Jesus to pray for deliverance from evil in some way, as we see in the Lord's Prayer: "Deliver us from evil." Some, including many among the laity, have a special charism in this area.

In our view, it would be unwise for some persons to pray over others for deliverance, such as those suffering from severe depression or exhaustion and people experiencing a vulnerable period in their lives. Of course, it goes without saying that those struggling with regular patterns of serious sin should not be involved.

As we have seen, liberating people from the influence of evil spirits was a central aspect of Jesus' ministry. Such liberation can take place in simple ways, of which we are often unconscious at the time. A person might be delivered, for example, through an act of love, a word of truth, a time of worship, the reception of the sacraments, the reading of the word of God, an act of repentance or forgiveness, acts of humility, a time of personal prayer, the invocation of the Holy Spirit, or the fulfilling of duties. These are the normal means by which most people are protected and cleansed of the influence of evil spirits in day-to-day life.

At times people might make comments such as "Oh, I feel so much lighter" or " I have peace again." Or they may become aware of being more right with God or others. Yet they are unaware of what has taken place.

Experience has shown that sometimes these normal means of cleansing and liberation are not sufficient, and the influence of evil spirits needs to be addressed more explicitly. In our society, which has abandoned the relative safety of a Christian ethos and moral code, there are many developments that make people susceptible to the influence of demons. These include the breakdown of social norms regarding many areas of morality; the many forms of physical and emotional abuse, especially in childhood; corruption

---

18. Julian Wilson, *Wigglesworth: The Complete Story* (Bucks, UK: Authentic, 2002), 134.

of the entertainment industry, in particular in TV, film, music, computer games, and the Internet; and the growth of false religious groups and views, such as New Age, neo-paganism, atheism, the occult, witchcraft, and Satanism. It is astonishing to watch how quickly long-held clarity over certain tenets of morality are collapsing, as people wander blindly in the darkness, without the light of the gospel and the wisdom of the Church to guide them.

In the early Church, which was born into a pagan empire, it became necessary for catechumens to pass through a period of exorcisms before baptism. These were performed mostly by lay catechists. Still today, all baptisms contain a prayer of exorcism.

It is not unusual for us to find—in the middle of a simple prayer of blessing or intercession in prayer ministry—a deliverance need revealing itself, either in subtle or dramatic ways. It is my opinion, and that of many others in this ministry, that many people in our society need deliverance at some level. If societies continue in spiritual decline, I believe we will see deliverance once again becoming one of the major signs to the world of the kingship of Christ. In my opinion, it will not be only a "hidden ministry" experienced in the context of private appointments but will also be witnessed in public, as it was in many other periods in the history of the Church. It will be a sign to the world that Jesus is Lord.

Thus, the idea that one exorcist can deal with the growing needs for liberation in a diocese is as ridiculous as imagining that one dustman is enough for an entire city or one doctor for an entire town, especially when there is an advancing epidemic! This is a very important ministry, and it cannot be carried out by just a few priests and expert laity. It needs once again to be part and parcel of the normal ministry of all Christian communities of believers, as it was in the first centuries of the Church. Of course, those offering this ministry need to be trained, and their lives need to be in good order, with an established life of prayer. However, such people can be found. The Church needs sensible, levelheaded formation developed for local communities that helps people understand this area in a balanced way and equips them to grow and mature in it.

Deliverance of believers

The New Testament confirms that at times, believers may need prayer for deliverance. History provides many examples. One example from the New Testament is the deliverance of the man in the synagogue (which suggests he may have been a member of the congregation), who was controlled at that moment by an evil spirit. Jesus dealt with this through a simple command (Mark 1:21-28; Luke 4:31-37).

I had a surprising experience in a Miracle Healing Service in Romania. The service was in a local public theatre that seated nine hundred to a thousand people; it had a very large balcony holding hundreds of the congregation. The crowd was made up of Catholics, Orthodox, and Evangelicals. At the beginning of the service, I spoke about the power of the name of Jesus. As I did so, a woman with a demon ran to the front of the balcony and began screaming in English, "You lie! You lie! You lie!" (Her husband told us later that she did not speak a word of English.) I simply said, "Sister, we love you, and Jesus loves you," and she instantly became silent and fell back into her chair, and two members of the team prayed with her.

Everyone burst into loud applause and cheering. They knew that in those simple words, Jesus had taken control of the situation. We had no more interruptions from her the rest of the night. Glory to God!

Weapons in deliverance

I discovered the power of the cross in deliverance ministry many years ago, when I was still quite new at all this. I was in training with people more experienced than myself. On this particular day, I was called to give assistance in a very serious case.

The individual, a woman, was becoming violent and breaking the furniture. As I entered the room, the two women team members were calmly talking, and the woman with the demon was leaning up against the wall like a caged animal. I rather innocently drew out of my pocket a small crucifix that had broken off a rosary, saying, "Well, I've got this." As I held it up, the woman was thrown to the ground, away from the cross, and then lay crumpled in the corner. I was shocked and praised God.

A similar thing took place when I first administered holy water. The person with the demon began screaming very loudly. I discovered that evil spirits experience burning when holy water is applied.

Other weapons in this ministry include the holy name of Jesus, the Scriptures, blessed salt, invoking the blood of Jesus and the light of Christ, relics of the saints, the invocation of the help of the saints and angels, cloths prayed over by those with a special charism in this area, and the praise of God.

Holiness in deliverance

It has sometimes been said that one can only drive out a demon from someone else that one has defeated in one's own life. I think many people engaged in this ministry would agree with this statement. In our experience, this does not mean that one has to be a saint before God can use you. I would caution, however, that it would be highly foolish to attempt to deal with an area in which you yourself are having serious problems. That said, ordinary good people who are praying daily and love God and seriously try to live by God's commands in love can be effective in many cases.

Even so, people who are growing in holiness have a great advantage in this ministry, if they have faith for deliverance. And very holy people with faith for deliverance can see absolute wonders, in which the most severe cases are freed by one prayer or command or in which even their presence can utterly terrify demons. A priest I knew was on his way to pray with a person who had a demon, and the demon began protesting in fear about the priest's coming. Glory to God!

Physical healing through deliverance

Jesus often freed people from demons that were causing sickness—for example, the man with a "mute and deaf spirit" (Mark 9:25).

I remember the first time I saw a physical healing as a result of casting out an evil spirit. A very nice middle-aged Anglican woman who was suffering from a rare disease that was slowly killing her came for an appointment. This condition caused her body to always feel completely cold. Something in her nervous system was dying, and she was given ten years to live. To get some sense of heat in her body, she would have three scalding baths every day. These were so hot that her husband could not even put his hand in the water.

As we talked with her and prayed for discernment, two words came to my mind. I asked if these words meant anything to her. She answered that these words were almost exactly the name of the cottage she had been staying in when she first became sick. We knew we were onto something.

We began to pray, and after a minute or so, I simply and calmly commanded the spirit of that name to leave her and go to the feet of Jesus. Instantly the woman felt heat filling her whole body, something she'd not felt for years. She was completely healed of her incurable terminal disease, and months later, she told me that her doctor had confirmed her healing. Since that time, we have seen many healings as a result of casting out an evil spirit.

Deliverance from mental disturbance

Mental disturbances can have many sources, and it would be unwise to suggest that all mental problems come from the influence of demons. But as this chapter is about dealing with demonic influence, it would be an omission to say nothing about the wonderful changes that have come to some people's mental health through deliverance when the cause is truly demonic. The man whose demons named themselves "Legion" seemed to have the symptoms of insanity, but his condition had a spiritual cause (Mark 5:1-20).

Once a desperate mother brought her three-year-old son to me. He was completely out of control, and she was suffering from utter exhaustion. He ran wildly all over the room in a very disturbed manner, and it was impossible for either of us to get his attention in any way. It took her some time to catch him, and then she had to hold him very firmly in her arms. Every time I tried to put my hand on him to pray, he threw himself forcefully in the other direction. This was done in such a violent way that it took all the mother's strength to prevent him from escaping her grasp. She told me that he was like this all the time.

Quite unable to get my hand on any part of his body for prayer, I just placed it over him, following his movements the best I could. I prayed for healing and almost silently for deliverance, having discerned that this torment was very likely caused by demonic influence. There appeared to be no change at all in the boy, and he left as wildly out of control as when he had arrived. I heard nothing from them for three years.

Then one day, at a Catholic Miracle Rally in London, the mother approached me. Standing next to her, quietly holding her hand and looking up at me, was a perfectly behaved six-year-old boy. She explained who she was and proudly showed me her son. I could not believe my eyes. She said nothing had changed that day three years ago, but in the two weeks that followed, something remarkable took place. All his traumatic and disturbed behavior completely disappeared, and he became a happy and sane little boy, engaging in life like any other boy of his age. His life was transformed, and so was hers. Glory to God!

A friend of mine in another country was brought a woman who was violently out of her mind. She had to be fastened with ropes for her own protection and that of others, and she was in the charge of four men who struggled to control her. My friend had never dealt with such a severe case before. But after prayer and discerning that her problems were truly spiritual in origin, he proceeded to pray with her, and by the power of God, she was totally liberated in one session.

Multiple deliverances

At times Jesus liberated more than one person at the same time, as we see with the two demon-possessed men in Matthew 8:28-34. There were even times when he freed many possessed by demons (Matthew 8:16; Mark 1:32-34).

Sometimes at our events, we have a time praying for deliverance. And it is normal to witness many people delivered at the same time. There are often manifestations of various degrees of intensity but sometimes none at all. Usually between 20 and 40 percent of the congregation raise their hands at the end to confirm that they felt something leaving them. Often this number is considerably higher, up to 60 percent.

Degrees of Demonic Influence

Evil spirits can influence people's lives in a variety of ways, from temptations to possession, which may affect people morally, psychologically, spiritually, and sometimes physically. Serious discernment is often needed to discover what is going on and how to deal with the issue. In this area, different authors use different language to describe various levels of demonic influence. The language I have chosen may not, therefore, correspond with what is familiar to the reader, but this is not the most important thing. What matters most is an understanding of the subject so as to be able to help people appropriately.

The demarcation of where one criterion ends and another begins is also not always clear, and each category listed has various degrees of intensity. Demons can enter people through persistent indulgence in serious sinful patterns, through traumatic events, through contact with the occult, or at times through the influence of forebears. This is not a comprehensive list but rather a brief summing up of some ways the demonic can influence people.

Demonic Temptation

In traditional theology, there are three areas in which we must gain victory in the Christian life: the world, the flesh (our fallen nature), and the devil. There are many ways in which we are tempted, but when these temptations are not simply the result of our interaction with the world and our fallen nature, they can be the direct result of demonic activity. Often such temptations seem particularly strong and compelling.

At times, we make ourselves vulnerable to such attack because we have allowed ourselves to repeatedly fall prey to "normal" temptations in one area so that certain patterns begin to establish themselves. It is then possible for the demonic to take advantage of such a situation and establish itself in our lives. Such temptations can be occasional or persistent. In other cases, demonic temptations can be a one-time experience. Such temptations, it should be said, are not the preserve of weak people with patterns of serious sin. Even canonized saints were sometimes attacked with terrible demonic temptations.

Even so, in such situations, a short, direct prayer, prayed by the individual himself in the name of Jesus, can drive away the tempter. However, if such temptations become persistent and strong, it may be helpful to receive prayer from a person of faith in this area.

Affliction

Sometimes demons can bring influence into our lives through afflictions. These can come in many forms, such as obstructions and assaults, and are external to the person. There are extreme examples of such instances in the lives of the saints, including St. Pio of Pietrelcina and St. John Vianney, as well as in biblical characters like Job. This can include demonic visitations or demonic visions or the disturbance of material things, such as objects being moved, thrown around, or broken. If this should happen, prayers for protection and prayers of praise are very effective in halting them. The use of sacramentals, such as holy water, or invoking the holy name of Jesus or Scripture also have great power. If places are discerned to be severely infested by the presence of evil, the celebration of a Mass can be highly effective in banishing evil spirits.

Sometimes attacks can come in more subtle ways through the people around us, and we find ourselves attacked on many fronts simultaneously—our boss becomes vindictive, passersby become aggressive for no apparent reason, and so on. In some countries, attacks upon a person may be the result of curses put upon people by others. But the power of curses can be broken through prayer.

Also under this category of affliction come those illnesses that are the result of demonic activity and that are healed not through prayer for healing but by a prayer of deliverance.

Oppression

Demonic oppression seems to be experienced as an unpleasant weight upon a person emotionally or spiritually, and it may even be felt physically. Sometimes it is accompanied by depression. Of course, such feelings can come from natural causes, and discernment is needed. Often this kind of problem can be dealt with by a simple prayer commanding the oppressing spirit to leave. At other times, especially if the oppression is linked to deep emotional and psychological issues, it can take longer. But as these problems are dealt with, the enemy loses his grip, and with prayer, freedom comes.

Obsession

At this point, we find considerable differences of interpretation and use of language among authors. I am using the term here to refer to strong, demonically inspired, obsessive thoughts, temptations, and emotional and psychological torments.

Bondage or infestation

There is a category of demonic influence in which evil spirits have gained control of some aspect of the individual. This could be in any of the areas of the seven deadly sins, for example, or some other area resulting in a great lack of freedom. At this stage, we are no longer referring to an influence that is external to the person, yet is less than full possession. Even so, this kind of influence can, at times, be dealt with reasonably simply and quickly.

The example at the beginning of the chapter fits into this category. Recently I was in the United States, and we were in the middle of a time of inviting the Holy Spirit to minister to the people. A young woman who had appeared perfectly fine up until that moment suddenly began screaming uncontrollably and fell to the floor. It was clear to me this was not emotional in origin. I prayed for deliverance silently so as not to worry her, as she was young. As I continued to pray, she became calm and rested in the Holy Spirit.

After the event, she came up to me and thanked me, saying, "I feel so much lighter now." I'm not even sure she knew what had happened to her. This was quick and easy, but at other times, more serious manifestations can take place, and something of a battle may be required to gain victory.

Usually in bondages of this kind, the evil influence is not experienced all the time but rather operates mostly in a particular area of a person's life or in particular circumstances. This can be the case in otherwise normal people. Perhaps it shows itself in persistent or recurring irrational thoughts or reactions in an area of the person's life that prevent them from living in the joy and peace of the Lord. We have ministered to great numbers of people with such issues. Here is a testimony from one such person:

> I used to have regular feelings of hate for life. I was even afraid of eternal life because I hated life so much and couldn't stand the thought of keeping it for eternity. Once during ministry at a Cor et Lumen Christi event [when I was being prayed over], I went into a fetal position on the ground. I remember it was as if I were watching it happen. Damian rebuked a spirit in me, and I started screaming and kicking. Then there was great peace. For weeks afterward, I experienced an extraordinary peace in my body. The peace still remains decades later. I have not had those feelings of hatred for my life ever since.

I chose this example because such experiences are relatively common. But there are other examples in which the level of bondage is considerably more serious and influential in the person's life. Even so, the Lord of glory is bringing large numbers of people into a transformation of life through liberation from evil spirits. This is taking place through both gifted clergy and gifted laity, for which we praise God.

Possession

At times, the influence of evil spirits becomes so strong in the person that he or she becomes possessed. This is an experience of domination of the personality and/or the body, which can be temporary or permanent, and the degree of influence, while very strong, can vary. However, this is not the place for explanations of possession. Suffice it to say that the Church, through her members, has since the time of the apostles been effectively liberating the possessed by the power of the authority of Christ. Praise God!

Of course, in all these levels, discernment of what is causing the problems is needed. However, I will deal with this in the chapter on discernment of spirits (chapter 8). In this ministry, it is crucial to pray for the spiritual gift of discernment of spirits. If we don't have it, we must try to make sure that someone on our team does.

The Importance of the Word of Command

It is obvious to anyone who has been in this ministry for any length of time that in many cases, indirect prayers for deliverance are not adequate. In such cases, the direct command has more power and effect. In the New Testament and the early Church, this was the normal means of obtaining liberation for those suffering from demonic influence.

As the Church has nowhere forbidden the laity to use the direct command in deliverance ministry (private or simple exorcism), I want to give three main reasons from our experience why love demands, in many cases, the humble and faith-filled use of the direct command.

1. The direct command is often needed when a demon manifests in a person. This can be a moment of suffering and turmoil or confusion for the individual concerned—spiritually, emotionally, and sometimes physically. Such manifestations may cause the individual to experience humiliation, and in these circumstances, the indirect prayer may not be sufficient or immediate enough in its effect. In the process of liberation, the direct command is often the simplest and most effective weapon we have to save the individual experiencing prolonged and unnecessary suffering and humiliation at the hands of demonic powers in the process of liberation. So love demands that we use the most effective and swift means to free them.

2. The direct command is often necessary if there is a public demonic manifestation that invites unhealthy fascination or fear on the part of onlookers. I remember being in a ministry situation in which a woman standing in the front row exploded into demonic screaming

at such a volume and pitch that it dominated the entire auditorium. We had a group of young people helping with the worship ministry, who on seeing this became very afraid. I briskly walked over to the woman and, discerning the cause to be demonic, commanded the demon to be silent in Jesus' name. The screaming instantly stopped. People around the woman breathed a sigh of relief, and the devil was humbled before the power of Jesus. Alleluia! Everyone's faith in the power of the Lord grew in that moment. We proceeded, by God's power, to free the woman very quickly from that which was tormenting her. Those young people will never forget witnessing the authority of Jesus and the instant submission of the demonic to his power in that situation. Love for the bystanders sometimes requires the use of the direct word of command in deliverance.

3. The direct command is often necessary in public evangelistic gatherings when a spontaneous demonic manifestation takes place and the power of Christ over the powers of darkness must be demonstrated. This reveals the victory and saving power of Christ as Lord over all. Unbelievers present justifiably want to see if Jesus' power in his disciples is greater than that of the evil one. An effective word of command finishes all arguments and demonstrates that Jesus is not only a person of history and a prophet but also the Lord of lords; every power has been put under his feet. In the first centuries of the Church, the liberation of people from evil spirits was one of the primary signs that convinced pagans of the truth of the gospel. Love for unbelievers requires use of the word of command in many situations of spiritual confrontation.

How to tell when the spirits have left

Through discernment, the one leading the ministry or another working alongside the leader can tell if a spirit has left a person. This can be assessed by the person's responses to the sacred: a crucifix, holy water, the name of Jesus, and so on. Sometimes we can look to the experience or discernment of the person receiving prayer, but it is vital not to allow that person to steer the ministry. Fr. Gabriel Amorth testifies:

> At the end of the most difficult exorcisms, when I am confronted with total demonic possession, I pray the christological hymn of the

Letter of Paul to the Philippians (2:6-11). When I speak the words "so that all beings in the heavens, on earth, and in the underworld should bend the knee at the name of Jesus," I kneel, everyone present kneels, and always the one possessed by the demons is also compelled to kneel. It is a moving and powerful moment.[19]

Finally and most reliably, we know a spirit has left because of the fruits we observe in the person's life over the following days, weeks, and months.

Prayer for Deliverance: Several Approaches

There are several approaches to deliverance prayer (private or simple exorcism) used in various parts of the Catholic Church today. We here present three different ones. None are to be understood as the best or only model; rather, all are offered because they have produced good fruit in this area of ministry over many years. The practitioners who composed these models have great experience and wisdom in the area of deliverance and are in excellent standing with their local bishops.

I agree with the Fathers that the power to drive out devils is a spiritual gift available to all sincere, praying Christians who are living good lives. Even so, it should not be assumed that everyone is suitable to engage in deliverance as an ongoing ministry, especially when dealing with very serious situations. In such cases, the Lord provides an especially powerful charism. At all levels of this ministry, we need wisdom, compassion, and real faith.

If you feel called to engage in this ministry regularly, keep in mind that it will require a strong commitment to radical Christian living as well as love, humility, a life of prayer, and strong faith. Ephesians 6:10-20 tells us that those engaged in such a ministry require the "whole armor" of Christ. Some people find it helpful to pray this passage as a prayer. When we are called to put on the full armor of Christ, what that really means is that "half-baked Christianity" in this ministry won't do.

Demons are never to be our focus, even though we must learn some things about them and their activity so as to help those afflicted by them.

---

19. Fr. Gabriele Amorth, *An Exorcist Tells His Story* (San Francisco: Ignatius, 1999), 22–23.

Christ Jesus is our focus, and the more our lives are focused on him—living in his light and walking in generous love, humility, detachment, and holiness—the more effective we will be.

Deliverance prayer model 1

This model is from a Carmelite theologian and professor emeritus of spirituality at the pontifical Milltown Institute of Theology and Philosophy in Dublin, Ireland. The author makes it clear that this model is not proposed as a model for all: "I am not addressing people who have a powerful, acknowledged deliverance ministry. This is a charism of deliverance. They will know other ways."

His indirect model of prayer is for those "who are not powerfully gifted in this area and do not have much experience but are nonetheless inevitably drawn into deliverance matters for pastoral reasons."[20] He also endorses the freedom for believers who have a charism in deliverance to use the direct command if required.

1. "**Prayer of Praise.** We begin with a prayer of praise that celebrates the Lordship of Jesus. It is because of his victory that we are engaged in this ministry. We recall his death and resurrection by which he has overcome all evil. We give thanks for the ministry he has given to those who believe in him.

2. "**Prayer of Protection.** We are engaged in a difficult and dangerous ministry, one against very powerful forces. We therefore pray for protection for ourselves and for those around us. We pray in particular that the person to whom we are ministering may be protected, that they will not come to any harm because of our ministry.[21]

---

20. National Service Committee for the Catholic Charismatic Renewal in England, *Deliverance as Part of the Healing Ministry*, April 1992, 19.

21. I draw a parallel with crossing a road. Crossing the road is probably the most potentially dangerous occupation most of us will engage in if we do not take sensible precautions. However, it would be ridiculous to stand on the pavement trembling for fear that we are likely to be killed every time we are about to cross the road! No, if we take wise precautions, we can step out confidently, keeping alert as we progress, and we will arrive safely at the other side. Yes, there are hazards in ministry, but if we are sensible and humble, ministering in faith and love, we can be in peace.

3. "**Scripture.** There is power in the word of God against all evil. But it has also great power for healing. We read God's word to strengthen the faith of the person in need, to strengthen our own faith. A few words of explanation of the scripture passage are appropriate here to focus on the main point of the Lord's word.

4. "**Intercession.** We pray for the strength needed for the person. We invoke Mary, the angels, the holy Michael and the saints to intercede for us. We recall the power of the Eucharist celebrated throughout the world even as we now pray, and we join spiritually in its offering. We present ourselves as weak and helpless in ourselves, but strong in faith and in the name of Jesus.

5. "**Prayer for Healing and Deliverance.** Healing prayer is an essential part of all deliverance ministry. It should certainly follow the actual deliverance prayer, but it will often be necessary at the beginning also to help the person to let go of sinful attachments, of resentments, and of what binds them: it is often necessary to help the person to reach out in freedom to the gift the Lord is offering."[22]

The actual deliverance prayer should normally be deprecative, that is, directed to the Father or Jesus or in the name of Jesus, to set the person free. In shaping our prayer this way, we follow the lead of the revised liturgy. It is a prayer in faith that God, through Jesus Christ, will liberate the person. In some circumstances, it may be appropriate to add a silent imprecatory prayer of direct command to the evil spirits to depart, but this may not be necessary.

After the deliverance prayer, further prayer for healing may be appropriate, so that the person may come into full freedom, with all blockages removed.

If there is a priest present at the deliverance session, it can be helpful to have the whole process within a celebration of the Sacrament of the Sick. In this case, the deliverance prayer can be said at the imposition of hands.

---

22. *Deliverance as Part of the Healing Ministry*, 21–22.

6. "**Prayer of Blessing.** With deliverance, the person is set free. But we have to avoid the situation described by Jesus:

> When the unclean spirit has gone out of a man, he passes through waterless places seeking rest, but he finds none. Then he says, "I will return to my house from which I came." And when he comes he finds it empty, swept, and put in order. Then he goes and brings with him seven other spirits more evil than himself, and they enter and dwell there; and the last state of that man becomes worse than the first. (Matthew 12:43-45)

We must always pray a blessing prayer that will invoke God's love and the power of the Holy Spirit on the person. A prayer for baptism in the Holy Spirit is very appropriate.

This rite may seem long, but it need only take about ten minutes. The all-important thing is not what we do but the power of God that we call down on the person in need. It is the quality of our faith that counts."[23]

Deliverance prayer model 2

Unbound Ministry is an approach to deliverance and healing developed by Neal Lozano and made popular through his book *Unbound: A Practical Guide to Deliverance*. Lozano describes Unbound as "a safe, loving, effective model of deliverance prayer that helps people to respond to the good news of the gospel and apply the truth to their lives by using five basic responses called *the Five Keys*. The focus of the model is on deep listening to a person's heart and story." The following is a description of the Five Keys of Unbound Ministry.

Key One: Repentance and Faith

Our greatest deliverance is in embracing the grace of baptism, turning from sin, and turning to the Lord. With the first key, we participate in ongoing repentance and expressions of faith as the hidden sins of our heart are revealed. "*Lord, I surrender to you . . . . Forgive me for . . .* "

---

23. Ibid.

Key Two: Forgiveness

If we want to be like Jesus, we need to forgive from the heart. Now, by faith, we pronounce forgiveness in necessary areas. Expressions of forgiveness are most powerful when they are specific and rely upon the power of Jesus' name. "*In the name of Jesus, I forgive . . . for . . .*"

Key Three: Renunciation

Renunciation is an expression of repentance and a declaration before the kingdom of darkness that I no longer make a home for sin, deception, and the power behind them in my life. In this key, we renounce the lies and deceptions that have been buried in our hearts and thoughts. "*In the name of Jesus, I renounce . . . fear . . . , anger . . . , the lie that I don't belong . . .*"

Key Four: Authority

In Christ, we have authority over our enemies who seek to destroy us. We can take our stand against them through repentance, forgiveness, and renunciation and then declare the truth of their defeat by saying, "*In the name of Jesus, I command any (or every) spirit that I have renounced to leave me now.*"

Key Five: The Father's blessing

Every blessing that the Father spoke to Jesus is ours. The Father reveals to us who we are as we come before him in the Son. With the fifth key, we listen to receive his blessing, and we are healed. To be free means that the obstacles to the gifts that have been waiting for us are removed, and the Father's love and affirmation are made real to us in Christ.[24]

Deliverance prayer model 3

This is a prayer for deliverance from Francis MacNutt of Christian Healing Ministries, Jacksonville, Florida.

---

24. Used with permission of the author, Neal Lozano, *Unbound: A Practical Guide to Deliverance* (Grand Rapids, MI: Chosen, 2010).

1. *"In the name of Jesus Christ, . . . "*

We cast these spirits out, not by our own authority, but by the power of the name of Jesus Christ. (The "name" really means the "person" of Jesus Christ.)

2. *" . . . I command . . . "*

It is no polite request we make of the evil spirits; we use authority. If there is doubt or hesitation in your voice, the spirits will pick up on your fear and try to further intimidate you ("We are stronger than you are"; "You will never get us out"; etc.). Believe fully in the authority of Christ to drive the spirits out. True it is that you cannot do it, but Jesus Christ within you will free the captive.[25]

3. *" . . . you spirit of _____ . . . "*

When possible, identify the spirit by name (for example, spirit of hate, spirit of lust, etc.).

4. *" . . . to depart . . . "*

This part of the command is self-explanatory.

5. *" . . . without doing harm to _____ [name the person by first name or entire name] or anyone else in this house or in her family, and without making any noise or disturbance . . . "*

There have been times other people have been attacked (or even entered) by the spirits as they leave. Sometimes, too, pets in the house have been invaded and behave strangely afterward. You can avoid all this by praying for protection before and during the deliverance.

Evil spirits like to create uproar and frighten you off by ugly and sickening performances, so command them to be quiet and not to create any

---

25. If you feel that your faith is too weak, you may be right. Let someone else lead the prayer, for no amount of bluffing will make us effective. We should pray for greater faith, and the Lord will surely hear us, as this is his certain will for everyone. However, judging our faith by our feelings is not always accurate. While we may feel that our faith is poor, it can still be enough for the job at hand.

disturbance. This will lead to a peaceful deliverance or, at the very least, cut down on any violent or noisy displays.

6. *"... and I command you to go straight to Jesus Christ, to dispose of you as He will. Furthermore, I command you never again to return."*

... Occasionally, you do not have to name the evil spirit, but simply, as you look into the person's eyes, command the spirit at whom you are looking to leave. You are already in contact with it, and you can tell it to go.[26]

Our own approach includes various elements found in these models, depending on the situation and the level of demonic influence we are dealing with. At times processes such as these are helpful, but at others a simple command, as in the Gospels, is all that is required.

It is always best to do this kind of ministry at least in pairs, which should be of mixed gender. A deep and regular life of prayer and fasting is very important for all those regularly engaged in this ministry.

I have seen firsthand how wonderful and life changing this ministry can be. We give God thanks for the authority he has given to his children, and we pray that this ministry will be fully restored to the whole Church.

---

26. Francis MacNutt, *Deliverance from Evil Spirits* (Grand Rapids, MI: Chosen, a division of Baker Publishing, 1995), 173–175. Used with permission.

CHAPTER 7

INNER HEALING

"The Spirit of the Lord is upon me
because he has anointed me to preach good news to the poor.
He has sent me to proclaim liberty to the captives."
—Luke 4:18

It is not clear to me that the inner healing ministry was intended by St. Paul to be included in his phrase "gifts of healings" (1 Corinthians 12:9). Paul certainly does not mention it, and therefore, it could be argued that it is beyond the scope of this book. It seems almost certain that St. Paul and the New Testament in general, when speaking of healing gifts, mean physical healing. However, inner healing deserves a mention, in my opinion, because through the hands of those skilled and anointed by the Holy Spirit, a truly profound transformation can take place that is far beyond the natural powers of normal counseling and therapy or any well-developed human process.

As inner healing may be unfamiliar to some readers, let me begin with two definitions. Fr. Michael Scanlan defined it this way: "Inner healing is the healing of the inner man. By inner man we mean the intellectual, volitional and affective areas commonly referred to as mind, will and heart but including such other areas as related to emotions, psyche, soul and spirit."[1] And from John Wimber: "I define inner healing as *a process in which the Holy Spirit brings forgiveness of sins and emotional renewal to people suffering from damaged minds, wills and emotions.*"[2]

Inner healing can come about in various ways, as the following examples will show.

In one case, a young man sought prayer. The minister, after inviting the Holy Spirit, received an image of the man's father opening his arms and welcoming his son. This had been a real event in the young man's childhood but had been buried under negative experiences. The image touched something very deep in the young man, and he wept profoundly. From that day, a pattern of conflict with his father completely disappeared.

---

1. Fr. Michael Scanlan, *Inner Healing: Ministering to the Human Spirit through the Power of Prayer* (New York: Paulist, 1974), 7–9.
2. John Wimber with Kevin Springer, *Power Healing* (Kent, England: Hodder and Stoughton, 1986), 95, italics in original.

At a conference in England, a word of knowledge was given from the platform that there was a woman present, suffering from depression, who had been abused as a child, had tried to kill herself on three occasions, and still struggled with suicidal temptations. As soon as she heard this, the woman knew that the word of knowledge was for her. At the end of the service, she came forward for healing prayer. When she arrived, she looked as if she had a black cloud weighing on her head. She came to me and explained her situation. The sexual abuse had caused a very deep depression, which she had been suffering from for years and for which she had been prescribed a high level of antidepressants.

I invited the Holy Spirit to come upon her. As I did, I led her in a short prayer of forgiveness. I then encouraged her to remain in God's presence. As she engaged with the Lord, I prayed and told her to say the words "I am loved. Amen!" She seemed to withdraw into herself somewhat and shook her head.

I repeated: "Say, 'I am loved. Amen!'" With a great deal of effort, she forced out the first words: "I am . . . " Then such a terrible cry of broken-hearted pain came from her that she could not finish the sentence. But I knew that the Holy Spirit was leading me. "Say it again," I repeated. "I am loved," she mumbled with great difficulty. "And again." "I am loved. Amen," she said quietly. "Louder, please." "I am loved. Amen!" she repeated in a louder voice. "And again," I said.

People around me probably thought I was being somewhat harsh, but I knew what the Lord was doing. "And again, louder." "I am loved. Amen!" She said it clearly now. I continued getting her to repeat this until, after four or five more times, she was declaring it strongly. Even so, she was still in tears. When I felt prompted to do so, I brought the prayer to a close. We had prayed for only ten or fifteen minutes. I told her that when she felt better, she should go to her doctor and have him take her off her medication gradually, as she had been taking it for many years. The woman left, still weeping quietly.

Some months later, I received a letter from her. She wrote that when she had arrived at the conference, she had gone to confession for attempting to kill herself because of her mental anguish. Then she went through the healing prayer with me and went to bed still in tears. However, this is what happened the following morning: "I was filled with joy, and for the first time in a long while, I woke up singing, and the dark cloud and cluttered negative thoughts all lifted off me, as if someone had switched on the sun in my head. My heart was lighter, and something dark had left me."

When I saw the woman one year later, I literally did not recognize her because she was so completely transformed. Her doctor had confirmed her healing and brought her off her medication over a couple of months. She was a new woman.

At one of our Healing, Signs, and Wonders Conferences, we prayed for the outpouring of the Holy Spirit and physical healing but not specifically for inner healing. However, a woman gave this testimony the following day.

She had been in a car crash twenty years before, which caused her to have noises in her ears and tremendous pains and weakness in her body. She could hardly lift a bowl of soup. All these physical symptoms were healed. But more interesting for what we are discussing here is that the shock of the accident had left a deep wound in her emotionally. Every morning for the twenty years since the accident, she had woken up crying uncontrollably and urinating. Through the prayer, God reached deep into the emotional wounds from that car crash and healed everything. After all the years of suffering and humiliation, she was free. How beautiful is the healing love of God!

As I have shared, the inner healing process can be the result of seeking prayer and then being helped by someone with skills and anointing in this area. It can also happen through a prophetically inspired word, as with the suicidal lady. And it can happen simply by being in the presence of God's power in a healing or Holy Spirit service, in which no one is actually praying for these issues.

We also find that inner healing can happen gradually. As people come regularly for general prayer, their hearts are healed by the enfolding presence of the Lord and his love and the prophetic words of encouragement and comfort from the team ministering to them. At other times, inner healing can be a simple process of ongoing forgiveness. One chooses to regularly release forgiveness to an individual, often with no feeling, until one day it is complete, and freedom comes.

Common Elements of Inner Healing

Inner healing can, of course, take place in an appointment situation with various Christian healing ministries. In such contexts, the inner healing process often involves the following:

- The recognition and ownership of an unhealthy or harmful pattern of thought, emotions, or behavior.

- The discernment that the roots of this are to be found in past events, either real or perceived.

- The need to forgive others or ourselves. Forgiveness can be instant or a process over time. People have to be helped to see that unless they choose to forgive, they can remain victims. Forgiveness is a decision that may not, at the beginning, be accompanied by feelings of forgiveness. But if these do not come at once, they may follow as forgiveness becomes deeper over time.

- The need to repent. This releases us from the burden of guilt and shame, opening us to God's transforming mercy.

- The identification of the event or events that created the inner wound. This identification could come by way of a memory or a revelation given by the Holy Spirit to the individual or another through a word of knowledge. (It should be noted that if we receive a word of knowledge, assuming it is accurate, we should discern carefully when we are to share it. God may want us to know something to help us in our approach to the ministry, but the person may not yet be ready to face it. Some experiences are so painful that the person cannot bear to think about them or is unable to remember them, because the mind buries them in order to cope with the associated pain. In this situation, make a note of the word of knowledge, and pray privately until such a time as it is appropriate to share it.)

- A release of emotions, which have sometimes been pent up for many years, such as anger, fear, sorrow, or loss, is sometimes experienced. In a ministry session, it is important to agree on a way of expression with parameters. Often the release of emotions is necessary to allow the deeper issue to become clear. Anger, for example, is always a secondary emotion. It should be remembered that a release of emotions does not of itself ensure inner healing. If causes are not dealt with, there will continue to be emotional problems.

• An experience of God's presence and/or truth (erasing the "root lie"— see below) in the past event and/or a new sense of peace and freedom. In inner healing, we are not trying to erase a painful memory or event; we are seeking its transformation.

• Prayer for restoration, the in-filling of the Holy Spirit, and reception of the truths of God's love deeply in the heart and mind.

• Post-prayer direction (including perhaps a word of wisdom and/or knowledge).

We do not give a rigid order to this process because experience tells us that God is not constrained by a particular pattern or structure. While forgiveness is almost always required, a release of emotions, for example, might not be. However, the above are normally parts of the inner healing process.

The root lie

Painful past events can send "lying echoes" through our lives, which skew our perceptions and cause exaggerated, inappropriate, or unhealthy reactions. Inner healing takes place when God's love, forgiveness, and truth are applied to the "root lie" and erase it.

The trauma of a bad car crash, for example, might cause an irrational fear of driving because of the root lie that says, "Be afraid; this will happen again!" Abuse imbeds the lies "I am vulnerable" and "I am worthless." The related emotional pain or reaction somehow feeds on the root lie. Once this lie is overthrown by God's truth and love in a spirit of forgiveness, freedom comes.

In this ministry, we witness in a powerful way how the truth, spoken in love, sets people free and lays solid foundations for living the life in the Holy Spirit.

A Model for Inner Healing Prayer

Here is a very simple model for inner healing that can be used to great effect by those with little or no training in this field:

1. Get into pairs.

2. Decide who will receive prayer and who will pray.

3. The person receiving prayer then asks the Holy Spirit to reveal to him or her any event that needs healing or any person who needs forgiveness.

4. Allow the Holy Spirit to bring to mind something or some person from the past that needs forgiveness.

5. It may be that some emotions surface at this point. (It's okay to feel these—emotions are amoral.)

6. Then, when you feel that you can (and it is necessary to use the will), pray the following prayer: "In the name of Jesus, I forgive _____ for _____. I pray that they be released from all negative consequences resulting from this sin, and I ask you, Jesus, to bless them with your joy, peace, happiness, and love. May they prosper in every way. Amen."

During this process, the other person simply prays silently or in tongues, perhaps giving some gentle nonverbal comfort (such as a hand laid gently on the person's back). In this model, do not use words of knowledge or in any way direct the process, other than helping the person through each stage at the appropriate moment.

Part III
Other Spiritual Gifts

CHAPTER 8

DISCERNMENT OF SPIRITS

It is my prayer that your love may abound more and more,
with knowledge and all discernment.
—Philippians 1:9

Discernment of spirits has served many roles in the life of the Church. It is essentially the gift to recognize when something is of God, humanity, or the devil. The word *discernment* has the sense of sifting or sorting between one thing and another, as in sifting wheat from chaff. The Fathers of the Church often used the term *discrimination*. Discernment or discrimination has been highly prized through the ages as a sign of spiritual maturity.

There are several instances in the New Testament where we see the gift of discernment of spirits. John the Baptist openly rebuked the Pharisees and Sadducees, who had apparently come to receive baptism in good faith. Discerning their hypocrisy and the real condition of their hearts, he called them a "brood of vipers" (Matthew 3:7).

On a number of occasions, Jesus used similar bluntness. When Peter contradicted the Lord's intention to go to Jerusalem and face the cross, Jesus responded, "Get behind me, Satan! You are a hindrance to me: for you are not on the side of God, but of men" (Matthew 16:23).

At times, as we have seen, when Jesus was healing, he simply commanded the person to be healed. On other occasions, he discerned the cause of the sickness as an evil spirit: "You mute and deaf spirit, I command you, come out of him, and never enter him again" (Mark 9:25). And it is clear that Jesus could discern the spirit motivating Judas, while this was hidden from his disciples (Matthew 26:21).

The devil quoted Scripture to Jesus, none of which was untrue in itself, only wrongly applied from a sinister motive. Judas' plea against the extravagance of very expensive nard being poured on Jesus' feet sounded reasonable at face value, but it was motivated by Judas' love of money (John 12:3-8). The discernment of spirits uncovered the reality.

In the Book of Acts, St. Peter discerned the spirit motivating Ananias and his wife, Sapphira, when they attempted to deceive the apostles with a false show of total sharing while holding back some of the money they had acquired. Peter declared, "Ananias, why has Satan filled your heart to lie to the Holy Spirit and to keep back part of the proceeds of the land?" (Acts 5:3). So serious was the deceit that the Lord struck them dead.

The Role of Discernment of Spirits

Discernment of spirits for prophecy

In the writings of St. Paul, the gift of discernment of spirits is often linked to discerning the origins of prophecy. Prophecy is inspired speech, and Fr. Francis Sullivan expresses the view of many biblical scholars that in discerning the origins of prophecy, discernment of spirits plays a vital role. He draws our attention to the fact that when Paul exhorted believers to "let two or three prophets speak, and let the others weigh what is said" (1 Corinthians 14:29), "the Greek word translated 'weigh' is a verbal form of *diakrisis*," the same word used for "discernment."[1]

Some basic disciplines help in our discernment of prophecy, such as knowledge of the Bible and of orthodox doctrine. But truth can be spoken with a completely wrong motive and from a wrong spirit. As noted above, when Satan tempted Jesus in the desert, he quoted Scripture but with malicious intent. Such "prophecies" produce negative results or confusion.

As we have already said, some so-called prophecies are simply pious sharings that are not inspired by the Holy Spirit. Others that are wrong might be innocent mistakes. We need to be alert but kind. False prophecy cannot be ignored but must be corrected if it misleads. Mistakes must be handled with patience and encouragement. With so many "prophetic" voices without and within the Church today, discernment is an indispensable gift in helping people correctly identify the genuine, life-giving, prophetic voice of the Holy Spirit.

Discernment of spirits in spirituality

Many of the saints and holy men and women down through the ages have exercised the gift of discernment. The Desert Fathers were renowned for their discernment of spirits, and they taught of its importance in the

---

1. Sullivan, 105.

Christian life. Some elders visited St. Antony of the Desert to ask him which is the greatest of all virtues. Antony concluded his answer with the following:

> "The light of the body is the eye; if therefore your eye is pure, your whole body will be full of light. But if your eye is evil, your whole body will be full of darkness" (Matthew 6:22-23). And this is just what we find; for the power of discrimination, scrutinizing all the thoughts and actions of a man, distinguishes and sets aside everything that is base and not pleasing to God, and keeps him free from delusion . . . [and] is the mother of all the virtues and their guardian.[2]

The teaching of the Desert Fathers was systematized by St. Cassian (360–435), who wrote extensively on discernment of spirits in the spiritual life, which he referred to as *discretio*. Speaking of monks who fall due to lack of discernment, he states:

> There is no other cause of their fall, except that not being formed by the ancients, they could not acquire this virtue, by which they can distance themselves from two contrary excesses. It teaches them a royal way that does not allow them to stray to the right, seeking a foolish presumptuous virtue or exaggerated fervour which would go beyond a just temperance, or to the left, towards slackness and vice under the pretext of right ordering of the body, which leads to lazy torpor of spirit.[3]

Throughout the history of the Church, the gift of discernment of spirits has had a very important place in the guidance of souls, and continues to do so. In Ignatian spirituality, it is the gift to know what spirit is the source of movements within the soul—what is prompting thoughts, desires, emotions, imaginings, inclinations, feelings, visions, sensory experiences, darkness, illuminations, locutions, and consolations.

It is important to remember that discernment of spirits is about identifying what is coming from God as much as knowing what is coming from

---

2. St. Nikodimos and St. Markarios, compilers, *The Philokalia*, volume 1, trans. G.E.H. Palmer, Philip Sherrard, and Kallistos Ware (London: Faber and Faber, 1983), 99, 100.
3. A Carthusian, *The Call of Silent Love: Carthusian Novice Conferences* (Herefordshire: Darton, Longman and Todd, 2006), 119.

elsewhere. In discerning a vocation or calling, the Ignatian Spiritual Exercises have proved a very valuable tool. While Ignatian retreats are common, the discernment of spirits in ministry is rarely taught.

Discernment of spirits in ministry

There is a grace of discernment of spirits that God gives for the exercise of ministries, but it is especially helpful in charismatic ministry. Those unfamiliar with the practice of regularly allowing the Holy Spirit to prompt them tend to take the approach of faithfully doing their best in their ministries with the intent to love others and do no harm. This is a very noble approach, but it does not perhaps allow sufficient room for the Lord's specific guidance and promptings. People feel prompted to do a wide variety of things when ministering to others, with very mixed results. Those familiar with the possibility of allowing the Spirit to lead them in their daily actions are generally more attentive to his intervention.

Learning to be sensitive to promptings that are genuinely of the Holy Spirit is obviously a tremendous asset in all areas of ministry. Such Spirit-led discernment can save us a lot of time and human effort and enable us to work with what often feels like surgical accuracy, pinpointing exactly God's purposes in a certain situation. It saves us from going down blind alleys, following flawed human ideas, and being led into deception and even deeds opposed to the Lord's plans.

Discernment of spirits in prayer ministry

In prayer ministry, there are indicators of God's presence and action upon or in a person being ministered to and in the minister. Identifying these can be tremendously helpful. However, almost all of these signs can be produced consciously or subconsciously by the individual, and on rare occasions they can be simulated by the devil. Once again, the gift of discernment of spirits goes further than learned skills, enabling the minister to see with an assurance what spirit is at work and to discern God's purpose and the appropriate response. Cooperating with the Lord's agenda yields wonderful fruits.

Discerning mysteries

Discernment of spirits also enables a perception of a mystery at a depth of understanding that is beyond our natural powers. An example of this is St. Peter's discernment of Jesus' true identity: "You are the Christ, the Son of the living God" (Matthew 16:16).

Fr. Bentivegna points out in his interesting summary of St. Augustine's teaching on charisms that the gift of discernment of spirits is important: "When things, besides being superior to our human knowledge, are not naturally conceivable, 'Only the man who, among the gifts mentioned by the apostle, has received the charism of discernment of spirits is able to know these things in the way they should be known.'"[4]

The discernment of spirits by the good thief is an extraordinary manifestation of this grace. The first thief cries out, "Are you not the Christ? Save yourself and us!"(Luke 23:39). This is clearly a temptation to Jesus to abandon giving his life for the world. The good thief, however, even in his agony, discerns the origins of this plea and rebukes the first thief (Luke 23:40). Through discernment of spirits, he knows that the spirit prompting the other man is from the devil, not God. He says, "Do you not fear God, since you are under the same sentence of condemnation? And we indeed justly; for we are receiving the due reward of our deeds" (verses 40-41).

Could the good thief be speaking on behalf of all humanity, for whom suffering and death are the just punishment for sin? He then makes an extraordinary declaration about Jesus: "This man has done nothing wrong" (verse 41). What a remarkable revelation! By this phrase, he announces Jesus as the sinless one.

The good thief's third discernment is about who Jesus really is and what he is accomplishing. In contrast to the other thief, he does not try to tempt Jesus to escape the cross. He understands (even as the apostles did not) that the cross is a necessary passage for Jesus into his glory and the means by which he himself will be saved: "Jesus, remember me when you come into your kingdom" (verse 42, NRSV).

The good thief discerns not only Jesus' sinlessness but also his kingship and power to save through enduring the cross. In that moment, he alone in all the earth, with the Virgin Mary, discerns clearly the identity, purpose, and glory of Jesus on the cross. With such discernment and faith, it is no

---

4. See Bentivegna, "The Witness of St. Augustine," 31.

wonder that Jesus can promise him, "Truly, I say to you, today you will be with me in Paradise" (verse 43).

That some are granted such penetration of mysteries through discernment of spirits does not mean that only those who have this gift can know anything of God. Rather, it means that a special and even privileged perception of the mysteries of God and the spiritual world is granted to some from time to time.

Discernment of good and evil in unexpected places

St. Augustine notes that it is easy to recognize evil when it is plainly in sight, but it requires discernment to detect evil when something or someone appears good:

> It is not a great thing to recognize as an evildoer one whose actions are openly against morals and the rule of faith; in such a case there are many who are able to discern. One who has the charisma of discernment, over and above this, is able to notice quite swiftly if one, who at first sight looks still good, is, in fact, an evildoer instead. An intelligence which is enlightened by this gift is enabled to judge the quality and dimension of the harm that can be received by our soul from things that appear good while they are the opposite. . . . And so one who has the charism of discernment assuredly understands when something evil is concealed even in those who have a good reputation among the righteous.[5]

Alternatively, the charism of discernment enables us to discern goodness in unexpected places. Jesus was able to discern not only evil within people's hearts but also goodness concealed there—for example, with Matthew the tax collector and Zacchaeus.

This gift to see God's intention in people and situations, and the grace to affirm it, is tremendously important. I once heard a great leader remark that, very often, we don't accept the revival God sends because it's not the one we expected. Often we think that God should respect our idea of how things should be done. Sadly, this can be tremendously limiting. It can

---

5. Augustine, Commentary on the Beginning of Genesis, chap. 12, in Bentivegna, "The Witness of St. Augustine," 31–32.

"cause us to jump to wrong conclusions and shut off possibilities based on our assumptions.

All new movements in the Church have been misunderstood and even persecuted or maligned. This has been true from the early monastics and Franciscans to the new movements in today's Church. While the papacy's history isn't perfect, popes were often the ones graced with the gift of discernment of spirits. Many have recognized God's hand at work in new, immature movements and defended them, even while people were panicking and protesting.

Having new eyes in discerning ministries

In a post–Vatican II era, with a renewed theology of charisms and with the growing involvement of the laity, God is offering his Church a marvelous opportunity. The Church needs to make real space for the development of personal ministries, not only those originating from the ordained ministry and the corporate charisms of religious orders. We also need to welcome ministries developing from the personal charisms and spiritual gifts of all the individual members of the Church. Learning how to allow such gifts to grow up—from their first immature efforts to an intermediate stage and finally to maturity—requires patience on the part of the Church, so that the good that God is doing can be retained. The following passage from the Catholic Catechism, while applying to bishops, is also applicable to all those in leadership in the Church: "'Their office [is] not indeed to extinguish the Spirit, but to test all things and hold fast to what is good' [*Lumen Gentium*, 12], so that all the diverse and complementary charisms work together 'for the common good' [1 Corinthians 12:7]" (CCC 801).

In this area, we can learn much from mature Catholic charismatic communities, various charismatic ministries in the Church, as well as charismatic churches. While the Catholic Church has a deep doctrine of the priesthood of all believers, many of these churches seem to live this more dynamically. They see all the laity as ministers of the kingdom in the power of the Holy Spirit, with a mission mandate different from but complementary to that of the pastors. They expect the laity to exercise charismatic gifts as part of the mission of the local church, and they are often experienced at recognizing the charisms of their people.

Discernment in discipleship

There are two errors we can fall into regarding discernment in discipleship. On the one hand, we can be so focused on the urgency and success of our mission that we release people with weak foundations—in character, prayer, and ministry training—without enough formation. This can result in people loving the mission more than the Lord himself, bringing harm to others, or experiencing moral failures.

On the other hand, people can be made to go through so much formation before being entrusted with anything that they lose their fire and become discouraged. In some circles, stressing the need for discernment has become an excuse for holding people back and stunting growth. Such behavior commonly has its roots in insecurity, fear, or envy on the part of the leader. Often unconsciously, some leaders fear that if someone else grows and their gifts are recognized as genuine and appreciated, this may leave them less room to exercise their own gifts. The gifts of others are then quenched under the pretext of the need for careful discernment and prudence. Ironically, such unredeemed attitudes are certain to weaken the leader's own spiritual gifts.

Those of us who are leaders need to commit ourselves to identifying, forming, and releasing people in the spiritual gifts and ministries the Lord is giving them. This is not always easy. Many weaknesses may be present alongside gifts. While offering encouragement, pruning is also part of a responsible approach to discipleship. Sometimes the people we find most difficult to accept, disciple, and mobilize are younger versions of ourselves.

There are many contexts in which a strong leader emerges and is unable to nurture other new leaders because it often just feels like too much hard work. Yet in my journey, I have realized that "there is no success without successors." What father would want to hold back his own children? True, a good father also disciplines and prunes, but he does so eager that his children might produce more fruit.

When we picture the process of pruning, many of us imagine a tree being cut back. When Jesus speaks about pruning, he refers to a vine. For a vine to be most fruitful, it must not be allowed to grow haphazardly but must be directed along a trellis or fence or linked to neighboring vines. When we prune a vine, we do so in a way that gives it direction. We want more of it exposed to the sun, causing it to bear more fruit.

Discernment of spirits, in relation to ministries, should always be directed to helping people grow in the right direction and bear greater fruit. Some people have a special charism of knowing what other people's charisms will be. This can, alongside other forms of discernment, help enormously in facilitating people's growth.

Discernment of spirits in deliverance ministry

Some people have a gift of discerning the presence of evil spirits. This gift can come in a variety of ways. It may begin as just a "hunch," a sense of the presence of evil. There may be an inner sense of unease, the feeling that something is not right. Sometimes there is a feeling of oppression or darkness, an unnatural coldness, a sense of threat, or strange odors. Often gifted people cannot identify how they "know" something, but events prove them correct. Certain physical reactions in the person troubled by demons, especially in response to the sacred, can give away the presence of evil.

On occasion one looks at a person and "sees" a particular spirit "upon" him or her. In our experience, this is not usually seen in the form of a person but rather a characteristic or effect. Some people occasionally see an embodiment of an evil spirit.

Some people are strongly gifted in this area. I worked with a Catholic layman whose charism of discernment of spirits in deliverance was amazing. A person under the influence of demons, who was going through the process of deliverance, testified afterward that as soon as he felt a particular spirit rising up within him, even if there was no external manifestation of its character, this man would almost instantly know its name. He would then address it with tremendous power, causing the spirit to scream in terror or to propel the individual across the floor before leaving him or her.

This kind of "surgical" discernment of spirits is, of course, tremendously helpful in speeding up the process of deliverance, which greatly benefits the sufferer. In deliverance ministry, there are common signs of demonic activity, as we have already related, and these are good to learn. But it is only the activation of the gift of discernment of spirits that brings a deep assurance of whether something is actually caused by the demonic.

When I was in my twenties, I was at a very large conference for five thousand leaders, given by John Wimber. His teaching style was very low-key. As he taught, we all followed attentively in our booklets. Suddenly he became silent; then with force but unemotionally, he commanded a spirit to be gone.

Instantly a woman sitting in the audience was thrown up in the air from her seated position, landing in the row behind. She remained slumped there in complete silence for the rest of the session.

John looked down at his notes and apologized, saying, "Sorry about that; I was getting some [demonic] interference," and continued his teaching in the same tone in which he had left off. This combination of sharp discernment of spiritual activity, biblical authority, and zero hype left us sitting and staring with our mouths open.

Growing in the Gift of Discernment of Spirits

As I emphasized previously, spiritual gifts cannot be produced simply with training and effort, and this is true of discernment of spirits. God has to grant the gift. However, there are ways to grow in discernment generally, and those who pursue discernment seem to be more open to receiving the free gift of discernment of spirits.

Growing in general discernment does not take place primarily by developing an "eye" for what's wrong; rather, it can be described as a spiritual instinct that grows as a side effect of living deeply immersed in the things of God. In the past, bank employees were trained to spot fake bank notes not by studying the forgeries but by continual exposure to authentic notes. This imprinted so deeply in their minds the correct image of the notes that any variation would be quickly identified.

Like all spiritual gifts, discernment of spirits is a gift that often begins in a small way, requiring us to be sensitive and very attentive. If we respond appropriately, with mercy and courage, in love, most likely the Lord will increase its fruitfulness in our lives. While it should be remembered that it is possible for even the most gifted to be mistaken at times, this gift can be remarkable in its manifestation and is of inestimable value in the Christian community.

CHAPTER 9
THE GIFT OF TONGUES

I thank God that I speak in tongues more than you all.
—1 Corinthians 14:18

While there appears to be no evidence of the gift of tongues in the life of Jesus, the gift is mentioned at the end of Mark, in chapter 16, when the risen Jesus says,

And these signs will accompany those who believe: in my name they will cast out demons; they will speak in new tongues; they will pick up serpents, and if they drink any deadly thing, it will not hurt them; they will lay their hands on the sick, and they will recover. (Mark 16:17-18)

The gift of tongues was also central to the Pentecost event and clearly a common occurrence in the life of the early Church. In this chapter, I will explain the various ways in which this gift is expressed.

Speaking Known Languages Miraculously

First, there is the miraculous speaking in a language that one has not learned. At the beginning of this book, I referred to my own experience of speaking in Spanish, a language I did not know, and having it translated by someone who heard it. While this has happened several times among members of our community, we couldn't describe it as a regular occurrence. However, some have spoken in German, Italian, Spanish, French, and Gaelic without knowing these languages.

On a healing outreach some years ago, a member of my team was praying over a woman from Ireland, and as she prayed, she unknowingly repeated, "My dear daughter, my dear daughter," in Gaelic. As one can imagine, the woman being prayed with was profoundly touched, knowing that my friend knew no Gaelic at all. Just a few weeks ago, one of our members was on a retreat, and each day when she was praying in tongues, someone nearby told her she was speaking in a real language—one day Spanish, the next Italian, and the next French!

Some of the saints spoke regularly in languages they had not learned or were understood while speaking in their own language to people of another tongue. Such is the case of St. Vincent Ferrer—the great Dominican, wonder worker, and evangelist—who preached in his own Valencian dialect of Spanish while being understood in the native language of the congregation.

Missionaries today are having similar experiences. The evangelist Surprise Sithole was traveling mostly by foot in Mozambique and Malawi to preach the gospel in villages and areas that were non-Christian. He tells of how he was on the island of Chikusi and somehow found himself preaching in the Chichewan language, which he had never studied. When the people witnessed this, they were converted to Christianity. What is so interesting is that this evangelist has not lost the ability to speak the language but still speaks it today!

Praying in Tongues

The second expression of the gift of tongues is mentioned by St. Paul in some of his letters. This is the gift of praying in tongues, also referred to as praying in the Spirit (1 Corinthians 14:15). Paul gives clear guidance about how this gift should not dominate Christian gatherings in a way that excludes the exercise of other gifts, especially prophecy. It is clear that in the Corinthian church, Paul needed to rebalance an approach to tongues that had become unhelpful, but it is important to draw from these texts his positive teaching and assumptions about the gift of tongues when it is used appropriately.

Paul explains that this gift is highly important to him personally, writing, "I thank God that I speak in tongues more than you all" (1 Corinthians 14:18). For "if I pray in a tongue, my spirit prays," (14:14) and "he who speaks in tongues edifies himself" (14:4)—in other words, builds himself up in the spirit. Paul expresses his belief that every Christian can speak in tongues: "Now I want you all to speak in tongues" (14:5). The apostle is adamant that praying in tongues should be part of the Christian gathering: "Do not forbid speaking in tongues" (14:39).

Paul also encourages us to pray in the spirit and pray with our mind, to sing in the spirit and sing with our mind (14:14-15). He refers to praying and speaking in tongues as "the tongues of angels" (13:1). Praying and especially singing in tongues can be a sublime and powerful experience, especially when expressed with others. It can cause an experience of deep supernatural unity and harmony among those gathered. At times it is so beautiful that one's spirit seems to fly. Often immediately afterward, a profound peace descends, along with a deep sense of God's presence. For this reason, praying and singing in tongues can be a powerful aid to recollection in group prayer and after the reception of Communion.

Often it appears that those exercising the gift of tongues do so at will and that it is therefore a merely human activity. As spiritual gifts cannot be exercised simply when one wishes, this understandably leaves us with a question: how can such praying in tongues be considered supernatural? I have always taught that it is not the particular sounds that a person makes that authenticates the gift of tongues as a true form of prayer, but the disposition of the individual's heart. By a comparison with the gift of tears, Sullivan gives a helpful explanation with which I agree:

> I would suggest the relationship between the gift of tongues and the 'gift of tears'. In both cases, I believe, it is a question of the activation of a natural capacity. Obviously, everyone has the natural capacity for tears; in my opinion everyone also has the latent capacity for glossolalia [at least the physical mechanics]. The 'gift' does not consist in either case in the imparting of a new physical capacity. Further, just as not every kind of weeping qualifies as the 'gift of tears', so also, in my opinion, not every kind of glossolalia qualifies as the charismatic gift of [praying in] tongues.
> When does weeping qualify as the 'gift of tears'? It seems to me that it is when both signifies and intensifies such an attitude as contrition for sins, compassion with the suffering of Christ, or joy in the experience of consolation…I believe that something analogous to this can be said about tongues. Speaking in tongues is a real gift of grace, a charism when it has a similar quasi-sacramental kind of efficacy, both to signify and to intensify one's attitude of prayer. (Sullivan, 144-145)

Tongues as jubilation

Praying in tongues continued for many centuries in the Church as part of the broader experience of "jubilation," which is the term used by the Fathers to describe wordless vocal prayer and songs. Almost all the major Fathers of the Church speak about jubilation, among them St. Augustine of Hippo, St. John

Cassian, St. Ambrose of Milan, St. Peter Chrysologus, St. John Chrysostom, St. Gregory the Great, St. Isidore of Seville, and the monk Cassiodorus.[1]

Describing this spoken or sung wordless prayer, St. Augustine wrote that one "does not utter words; he pronounces a wordless sound of joy, . . . expressing what he feels without reflecting on any particular meaning; to manifest his joy, the man does not use words that can be pronounced and understood, but he simply lets his joy burst forth without words."[2]

This gift of jubilation, including wordless spoken and sung prayer, was not reserved for private use but had a place in the Mass for the first eight centuries of the Church. "During the celebration of Mass, as the congregation and choir sang the last alleluia, the people moved into exuberant wordless singing."[3]

Beyond human structures

In many circles, praying in tongues has been a blessing, and in others, a subject of bewilderment or even ridicule. What seems to confuse people most is the idea of its not being understandable. What could be the point of that? But that is the whole point! As St. Paul writes, "One who speaks in a tongue speaks not to men but to God; for no one understands him, but he utters mysteries in the Spirit" (1 Corinthians 14:2).

Praying in tongues is a form of praying in the Spirit. Its gift is precisely that it breaks beyond human structures and concepts. It is not antirational but trans-rational. In the mystical tradition, God at certain times gives gifts of prayer that are higher than human concepts. We communicate with him on a plane beyond human words and intellectual structures, Spirit to spirit. While it would be incorrect to assume that all praying in tongues represents this level of mystical prayer, tongues do facilitate a different way of relating to God. The gift calls forth a cry of love, joy, wonder, and praise that isn't limited to our human forms of communication.

This may seem strange, but actually we all express ourselves in similar ways in normal life. How many of us sink into a nice hot bath and let out a deep "Ahh!" expressing our feelings far more adequately than "This bath is nice and hot"? Or when our child wins a race at primary school, we let out a cheer. A cheer is not a word but a free and effective communication of what is happening in our hearts. How many of us, when shutting a door on

1. See Ensley, 8–14.
2. St. Augustine, *Ennarationes in Psalmos*, 99, 4, PL37, 1272, quoted in Ensley, 8.
3. Ensley, 14.

our finger, respond with "I've shut the door on my finger; that was stupid of me, and it's very painful"? More likely, we say, "Oww!" These are all examples of expressing what is going on within us verbally but without words.

Praying in tongues, at its simplest level, is the same as this. But do not think it is only this. Praying in tongues can be experienced at the highest level of mystical prayer, as has been the case with some of the saints. The authentication of praying in tongues is not how clever or fluent it sounds, although fluency does seem to increase over time, but whether it is expressing something deep within us toward God. As St. Augustine wrote, "Through this means, the feeling of the soul may be expressed, words failing to explain the heart's conceptions."[4]

Praying without ceasing

The call of the Bible to "pray constantly" (1 Thessalonians 5:17) is an extraordinary invitation. St. Augustine says that "if you wish to pray without ceasing, do not cease to desire."[5] But often we need something to fan the flames of this desire and give it expression. In the history of the Church, the Jesus Prayer said repeatedly has served this purpose wonderfully for innumerable souls. But praying in tongues has also greatly helped many people in their desire to pray ceaselessly. This is because it does not always require the engagement of the mental faculties but only the raising of the heart to God, so one can practice it easily while going about other duties in life.

Prophesying in Tongues

The third form of the gift of tongues is prophecy in tongues. This occurs when a person is inspired to speak out a message in tongues in a public gathering. Normally, this speech is not in a known language but rather in sounds with no known logical structure.

Paul makes it clear that this kind of speech from an individual should be shared in an orderly way when the Church comes together, and it should be accompanied by an interpretation (1 Corinthians 14:26-27). This interpretation is not usually a translation but the gift of understanding the message

---

4. St. Augustine of Hippo, *Commentary on the Psalms*, as quoted by Terry Donahue, "The Gift of Jubilation," sfspirit.org/articles/9709/article1.htm.
5. St. Augustine, Exposition on Psalm 38, 13.

of the Spirit that was given in the unknown tongue. Like all expressions of the gift of tongues in Christian gatherings, prophesying in tongues is not beyond the control of the person speaking and thus can be exercised in a disciplined way.

Tongues can facilitate the other gifts

It has been the experience of millions of people that the gift of tongues facilitates a greater operation of the other spiritual gifts. For example, praying in tongues often seems to open up our spirits for the activation of prophetic gifts. It is not insignificant that the vast majority of people with developed healing ministries in the Church today also pray in tongues. Prayer in tongues, as well as being a gift that flows from an encounter with the Holy Spirit, seems to attune one to the touches and movements of the Spirit and opens the soul to be more receptive to the Lord in every situation.

A Deeper engagement in the Mass

A few years ago, I was unhappy with the level of my attention and desire when attending Mass. Having experienced extended praying in tongues as a helpful tool in attuning myself to the Lord's presence in other contexts, I decided to pray in tongues silently throughout the entire Mass each day, except at the responses. (It should be noted that this was truly silent prayer, not whispering, which would be an annoying distraction to others.) I experienced an amazing breakthrough. Daily Mass, which I have always loved, became something much more powerful and profound for me, and this has remained so for some years now, thanks be to God.

Today my interior prayer at Mass, unless the words of the Mass or readings provoke some other response, alternates between praying silently in tongues and the interior Jesus Prayer. Both forms of prayer, rather than being distractions from the words and actions of the Mass, magnify its meaning and power in my heart. While this approach may not suit everyone, others who have incorporated it have found similar results.

So the gift of tongues, while appearing foolish to many, can be a tremendous gift in our personal prayer, corporate worship, liturgy, prophetic service, proclamation, and ministry. Often referred to as the least of the gifts, it can, through its very humility, facilitate great things in the life in the Spirit.

CHAPTER 10

FAITH

"All things are possible for him who believes."
—Mark 9.23

This chapter is the shortest in this book. This is because faith has been referred to in many of the previous chapters. However, it deserves its own chapter because faith is, in some ways, the key to greater power in the operation of all the spiritual gifts.

The faith that St. Paul speaks of in 1 Corinthians 12 as a spiritual gift is not "saving faith" or justifying faith. Neither is it faith in particular doctrines. Rather, this is the faith that makes things happen.

It is amazing that Scripture says the same thing about God who is omnipotent—"For with God nothing will be impossible" (Luke 1:37)—that it does about faith: "All things are possible to him who believes" (Mark 9:23).

The Power of Faith

The discovery of the need to pray for greater faith completely transformed our experience of the supernatural in our ministries. This was revealed to me in a rather dramatic way.

Many years ago, after seeing a priest from the Divine Retreat Centre in Potta, India, preaching on faith and ministering in miracles, the Lord prompted me to pray for the gift of faith for greater miracles. I committed to doing so each day for a week when ministering at a family conference. At the end of the conference, God prompted me to pray for a woman with a chronic condition that kept her in an electric wheelchair. I stepped out based on only the smallest feeling of faith. I knew I must pray for her although all my emotions were screaming, "She won't be healed—you're going to look like a fraud. God's never used you to heal anyone in a wheelchair before!"

I took what felt like a great risk and acted with the tiny faith I had. The woman was wonderfully healed; she ran around the hall and was still walking twelve years later. This experience was a watershed moment for me and embedded in me a principle about faith that has helped release a new level of miracles in my life.

People often think that they must be content with the level of faith they have for God's supernatural intervention in their lives, in the same way we have to be content with some attribute of birth, such as freckles or big feet. We often hear people say, "Well, I don't have faith for that," or, "Well, you're just gifted with more faith." But Jesus did not accept such thinking.

In fact, one of the only times Jesus got really angry was when his disciples displayed a lack of faith for deliverance of a boy with an unclean spirit: "O faithless and perverse generation, how long am I to be with you? How long am I to bear with you?" (Matthew 17:17). The reason Jesus was angry with this lack of faith was, in my opinion, because unbelief mysteriously shuts out the works of the kingdom and leaves people without help and suffering needlessly.

Jesus proclaims such incredible things about faith that, ironically, it's difficult to believe he actually means what he says. But the truth is, he does, and those who dare to believe him have access to astonishing possibilities. In our experience, five minutes of faith can achieve what years of interceding with only a vague hope failed to accomplish. Faith is the key that opens the door to the world of miracles. Most people pray with hope. However, the promises of Jesus do not relate to hope but to faith.

In my journey pursuing the promises of Jesus for the miraculous to confirm the gospel message and demonstrate the presence of the kingdom, it was when I began praying for an increase of faith for specific things that I experienced a shift to another level.

If I were to ask you if you believe miracles are happening in the Church today, you would probably answer that you believe they are. If I were to ask you whether you are regularly performing them in your own life, you would most likely answer that you are not. People often tell me about their failures and disappointments when praying for the sick. They say, "I don't understand it, Damian, I've prayed for lots of people, and they just don't seem to get better. I do believe God can do it, so why doesn't he?"

My response is simple. You are confusing two kinds of faith. The faith you have is what I call "creedal faith"; in other words, you believe *in* something. You believe that miracles are possible today. That is good, but it is only an intellectual assent to the possibility of miracles happening today. The gift of faith is the gift to believe *for* miracles to happen today; it is an empowerment of the Spirit to make miracles happen.

Steps for Increasing Our Faith

The question naturally arises, "How can I increase my faith?"

1. **Repent.** First, we have to be brutally honest with ourselves and acknowledge the poverty of our faith, which is revealed by the level of the supernatural results we see—no more, no less. Facing this, our response must be to repent. Even though we see much through God's mercy, until we see all that Jesus promised, we continue to repent for the smallness of our faith.

2. **Feed faith.** Much of society, and often even our own experience of Christianity, has taught us to doubt the supernatural interventions of God. The answer to this state of affairs is to feed and water our faith by reading about miracles, watching film clips of miracles, listening to stories of miracles, and attending events where miracles happen through respected Christians. Get alongside ministries that are experiencing them. Filling our minds in this way helps cram out the doubt, so that when we next find ourselves in a situation that requires a miracle, we are well prepared to believe for one. Also, we need to fill our minds with the promises of Jesus in the Bible about faith and miracles in the lives of believers.

   All of this is preparation for creating an atmosphere in which faith can be welcomed and cultivated.

3. **Pray for faith.** Faith for miracles, whether big or small, is a gift from God and his work in us with which we collaborate. It is not something we can create by our own efforts, for Jesus is the author and finisher of our faith (Hebrews 12:2). Understanding that we cannot create faith ourselves, we then "beg the Lord to increase our faith" (CCC 162; cf. Mark 9:24; Luke 17:5; 22:32). I found that interceding for an increase of faith by naming things specifically was very helpful. We don't just ask, "Lord, increase my faith for physical healings," or, "Increase my faith for higher levels of prophecy" or greater miracles. Instead, we need to be specific in our requests, and the Lord will help us build toward greater levels of faith.

   If you've never seen a healing through your prayers, it's normally better to start by praying to free people from aches and pains rather than from their wheelchairs. Then when you have seen some results, give praise and thanks to God, and pray for your faith to increase.

The same process is true of other spiritual gifts. If you try to minister too far above your faith level, your failures are likely to leave you discouraged, and those you pray for won't be helped. It's much better to grow in steady steps.

However, I do not want to give the impression that this process must take a long time. If people are faithful and pray regularly, they can grow considerably in a few months or even in a few weeks. Occasionally the Lord surprises us, and we take a big leap. But this is unusual; most people grow in stages. If we are faithful ("faith-full") in little, God will trust us with more.

4. **Step out in faith.** The fourth element may seem obvious but must be stated: we actually have to take a step in faith. Especially at the beginning, such steps are often accompanied by trepidation and even real fear. We may be tempted to believe we are acting out of pride and presumption. All we can do, after preparing well, is step out as we feel led, always treating with respect the one to whom we are ministering and trying to keep the focus on Jesus.

The Catholic Catechism says, "Faith is a personal act" (CCC 166). Occasionally a feeling or sense of great confidence or certainty comes when we exercise a spiritual gift, but in my experience, this is rare. If I only acted when I had a feeling of faith, I would have seen a tiny number of people healed, delivered, or receiving accurate prophecies, rather than, by God's grace, the huge number who have. In my experience, faith comes with just enough conviction to act, and only occasionally is there no sense of risk.

The same is true for prophecy. Don't start by trying to prophesy details in depth; rather, start with smaller things and thank God for successes. In time and with God's help, you'll grow.

A step of faith is the moment when my love for another person has to get the better of my fears of failing or looking foolish. My experience is that even if we fail, if we have acted in love, the person feels blessed that we tried. When we see dramatic results, people are often changed forever.

As I have said, this gift of faith has incredible effects on all the spiritual gifts. My wife, Cathy, for example, received an amazing grace in the area of intercession. Over a two-year period, she kept a record of her intercessions, and she received everything she prayed for. It is important to point out that she is very disciplined in listening to the Lord about what she should pray for and doesn't just pray for anything.

Faith is born of revelation, and revelation is given mostly through prayer. We can do all the reading and research we like, but if we don't pray, the revelation never really takes root, and the gift of faith remains an occasional event in our lives rather than a regular feature of our ministries and lifestyle.

Exercising faith is like wearing a pair of bifocal glasses. Most of us are used to using the upper lens of faith for distant things, such as the joy of heaven after death. But we are poor at using the lower lens of faith for things close to us, in day-to-day life. God wants us to open our eyes through the charism of faith so that we see everything with his perspective.

I believe that growing in faith is an obligation of love, because it releases into people's lives the resources of heaven that would otherwise be out of reach. As St. John Chrysostom declares, faith "is the mother of the miracles."[1]

---

1. St. John Chrysostom, Homily 29 on 1 Corinthians, *Nicene and Post-Nicene Fathers of the Christian Church*, vol. 12, ed. P.H. Schaff (Grand Rapids: Eerdmans), 172, quoted in Pat Collins, CM, *Expectant Faith* (Dublin: Columba, 1988), 98.

CHAPTER 11

MIRACLES

Nevertheless, just as besides the grace of faith, the grace of the word is necessary that people may be instructed in the faith, so too is the grace of miracles necessary so that people may be confirmed in their faith.
—St. Thomas Aquinas[1]

Miracles are part of the great supernatural heritage of the Church down through the ages, as the following story about St. Vincent Ferrer shows.

On an occasion when St. Vincent was preaching to thousands in Salamanca, he suddenly stopped and said, "I am the Angel of the Apocalypse and am preaching Judgment!" Then he directed: "Some of you go near St. Paul's Gate, and you will find a dead person borne on men's shoulders on the way to the grave. Bring the corpse hither, and you shall hear proof of what I tell you."

The men went on their errand, the multitude waited, and soon the bier was brought with a dead woman upon it. They raised the litter and set it up so all could see. St. Vincent bade her return to life, and the dead woman sat up.

"Who am I?" Vincent asked her.

She answered: "You, Father Vincent, are the Angel of the Apocalypse, as you have already told this vast assembly."[2]

Today we are living in an era in which miracles are multiplying at an extraordinary rate among God's people.

As I mentioned in the first chapter, the New Testament word for *miracle* is *dynamis*, meaning "deed of power." These deeds of power are signs that point us to Jesus. They are startling manifestations of the glory of God in our midst. Other words used in the New Testament to refer to miracles are *semeion*, meaning a sign authenticating God's messenger (Matthew 12:38; John 2:23 and 20:30), pointing us to Jesus; and *teras*, which is only used alongside *semeion* in the phrase "signs and wonders" (Acts 2:22; Romans

---

1. St. Thomas Aquinas, *Summa Theologica II*, IIae, 178, art. 1, reply to obj. 5.
2. Hebert, 169–70.

15:19). A miracle is "a sign which is a summons. Its promise appeals to the element of man which daringly strives to attain the full future of his existence."[3] And while a miracle has great attractive power, it is "a sign which invites, but does not compel, . . . a seed which bears fruit according to the type of ground in which it is sown."[4]

The list of supernatural acts possible in the lives of believers has been discussed at some length already. It includes healing miracles, casting out evil spirits, supernatural revelation of knowledge in prophecy, miraculous tongues, and so forth. The promises of Jesus regarding spiritual gifts in the lives of believers are not limited to these. So what can "the gift of miracles" mean in this context?

Some, like the famous biblical scholar William Barclay, suggest it refers specifically to the power to cast out evil spirits,[5] which Jesus calls a miracle (Mark 9:39). But it seems to me that while driving out spirits may be included, it is not all that St. Paul has in mind when he speaks of the gift of "the working of miracles" in 1 Corinthians 12:10.

We know that healing and deliverance from demons are not the only miracles seen in the New Testament. Others include the changing of water into wine (John 2:1-11), the multiplication of food (John 6:10-13), walking on water (Matthew 14:25-32), authority over the elements and creation in general (Matthew 21:19), resurrections from the dead (John 11), manifestations of God's glory (Matthew 17:2), and acts of judgment (Act 13:11).

Jesus makes it clear that he expects other kinds of miracles to take place in the lives of his followers. For example, after cursing the fig tree (Matthew 21:19), which withered at his words, Jesus tells his disciples that if they have faith, they will "do what has been done to the fig tree" (21:21). With faith, such miracles are not beyond the reach of believers, for "all things are possible to him who believes" (Mark 9:23).

In the feeding of the five thousand, Jesus challenges his disciples to perform the miracle of feeding the crowd in the deserted place: "You give them something to eat" (Mark 6:37). Can you imagine the disciples' faces at this

3. Johann Baptist Metz, "Miracles," in Karl Rahner, ed., *Encyclopedia of Theology: A Concise Sacramentum Mundi* (London: Burns and Oats,), 964.
4. Louis Monden, "Miracles of Jesus," in Rahner, *Encyclopedia of Theology*, 965, 966.
5. William Barclay, *The Daily Study Bible*: *The Letters to the Corinthians* (Louisville, KY: St. Andrews Press, 2002), 110.

challenge? And events show that they missed the chance Jesus was offering them.

This expectation of Jesus recurs when Peter is *called* across the water. Most of us, when remembering this story, think only of Peter's failure. But consider the fact that Jesus was so far away on the waves that the apostles were unable to recognize him; the distance must have been at least a hundred yards. Peter must have walked a considerable way on the water before beginning to sink, because as he did, the Lord was close enough to reach out and save him. And what were Jesus' words to Peter? Not "Who do you think you are, trying something like that? Are you full of pride?" No, rather Jesus is disappointed for Peter, saying, "O you of little faith, why did you doubt?" (Matthew 14:31). In other words, "If only you had kept on believing, you'd have made it!"

Peter had grasped something important that the other disciples had missed. When he saw Jesus walking on the water, he realized that it was an opportunity to do what Jesus was doing, and he took it. Later Jesus confirmed Peter's understanding: "He who believes in me will also do the works that I do" (John 14:12). What is also sometimes overlooked is the fact that the two of them must have walked together on the water all the way back to the boat. Not much to be ashamed of there, Peter!

In the account of the storm during which Jesus was asleep and the terrified apostles woke him, the Lord's response was "Where is your faith?" (Luke 8:25). Perhaps some might suggest this call to faith was simply a call to trust that God would protect the apostles in the storm, but if this were true, Jesus would have demonstrated it by putting his head again on the pillow and going back to sleep. Alternatively, he might have sat with them in the storm and exhorted them to trust while the storm continued to rage around them. He did not do either of these things but rather exercised spiritual authority over the storm, commanding it to be calm.

It seems clear that Jesus expected his disciples to exercise faith to do what he did. If we find this difficult to accept, many of the saints did not. They took Jesus at his word. There are many records of various saints walking on water, calming storms, and exercising incredible power over the elements.

It is interesting to note that while Jesus could work no miracle in his hometown because of the lack of faith, he never had this problem when performing a "nature miracle." The free will of human beings means that they can refuse his purposes, and unbelief can be an obstacle. But in nature miracles, this possibility does not exist. One might respond, "Sure, but the laws of nature are obstacles!" But these same laws of nature are obstacles in healing miracles too, and that hasn't prevented multitudes of healing miracles.

It seems to me that nature miracles should, in one sense, be "easier," because they depend only on the faith of the person praying or acting. I say this as a person who aspires to see the Lord perform nature miracles and prays for their increase in the Church. It is my conviction that we are going to see a great rise in nature miracles as Christians grow in their faith and grasp the truth of who they are in Christ and their relationship of authority over the material universe.

Power over the Elements

As I mentioned, there were many saints who lived this reality. Lest we think that such claims are simply myths from ancient history, there are many examples among modern Christians. The Coptic Pope St. Kyrillos exercised authority over the elements on many occasions.

> In 1964, the Pope was at St. Mina's Monastery when there was a severe storm. The monks came to him asking for his prayers that the storm would end. He then raised his cross and said, "Put the air of the heavens in a good mood." The storm became so calm that there wasn't even a breeze. The Pope then said, "St. Mina, when we asked you to calm the storm, did you have to stop the breeze as well?" Then a gentle breeze surrounded the area and all were astonished.[6]

But such things don't happen only to saints. When my son was a small boy, he experienced his prayers affecting the weather rather dramatically.

> There were two very similar occasions that took place while I was attending primary school (over fifteen years ago, when I was aged nine), so the stories might have blurred together somewhat in my mind. I'll report as well as I can remember.
> It was raining heavily. We wanted to go outside and play. We hadn't expected it to rain so hadn't brought in toys. Someone suggested I pray. I went over to the window, and some members of my class gathered around me. I looked outside at the pouring rain and

---

6. Fr. Rafael Avva Mena, quoted in Ata and Mena, 29.

dark clouds, then closed my eyes to pray. The room became quiet. One child spoke or laughed, and the teacher hushed them. After what must have only been ten or fifteen seconds, I opened my eyes, and instantly for all to see, the heavy downpour of rain in a moment became a slight drizzle, then stopped completely.

It might sound insignificant reading such a report, but every child there knew what had happened. Now happy that we could play outside, we went to the cloakroom. Some in my class were clearly in a bit of a state of shock. Some started calling me "miracle boy," and others started bowing down to me. I remember being very disturbed, even though I found such responses amusing. I also remember trying to remind them that they shouldn't bow down to me but to God.

As I said, this happened twice. On two separate occasions I was asked to pray, and the heavy rain stopped within moments of finishing the prayer. What is interesting is that a couple of years ago, I bumped into one of my old primary school friends at a local pub, and he reminded me of the story. "Do you remember, John, when you prayed for the rain to stop . . . and it did?" People remember moments like that.

Manifestations and miracles of fire

The most famous manifestation of fire is that of Pentecost (Acts 2:3), but we all remember Moses' experience of the burning bush (Exodus 3:2-4) and the pillar of fire that led the Israelites by night across the desert (Exodus 13:21). Elijah's ministry was also confirmed by dramatic manifestations of fire (1 Kings 18:38; 2 Kings 1:10).

Once again we see biblical experience continued in the lives of the saints and figures from Church history. One of my favorite stories is of a Desert Father known as Joseph of Panephysis:

Lot went to Joseph and said, "Abba, as far as I can, I keep a moderate rule, with a little fasting, and prayer, and meditation, and quiet: and as far as I can I try to cleanse my heart of evil thoughts. What else should I do?" Then the hermit stood up and spread out his hands to heaven, and his fingers shone like ten flames of fire, and he said, "If you will, you can become all flame."[7]

St. Patrick, in a confrontation with a magician, accepted a king's challenge to a contest through fire. Patrick put his own cloak around the magician and took the magician's cloak and put it around one of Patrick's brothers, Benineus. Then Benineus and the magician were put inside wooden constructions, which were set on fire. Patrick prayed before the watching multitude. In an hour, the magician was burned to death, but Patrick's cloak, which had been around him, was untouched by the fire. Benineus, on the other hand, had stood unalarmed within the fire and came forth unscathed, but the cloak of the magician was destroyed.[8]

Extraordinary Healings

Metal healings

There have been increasing reports in some healing ministries of metal inserts being affected by prayer or simple commands in Jesus' name in a remarkable way. We have had many incidents of this; here is just one of them, from a man named Ray.

> In 1973, I was knocked off the pavement in Johannesburg by a drunken hit-and-run driver. I was told by the doctors that they might have to amputate the arm, but . . . they saved it by the insertion of metal pins and plates. I was told that I would never have . . . "pronation and supination," which simply means being able to turn your arm from the elbow down to the wrist. . . . I couldn't write, other than to sign my name. I couldn't put my hand palm down, which makes things very difficult. I had to type with one hand. Many years later, I was x-rayed at the RLI [Royal Lancaster Infirmary]. The radiologist found to her amazement that the metal

---

7. Benedicta Ward, *The Desert Fathers: Sayings of the Early Christian Monks* (New York: Penguin, 2003), 131.
8. Muirchu maccu Machtheni, *Saint Patrick: His Writings and Life*, ed. Newport John Davis White (London: Society for Promoting Christian Knowledge, 1920), chap. 20, pp. 90–91.

was now covered with bone marrow, so my forearm is a solid lump with a piece of metal from the elbow.

Ray then attended one of our Miracle Healing Services, at which I commanded arms to be healed in Jesus' name. Ray describes the moment of his healing.

I was emotional. Tears welled up in my eyes. I realized something was happening, but I didn't know what. But then total astonishment. "... Look! ... Look!" And I'm still astonished. What amazes me about this transformation is the fact that this cure is medically and scientifically impossible. It cannot happen, but it has ... ! I know what I couldn't do before and what I can do now. It's absolutely wonderful!

... Well, clearly Damian Stayne didn't do it on his own. ... He isn't God, and neither is he a surgeon, so he couldn't have done it. So that leaves only one answer, doesn't it? If he'd said, "Be healed in Damian Stayne's name!" nothing would have happened. No; he said, "Be healed in Jesus' name." ... I can't explain it other than the obvious. Stunning! It's clearly supernatural; there's been a divine intervention. That's the only possible conclusion. You can talk about hyping yourself up and confidence and that sort of thing, but we're talking about a lump of metal here. This is impossible.

... Well, we're not charismatics. Just ordinary Catholics who go to church and love the Lord. I'm not easily impressed. ... It's got me thinking. ... What more is possible?

... I'm going to tell people about this until the day I die.[9]

We have seen several similar healings in which the metal would have to bend for the result to be achieved! Just the other week, we had two people in one service whose metal inserts changed radically after the prayer. One woman related how a metal plate in her wrist, which had been sticking out, had shrunk during the prayer and word of command. The mother general of an order of nuns was one of the pair who had laid hands upon the woman as I commanded healing from the stage. She had seen and felt

---

9. "Send Forth Your Spirit, O Lord, and Renew the Face of the Earth," *The Voice*, Catholic Paper of the Lancaster Diocese, UK, July 2014, 8.

the plate before the prayer. It was very amusing seeing her shocked and delighted face afterward.

There are two men I know who also see such healings in their ministries. In many cases, they have x-rays that show the metal inserts completely vanished. I have a copy of two of these x-rays, clearly showing the presence of the metal insert before the prayer for healing and its absence afterward. One of these men has prayed for 150 people with heart conditions and pacemakers. As part of the healing, the redundant pacemakers disappeared from their bodies!

Healing of blood

A young woman with leukemia attended a Miracle Healing Service I was leading in Hungary. She had been virtually forced to attend by a relative and went only under duress. A doctor on our team investigated the case. Here is the doctor's report.

> The patient's situation was deteriorating, and her doctor had advised her that she urgently needed a bone marrow transplant. However, because she was afraid, she kept postponing it. On the Friday before the service, she had an appointment with her specialist in which she received very bad blood results after many chemotherapy treatments. The doctors wanted her to remain in the hospital for another session of chemotherapy and wait for a donor for a bone marrow transplant. But the patient signed herself out of the hospital, accepting responsibility for this action. They urged her to return if there was any change (as they expected a negative deterioration).
>
> The next day, Saturday, she then attended the Miracle Healing Service, with no real expectation of receiving healing. When Damian led prayer for her category of sickness, she felt nothing and assumed nothing had happened. But that night she slept very well, which was unusual for her. She had no bleeding and no pains.
>
> The following day, she awoke from a good night's sleep and felt quite different. Because of this change, she obediently returned to the hospital that day to report this to her doctor, who she knew was to be on duty that day. She told her doctor she felt very different, and the doctor took a blood test. On the Monday morning, she was contacted and told to return to the hospital immediately.

The doctor told her there was some problem with the blood and another blood test had to be taken. They took another sample, and it came back as normal. Then a third, more detailed blood sample was taken, and the technician checked that the machine for testing the blood was not faulty. It was found to be functioning perfectly.

Two weeks later, a bone marrow biopsy was taken (this is the most certain way to diagnose leukemia) and the report came back normal with no signs of leukemia. It was at this point that it was noticed that the blood group type had changed. On discovering this, the doctor was astonished and immediately took a bedside blood group test to confirm the changes. Following this, the patient travelled to another town to check her blood type independently, where her sickness was not known. There too the result was completely normal and free of all leukemia.

Finally she was sent to a medical forensic expert. This is a person in Hungary who investigates unusual cases and has a legal role. This expert investigated all the medical documents confirming the findings and wrote up the final document summing up all her findings from the medical records and closing the case. This medical report, of which I have a copy, states original "Blood Type AB negative" and then later "Blood Type O." The medical report concludes: "Verdict: the thirty-four-year-old patient's healing cannot be explained medically."

When I received these results, I asked myself, "Why not just heal the old blood?" But it seems that for his own good reasons, the Lord wanted to do something even more extraordinary—change a person's blood type! Jesus is alive!

Tumors vanishing

When I was in northeast India, we ran a Miracle Healing Service attended by the archbishop. Sometime into the service, three men entered, two young and one older. The older man was extremely thin and was being carried by the other two. After I had used the word of command for the healing of cancer, one of the two younger men came to the platform and shared, "My father can swallow now."

"What's so marvelous about that?" I thought to myself. Then he explained that he and his brother had carried their father from the local hospital because he was dying of throat cancer. He had not eaten solid food for weeks because of a large tumor in his throat; he could not even swallow water. He was being kept alive via a drip.

After the service, the men took their father home, where he asked for a cup of tea, which he proceeded to drink without any problems. Then to his family's great surprise, he asked for some food. Then to their even greater astonishment, he proceeded to consume an entire meal in front of them. It was an incredible miracle for which we give glory to God.

In many countries, including England, we witnessed the Lord healing people of tumors up to the size of a fist. This was amazing. Then I saw a man in Uganda with a growth on his shoulder the size of a melon, and my heart went out to him for having to bear such a difficult condition. I begged the Lord to give us faith for the healing of such things.

Sometime later I was ministering in South Korea and prayed for cancers and tumors to vanish in Jesus' name. A woman came to the platform to testify that when she had arrived, she had stage-four cancer, with a very hard tumor in her stomach the size of a human head. Five minutes after the prayer and word of command for healing, her stomach was totally flat. We were left speechless! It seems that God is increasing not only the sizes of tumors healed at our events but also the numbers.

In one service in Africa this year, we had thirty-nine people testify to tumors shrinking or vanishing. Recently in Indonesia, at one of our Miracle Healing Services, fifty-one people testified that their tumors had significantly shrunk after the prayer and word of command, and others had tumors vanish completely. These included three tumors more than five inches wide, which completely disappeared in a matter of minutes. I received this testimony via Facebook just the other day, following our Miracle Healing Service in Poland: "My dad had an operation because he had been diagnosed with a bladder tumor . . . and now look how great is the Lord! My dad calls me and says that while he was on the [operating] table, six doctors were looking for and could not find a tumor! Dad called and thanks you, and the first thing he says is, THE LORD IS GREAT." Amen!

Paralytics walk

Of all the hundreds of lame people we have seen the Lord heal, there is one I consider particularly lovely. Back in Africa in a huge service, a pathetic-looking paralytic was brought by his family and laid on the ground near the stage. For a whole year, he had been paralyzed from the neck down. He was a desperately poor man. After the short prayer and command for paralytics to be healed, he simply rose up and came to the stage and walked up and down with tears streaming down his face. Over and over he kept repeating, "I can't believe it, I can't believe it!" and the people glorified God.

A lady came in her wheelchair with her husband, who is a medical doctor and a specialist in her condition, to a Miracle Healing Service I was leading in Lyon, France. She was dramatically healed. One year later, she and her husband attended a Miracle Healing Service that I was leading in Paris, and they both testified. She shared, "I was suffering from an incurable condition called Spondylarthropathie in my joints, spine, hips, jaw, thorax, ribcage, and feet. I taught my students from a wheelchair. After the prayer, you told us to do something we couldn't do, so I bent down and touched my toes, and then I started jumping for joy. He has turned my mourning into dancing."

Her husband then testified, "I can confirm. I have other patients like her. . . . What we believe goes far beyond what we understand. What I observed was that she was totally rigid. I had to help her get out of bed in the morning. I saw her suffer. And it's terrible when you're the doctor and you can't do anything for your wife. I saw her totally change. Now she runs faster than I do!" Jesus is alive!

Power over the Body

Extraordinary fasts

We have amazing accounts of miraculous fasting in the lives of many saints, in particular the Desert Fathers and Christian mystics. But perhaps one of the most incredible was that of Venerable Marthe Robin, who died in 1981. Marthe offered her life in perpetual intercession and lived a permanent fast for fifty years, consuming only the Holy Eucharist.

There is also the carefully documented case of Blessed Alexandrina da Costa, who lived an absolute fast for more than thirteen years, from March 27, 1942, until her death. Her sole nourishment was Holy Communion, which she received each morning. Here is the medical confirmation of the enforced surveillance in a hospital to uncover whether she was a fraud or genuine in her miraculous fasting:

> We the undersigned, Dr. C.A. di Lima, Professor of the Faculty of Medicine of Oporto, and Dr. E.A.D. de Azevedo, doctor graduate of the same Faculty, testify that, having examined Alexandrina Maria da Costa, aged 39, born and resident at Balasar, of the district of Povoa de Varzim . . . from 10 June to 20 July 1943 . . . at the Hospital of Foce del Duro, under the direction of Dr. Araujo and under the day and night surveillance by impartial persons desirous of discovering the truth of her fast. Her abstinence from solids and liquids was absolute during all that time. We testify also that she retained her weight, and her temperature, breathing, blood pressure, pulse and blood were normal while her mental faculties were constant and lucid and she had not, during these forty days, any natural necessities.

The certificate continues:

> The examination of the blood, made three weeks after her arrival in the hospital, is attached to this certificate and from it one sees how, considering the aforesaid abstinence from solids and liquids, science naturally has no explanation. The laws of physiology and biochemistry cannot account for the survival of this sick woman for forty days of absolute fast in the hospital, more so in that she replied daily to many interrogations and sustained very many conversations, showing an excellent disposition and a perfect lucidity of spirit. As for the phenomena observed every Friday at about 3 p.m. (i.e. her ecstasies), we believe they belong to the mystical order. . . . For the sake of the truth, we have prepared this certificate which we sign. Oporto , 26 July 1943.[10]

Levitation

One of the saints best known for levitating during prayer is St. Joseph of Cupertino (1603-1663), who experienced so many levitations that were

---

10. "Miracle of the Eucharist: Total Fast from Food in the Lives of the Saints," miraclesofthesaints.com/2010/10/miracle-of-eucharist-total-fast-from.html.

witnessed by his brothers in the Franciscan order and others that he is today amusingly regarded as the patron saint of air travelers! At times it was impossible to even mention the things of God to him without his being taken into ecstasy and levitation. Fr. Angelo Pastrovicchi's official biography of the saint, which was first published in 1767, states:

> Not only during the sixteen years of the Saint's stay at Grottella, but during his whole life, these ecstasies and flights were so frequent, as attested in the acts of the Process of beatification, that for more than thirty-five years his superiors would not permit him to take part in the exercises in the choir and the refectory or in processions, lest he disturb the community.[11]

Raising the Dead

Not only Jesus but also Elijah, Peter, and Paul performed the wonder of raising the dead. In the history of the Church, it would be virtually impossible to count all the resurrections that God has accomplished through his children. However, some stand out.

St. Vincent Ferrer's evangelistic ministry was constantly followed by countless miracles. On one occasion, a father brought a child to St. Vincent who had been cut into pieces by his mother, who had temporarily been struck with madness. Vincent knelt and prayed. "The pieces became united together, the body came to life again, and Vincent handed over to the father a living child. . . . Bishop Peter Ranzano claimed this as one of the miracles submitted in the canonization process for St. Vincent." A painting of the event hangs in the New Picture Gallery in the Vatican.[12]

In recent years, there seems to be an incredible increase in this type of miracle. I have three friends who have raised the dead. What an incredible thing to be able to say! There are famous examples with medical confirmation in some Christian ministries. Perhaps the most well-known took place under the ministry of Reinhard Bonnke, the great evangelist of Africa. There

---

11. Joan Carroll Cruz, *Mysteries, Marvels and Miracles in the Lives of the Saints* (Rockford, IL: TAN, 1997), 31, quoting Rev. Angelo Pastrovicchi, OMC, *St. Joseph of Copertino* (St. Louis, MO: Herder, 1918), 83–84.

12. Hebert, 170–171.

a man killed in a car accident was brought back to life. The miracle is verified by the doctors who were involved.[13]

Multiplications

In the Scriptures, we see Jesus multiplying the fish and loaves more than once. Multiplications of food had been seen in Elijah's ministry as well (1 Kings 17:7-16) and in Elisha's (2 Kings 4:42-44). There are so many stories of multiplications among the saints that it is difficult to choose which ones to relate. St. John Bosco has many lovely incidents of this that are recorded. I'll share just three here, one regarding essential provision, the other gratuitous, the last sublime.

Often Don Bosco would find that the supply of bread for the boys he cared for was inadequate, and God would multiply it. Here is the testimony of one witness:

> There were some fifteen buns in the basket—certainly no more than twenty. Unobserved, I placed myself on a step right behind Don Bosco and alertly watched his every move as he began to distribute the bread. The boys kept filing past to get their rolls from him. Some kissed his hand as he smiled and said a kind word to each. Each boy—some four hundred—received a bread roll from Don Bosco. When the distribution was over, I again peered into the basket. To my great astonishment, I saw as many rolls in it as there had been before, though no other bread and no other basket had been brought up.

On another occasion, on his arrival home after taking six hundred of the boys out, Don Bosco realized that he did not have enough horse chestnuts to give all the boys, as he had promised. Even so, he proceeded, from the few he had, to distribute to each one a generous portion. Miraculously, the horse chestnuts multiplied until all six hundred boys had been fed. Because the boys had all seen the small amount as they approached him for their portion, they all realized that a miracle had taken place and began shouting in unison, "Don Bosco is a saint! Don Bosco is a saint!" Every year afterward on that day, Don Bosco gave the boys horse chestnuts in celebration of the miracle.

---

13. The full story can be watched on You Tube, youtube.com/
watch?v=FPMMCZHqAHU.

Perhaps his most wondrous miracle of multiplication happened one day at Mass. It was discovered during the Mass that there were only a few hosts left in the ciborium. With a large crowd waiting to receive Communion, Don Bosco simply walked to the altar rail and began giving out the Body of Christ to each one of the large crowd of boys. Astonishingly, the number in the ciborium remained the same until each had received Communion![14]

Here is another multiplication story, this time from the Desert Fathers:

> [W]hen there was a famine in the Thebaid, the people who lived in the neighboring district, on hearing that Apollo's community of monks was often fed in a miraculous way, came to him as a body with their wives and children to ask him to bless them and give them food. The father, never fearing that there would be any shortage, gave to each of those who came sufficient food for one day. When only three baskets of bread were left and the famine still continued, he ordered the baskets which the brethren intended to eat that day to be brought out, and in the hearing of all the monks and the people said, "Is the hand of the Lord not strong enough to multiply these loaves? For the Holy Spirit says, 'The bread from these baskets shall not be consumed until we have all been satisfied with new wheat.' And all those who were present confirmed that the bread was sufficient for everybody for four months. And he did the same with oil and with wheat. . . . [T]hose who brought in the bread placed full baskets on the tables of the brethren, and after five hundred brothers had eaten their fill took them away still full.[15]

There have been famous occurrences of multiplications of food in many charismatic and Pentecostal missions. One famous Catholic example of modern times was at the Catholic mission in El Paso, Texas, under the ministry of Fr. Rick Thomas.

But multiplications have been occurring in the other churches too. For example, Iris Ministries, an evangelical charismatic organization serving the poor, has more recently seen the multiplication of Bibles and toys.

14. "Don Bosco: Miracles in His Life," salesians.org.za/index.php/bi-centenary/25-don-bosco-miracles-in-his-life.
15. Norman Russell, trans., *The Lives of the Desert Fathers* (Kalamazoo, MI: Cistercian, 1980), 76–77.

Manifestations of Glory

Transfigurations

Transfiguration is a miracle granted to some individuals and confirmed by reliable witnesses in Catholic, Orthodox, Coptic, and Pentecostal and Evangelical traditions. While this is not a miracle actually performed by the believer himself, it is a miracle that is granted to some. Almost always it appears on the faces or whole bodies of holy people.

St. Symeon the New Theologian (949–1022) often became so brilliant in light that even the holiest of monks in his monastery could not look upon his countenance, for

> his eyes would be blinded by the rays that were given off by it. . . . For since the grace of the Spirit had been distributed throughout his entire body, it made him fire, and the human eye could scarcely look at him when he was celebrating the liturgy.[16]

Maria Woodworth-Etter, the famous Pentecostal evangelist, often went into ecstasy while preaching, and her face would shine.

> She at such times is transformed in appearance, and the fashion of her countenance changes. Standing motionless for several minutes with the light of heaven streaming radiant in her face, she sees the unseen and invisible Lord.[17]

I witnessed this once on the face of a famous holy priest. He became so bright with light that I could not see all his facial features. A similar thing, although not so brilliant, happened to someone well known to me. He is a person of prayer, but as he was confessing to a friend his poverty in prayer, light shone from his face.

Transfigurations of various degrees prefigure the glory that all God's children will enjoy in heaven. They also manifest the reign of the kingdom of God on the earth in his holy servants.

---

16. Niketas Stethatos, *The Life of St. Symeon the New Theologian*, trans. Richard P.H. Greenfield (Cambridge, MA: Harvard University Press, 2013), 73.
17. Woodworth-Etter, 163.

Sometimes transfiguration and levitation take place at the same time; this was true of many saints. Here is an account of the hermit, founder, and evangelist St. Paul of the Cross, who died in 1775.

> He began, according to his custom, to have his countenance lighted up, brilliant rays flashing from his face; then his whole body began to tremble; then, as I believe, he perceived that he was losing the control of his senses, he clung with both his hands to the arms of the chair, and leaned his shoulders on the back of it; as soon as he had done this, he began to rise, together with the chair, and that to such a height, that I think he must have risen at least to the height of five or six feet. . . . [I]n this state he continued a very long time in most sublime contemplation. Finally he returned to himself, and, as the rapture passed away, a slight tremor took place all over his body, and gradually the servant of God, with the chair, descended and rested on the ground.[18]

A glory cloud

A cloud of glory (a luminous cloud) was seen in the tent of meeting erected by Moses (Exodus 40:34) and later filled the temple of Solomon (1 Kings 8:10-11). At the Transfiguration, a cloud of glory was seen by Peter, James, and John (Matthew 17:5). Glory clouds are not a charism, strictly speaking, as they are not performed through the person. But as they seem to attend certain ministries and individuals, I have decided to include them here.

Historically, a glory cloud usually takes the form of a luminous white cloud or mist surrounding or overshadowing a person or group. This manifestation was witnessed in the lives of many saints, such as St. Francis of Assisi and St. Symeon the New Theologian. St. Symeon's experience is rather striking, as it was not occasional but very regular in the last years of his life. "[W]e would often see a luminous cloud completely enveloping him when he was standing in the sanctuary at the time of the holy eucharistic prayer."[19]

Smith Wigglesworth, whom I have referred to before, had this experience on many occasions:

---

18. "Levitation and Ecstatic Flights in the Lives of the Saints," miraclesofthesaints. com/2010/10/levitation-and-ecstatic-flights-in.html.
19. Stethatos, 73.

Wigglesworth's holiness was graphically illustrated when, ministering in Zion City, near Chicago, Illinois, he arranged a prayer meeting for the ministers of the city. When they arrived, he was already in prayer, switching from English to divine tongues. As he continued, the others fell prostrate to the floor on their faces, and remained there for an hour, gripped by the power of God. Wigglesworth was the only one left standing and as he lifted his hands and voice to praise God, a cloud like a radiant mist filled the room.[20]

In addition to the classic glory cloud, there seem to be other kinds of manifestations around the world taking place in the air today. These include swirling clouds and clouds of "gold dust," or the air being filled with thousands of tiny explosions of light. Other striking manifestations include rain coming down indoors. A friend was present at a service in which it rained so hard indoors that the rain bounced off the stage! Recently a good priest told me he had been present at a Mass where the whole altar became soaked with water and blood.

Sometimes there is a greater release of supernatural power when the glory cloud is present. A lovely couple I know were running a mission in a small church in west Africa. The pastor had brought about eight people from the local deaf school, who sat on one side, and on the other side were three girls born deaf, blind, and mute. At a certain part in the service, the church doors blew open outwards, and a cloud entered the church. It moved down the center of the church slowly. Finally it arrived at the front, where it remained. In a few minutes, every deaf child had received his or her hearing, and those three blind, deaf, and mute girls were all completely healed!

This couple are two of the most unassuming, humble, kind people you could wish to meet. This experience was shocking to them, because they had never seen anything like it before in their ministry.

These are just a small selection of some of the miracles experienced by believers, many of which the Church has accepted as authentic. They do not include many other forms of miracles that are sovereignly granted rather than coming through the exercise of a charism of miracles. Eucharistic miracles, for example, in which the host turns into human flesh, fall outside this category.

---

20. Wilson, 84–85.

Miracles are signs and wonders that affirm believers in their faith and turn the hearts of unbelievers to the Lord. They reveal that the material world is subject to spiritual power, pointing humanity to higher realities and the divine. Miracles, like all other spiritual gifts, are not to be sought as trophies or ornaments to draw attention to ourselves. Rather they are to glorify God. They often produce a sense of wonder and amazement among the faithful and unbelievers alike. In our day, God, seeing our need, is increasing his miracles with great generosity.

Chapter 12

Ten Keys for Growing in the Anointing

"But seek first his kingdom and his righteousness."
—Matthew 6:33

In my experience of journeying with the Holy Spirit and growing in the spiritual gifts, ten keys have helped me come to the level of ministry the Lord, in his great mercy, has permitted me. Many people who started off with me in this journey, sadly, did not experience the growth in spiritual gifts that I have, because one or other of these keys was missing. Many of these people were more gifted than I and were also better people than I. I share these keys with you because without them, I would never have had the breakthroughs the Lord has allowed. I would undoubtedly have fallen into grave sin or become weird, and the gifts would have become disfigured or even lost.

Some of what I will share may appear obvious to you. However, let's remember that knowledge is not of much use to us if we aren't living it out. I encourage you, as you read, to examine yourself and cry out to the Lord, that he might help these keys find a place in your heart and way of life.

1. Absolute conviction

We need real conviction from the Lord through revelation (Ephesians 1:17-19) that these spiritual gifts are both available to us and critical to the health and growth of the Church today. We need to be convinced that they are not optional extras, like a sunroof or surround sound in your car, just for those "who like that sort of thing." Rather, they are part and parcel of the normal Christian life and indispensable in the mission of the Church (Mark 16:17-18). Without this God-given conviction, we will not persevere in the exercise of the gifts when times of testing come or when we experience misunderstanding from others. This is why it is important to know the teachings of the Bible and the Church on these matters and to have this knowledge inflamed in our hearts by the Holy Spirit.

2. Hope and desire

Without a real hope that God will grant spiritual gifts and grow them in us, we will not persevere in desiring them and in the exercise of faith for them (Hebrews 11:1). In our experience, it is vital to develop the kind of hope that arouses our hearts to "earnestly desire the spiritual gifts" (1 Corinthians 14:1). Hope is the foundation of our desire. The regular practice of thanksgiving is vitally important in keeping hope and desire alive.

The Old Testament tells us that it was when God's people failed to remember with gratitude the great works the Lord had done among them that they fell away from him (Psalm 106:7, 13, 21). Without hope we do not persevere, and it is only with perseverance that we bear fruit (Luke 8:15). This is why it is important for me to continue to read about and watch examples of others who have seen God do more in their lives in the area of spiritual gifts than he has done in mine. Such examples feed our hope and desires. Bigger hope and vision beget bigger desires, bigger desires beget bigger prayers, and bigger prayers beget bigger answers.

3. Faith

I have already spoken about faith, but let's remind ourselves about its importance once again. I have found it crucial over a long season to pray daily for an increase of faith in our exercise of the spiritual gifts. For some years, I did this each day. Even today, I prepare for events by praying every day, for at least a week in advance, for an increase of faith for the miracles of the Lord in ministry. We know that faith plays a key role in healing miracles and deliverance (Matthew 9:2; Mark 9:18-19).

Paul tells us that we prophesy "in proportion to our faith" (Romans 12:6). We need to pray for the grace to believe God's promises in Scripture. If we want to know how much faith we have for healing, for example, we can simply ask how many healings are taking place in our ministry. Our faith is measured by our results, not by our declarations or our daydreams.

To grow in faith, we need to exercise the little faith we have. As we do this, God, seeing our faithfulness in little things, will grant us greater gifts of faith. Faith grows by practice and in stages. There come moments of breakthrough, and these take us to new levels that enable greater manifestations of the Spirit's power.

As I have stated, I regard prayer for faith for the supernatural intervention of God as an obligation of love. Faith unlocks heaven's resources in people's lives. God is looking for people of faith to inherit his promises and to be channels of heavenly blessings on the earth.

4. Prayer and fasting

A deep life of prayer is essential if we are to grow in the fruitful exercise of the spiritual gifts. This, in practice, means an extended period of prayer daily and striving to "pray constantly" (1 Thessalonians 5:17).

It is very difficult to grow in the Christian life without a deepening life of prayer. If we do not mature in our relationship with the Lord and in Christian virtue, we can end up abusing spiritual power and leave a trail of bad fruit. People need to see Jesus' character in us as well as his gifts and power.

St. James tells us that we don't have because we don't ask (James 4:3). We have found that praying daily for spiritual gifts makes a great difference in their operation in our lives. For this reason, we encourage people to ask in a specific way. For example, I pray regularly that the Lord will use me to heal the blind, the deaf, the lame, and so forth and will grant me specific prophetic gifts. We have also discovered that regular fasting for an increased release and anointing in the spiritual gifts has contributed considerably to their effectiveness.

5. Purity

God is calling us to a pure life. St. Paul exhorts us, "Let us cleanse ourselves from every defilement of body and spirit" (2 Corinthians 7:1). He makes it clear that only those who purify themselves will be vessels of silver and gold set aside for special use in God's house (2 Timothy 2:20-21).

This requirement of purity extends to every area of our lives: the way we relate to and view others and ourselves, what we watch on TV and in movies, what we read, the music we listen to, the computer games we play, and how we engage with the Internet. If we want to grow, we may have to make some tough decisions in this regard. This may seem like a high cost, but in our experience, if we are in a place of faith and revelation that the Lord wishes to pour out these gifts, such decisions are a small price to pay for the Lord's great anointing.

Each of us needs to develop a strategy for purity in our lives so that the devil can't outwit us. The first strategy is to be able to name our hidden desires that are not pure and face up to our weaknesses. For example, I will never see a woman alone. I am very careful about the ratings of movies I watch, and I check reviews for sexual or violent content before watching.

I know of a bishop who was struggling with temptations on the Internet. He was determined to have victory, so he put his computer in the office and gave the key to his secretary. He then instructed his secretary to never allow him to be in the office alone. That man is going to go far in the kingdom and the grace of God.

Paul's advice in this area of temptation is never "Stand firm" but always "Flee!" (1 Corinthians 6:18; 1 Timothy 6:11; 2 Timothy 2:22).

6. Family

Many people have said, "God and his work first, then other things." I would prefer to express it differently: first, the love of God; second, the love of family; third, love of others through the ministry to which the Lord calls us. Jesus himself speaks about how some people break the law of honoring father and mother by giving to God what should be given to parents (Matthew 15:3-9). We could fall into the same trap with our time, resources, and affection. A common mistake among many good people in the Church is to give too much time and attention to parish and prayer group things and too little to spouse and children.

The reason family takes priority is because our family is our first mission field, the first people in our lives to whom God sends us. This does not mean, of course, that we are not sent to others as well; rather, it is a matter of ordering our priorities. My wife and children must know that they have priority in my heart before the other ministry or work that God has given me and that my daily time with them is a joy and is sacred to me. I can honestly say that I would rather be at home in our sitting room having family time than on a platform preaching and witnessing miracles. This gives my family a right sense of their value, not just to me but to God.

Those who get this wrong often find it is not only their family life that suffers; their ministries cannot satisfy them, and they become more vulnerable to temptations that can destroy them. We find that if our spouses and children feel they are first in our hearts after the Lord—and before the ministry—they become supportive and enthusiastic about the ministry and usually come to love the Lord deeply.

7. Humility

G.K. Chesterton wrote, "No man's really any good till he knows how bad he is, or might be."[1] The *Catechism of the Catholic Church* tells us that "*humility* is the foundation of prayer" (2559). It is crucial that we grow in humility if our exercise of the spiritual gifts is to extend the kingdom and not cause us or others harm. The greater the gifting, the greater the humility required.

It is a true grace to have loving friends who will, with kindness, tell us our sins, weaknesses, and blind spots. "Humility goes before honor," the Book of Proverbs tells us (18:12). And James states bluntly, "God opposes the proud, but gives grace to the humble" (4:6).

But it is not only self-knowledge that aids humility; praise and thanksgiving are also essential. Mary, who by grace had no personal sins to reflect upon to nourish her humility, was the humblest of all God's creatures. She remained humble through acknowledgment of her lowly state and the praise of God (Luke 1:46-55).

Humility is not something we can achieve ourselves, and it certainly has nothing to do with trying to look humble. There is almost nothing more repulsive than feigned humility. Humility is a gift of God, and we need to pray for it sincerely. I believe love must drive me to pray earnestly for humility, for without humility, God will not be able to trust me with all the gifts he wants to give me in order to bless others.

It is very helpful to pray that we may sincerely regard others as better than we are. This is not something that comes naturally to many of us; it involves a real change of perspective (Philippians 2:3). For years, I was great at seeing my good intentions and counting up others' failures! Humility does the reverse, counting up our own sins and counting up others' virtues. This does not lead, as one might think, to discouragement. Rather, it leads to a deep sense of gratitude and joy for God's mercy and the merciful love of those around us. It enables us to carry God's glory and power in reasonable safety. Humility is also proven and fostered by a spirit of thankfulness, obedience, and loving service.

---

1. G.K. Chesterton, "The Secret of Father Brown," in *The Complete Father Brown Stories* (Hertfordshire, England: Wordsworth Editions, 1992), 499.

8. Detachment

This is a virtue that is unpopular today, especially in the Western world, yet it is one that must be embraced. Of course, this means detachment from money and possessions, as the Bible makes clear. Jesus said, "How hard it is for those who trust in riches to enter the kingdom of heaven" (Mark 10:24). The *Catechism* confirms this: "The precept of detachment from riches is obligatory for entrance into the Kingdom of heaven" (CCC 2544). We must learn to distinguish between what we want and what we genuinely need, for we must be on guard against all kinds of greed: "A man's life does not consist in the abundance of his possessions" (Luke 12:15).

Every minister of power in the New Testament has dealt with attachment to money and possessions. Mary and Joseph left everything to flee to Egypt, to protect the young Jesus. John the Baptist lived a life of extreme simplicity (Matthew 3:4). The apostles "left everything" (Mark 10:28) and lived by a common purse, with Jesus and each other, before the crucifixion (John 12:6) and in the community of Jerusalem after Pentecost (Acts 4:32-37).

Even Cornelius, who presided over a large household, demonstrated a radical detachment, as the angel made clear: "Your prayer has been heard and your alms have been remembered before God" (Acts 10:31). Clearly, both his prayers and his alms must have been considerable to make him stand out, as it were, before the gaze of the Lord.

God wants us to enjoy the same freedom as St. Paul: "I have learned, in whatever state I am, to be content" (Philippians 4:11). It is clear that there are many members of the body of Christ who experience various degrees of aridity, sterility, or tepidness in the practice of their faith that is not from God. In such contexts, detachment from worldly preoccupations is needed, so that the heart can make room for God and his great love. A great experiential outpouring of the Holy Spirit is desperately needed to bring faith alive, to inflame people with the love of God and empower them for mission.

But in the spiritual journey, as people mature, it is not only material detachment that is required. We have to learn how to live detachment in the spiritual life as well. God in his kindness can grant many consolations to encourage and comfort us, and these are to be received with thanksgiving. However, there comes a time when the Lord has to wean us from attachment to these if we are to mature.

A good father might give his children sweets from time to time. But if children are given too many sweets, whenever they want it, they become spoiled, lose their appetite for substantial food, and end up with rotten teeth. The same is true in the spiritual life. We can't get to heaven on a diet of candy! We need meat and vegetables too—in other words, the purifying power of the cross. This expands our heart's capacity for consolations of a higher and more spiritual kind—mystical experiences of a quite different nature and incomparable in their depth of impact and fruit.

9. Community

The context for all charisms is the community of the Church (see CCC 951). Within the wider family of the Church, we all need a local context of prayer, love, and accountability. There the charisms can be nurtured and grow in a safe place, a place where we can make mistakes and learn. This may be a parish, a prayer group, or a community of some kind.

Without a context in which we feel loved and cared for, it is difficult to step out and take risks in the exercise of spiritual gifts in the initial stages. We all need a place to receive ongoing teaching and kindly correction so we can grow. Communities teach us to see the spiritual gifts in the context of love and provide us with a springboard from which to take these gifts into the other circumstances of our lives.

Communities also teach us to value the variety of spiritual gifts that complement our own, which fosters humility. History has shown that without a community context, it is easy for people exercising spiritual gifts to develop in an unhealthy way, focusing too much on themselves. The results can be self-promoting ministries, people acting in isolation and at times in unnecessary conflict with others. In one sense, it is true to say that we are not the discerners of our gifts and that it is the community that calls us forth (Acts 13:1-3).

Finally, community helps us to know we are loved not only for our function but for ourselves. This in turn profoundly improves the quality of our charismatic service.

10. Love

"Make love your aim, and earnestly desire the spiritual gifts" (1 Corinthians 14:1). As we stated in an earlier chapter, we seek the spiritual gifts precisely because we are making love our aim. We may have the most extraordinary gifts, but as Paul assures us, if we have not love, they will do us no good at all (1 Corinthians 13:1-3). Without love, the spiritual gifts become a moral, spiritual, and pastoral minefield. It is very good to earnestly desire the spiritual gifts, as Scripture tells us. But do not be fooled—the gifts in themselves will never bring you real joy. Only love brings joy. You may think how happy you would be if you possessed the gift of miracles, but let me assure you, without love even the miracles become boring.

If love is not your driving force, people become statistics. We either feel proud if the numbers are up or upset if they are down. Where is the joy in that? If we love and care for the people to whom we are sent, we rejoice with them over God's work among them, and their joy brings us joy. It took me a long time to really get this, but once I did, ministry became much more a source of joy to me and more about what Jesus was doing rather than what I was doing.

Jesus' love is what led him to exercise the spiritual gifts, and often when seeing people, he "had compassion on them" (Mark 6:34). Jesus came that our joy may be complete (John 15:11; 16:24), and that joy is completed by love. Make love truly your aim, and the spiritual gifts given to you will become sources of blessing to the Church and the world, as well as consolations for you.

Conclusion

We live in a world in which there are many confusing voices. On the one hand, proponents of radical new atheism, secularism, and materialism reject spirituality and the supernatural as irrelevant nonsense. On the other hand, there is a growing fascination among many with spirituality and the supernatural through New Age, the occult, witchcraft, and even Satanism, as well as violent radical expressions of religion. On both counts, demonstrations of supernatural gifts by Christians play a vital role. To one, they demonstrate the reality of a supernatural world that is denied; to the other, they manifest the incomparable power of the one true God and the lordship of Jesus Christ.

In such a climate, it is urgent that the Church "earnestly desire the spiritual gifts" (1 Corinthians 14:1), which God, in his providential love, is pouring out in our day. Such gifts, if received, will transform the Church's work of evangelization, empower her diverse ministries, and enrich her liturgy and prayer as in former days. We need a new commitment to offer formation in spiritual gifts in seminaries and parishes as a normal part of catechetical, theological, and ministry programs. God, it seems clear, desires to adorn his Church with these beautiful gifts, that she might become even more effective as the light to the nations (Isaiah 60:1-3).

If we can make room for the spiritual gifts and exercise them in love, humility, and joy, the Church will be greatly built up and the message of the gospel will be magnified throughout the earth, capturing the hearts of the multitudes looking for love and meaning and an encounter with the living God.

"Lord, renew your wonders in this our day as by a new Pentecost."
—Pope St. John XIII

"Grant to your servants to speak your word with all boldness, while you stretch out your hand to heal, and signs and wonders are performed through the name of your holy servant Jesus."
(Acts 4:29-30, NRSV)

Amen!

Damian Stayne's Ministry and Cor et Lumen Christi

If you are interested in knowing more about Damian Stayne's ministry and the life and mission of his community, Cor et Lumen Christi, or if you would like to attend one of their events or invite Damian or one of his team to lead an event in your area, visit the website coretlumenchristi.org.

Short videos of healings at the community's Miracle Healing Services can be found at coretlumenchristi.org/videos.php. Alternatively, search on YouTube "Damian Stayne" or "Cor et Lumen Christi." Or go to Damian's Facebook page, "Damian Stayne."

If you wish to support our life and mission, please go to our website and click on "Support Us." Thank you.

Recommended Reading

These books are recommended to you because they contain many helpful insights. While we cannot endorse every opinion or doctrine expressed in some of these books, all of them have within them real treasures that we have found greatly enriching.

Amorth, Fr. Gabriel. *An Exorcist Tells His Story*. San Francisco: Ignatius, 1999.

St. Bede. *The Age of Bede*. Translated by J.F. Webb. London: Penguin, 1965.

Carty, Rev. Charles Mortimer. *Padre Pio: The Stigmatist*. Rockford, IL: TAN, 1973.

Collins, Fr. Pat. *Expectant Faith*. Dublin: Columba, 1988.

———. *Gifts of the Holy Spirit and the New Evangelisation*. Dublin: Columba, 2009.

Cooke, Graham. *Developing Your Prophetic Gifting*. Grand Rapids, MI: Chosen, 2003.

Hebert, Fr. Albert J., SM. *Saints Who Raised the Dead*. Charlotte, NC: TAN, 2012.

International Catholic Charismatic Renewal Services. *Baptism in the Holy Spirit, Jubilee Edition*. Vatican City: ICCRS, 2017.

Lozano, Neal. *Resisting the Devil: A Catholic Perspective on Deliverance*. Huntington, IN: Our Sunday Visitor, 2010.

MacNutt, Francis. *Deliverance from Evil Spirits: A Practical Manual*. Grand Rapids, MI: Chosen, 2009.

———. *Healing*. Notre Dame, IN: Ave Maria Press, 1999.

———. *The Power to Heal.* Notre Dame, IN: Ave Maria Press, 1977.

McManus, Fr. Jim, CSSR. *The Healing Power of the Sacraments.* Notre Dame, IN: Ave Maria Press, 1984.

Petts, David. *Body Builders: Gifts to Make God's People Grow.* Mattersey, England: Mattersey Hall, 2002. Available from davidpetts.org.

———. *Just a Taste of Heaven. A Biblical and Balanced Approach to God's Healing Power.* Mattersey, England: Mattersey Hall, 2006. Available from davidpetts.org.

Pytches, David. *Come, Holy Spirit.* Hodder Christian Paperbacks.

Sacred Congregation for the Doctrine of the Faith. *Instruction on Prayers for Healing.* This can be found at the Vatican website, Vatican.va. The theological part is wonderful, but the disciplinary norms have been widely misunderstood because of problems of interpretation. Thus I suggest reading this document alongside the booklet *Prayer for Healing,* produced by International Catholic Charismatic Renewal Services in consultation with the Pontifical Council for the Laity, (ICCRS, 2003), which is valuable and gives a clear interpretation of the disciplinary norms.

Scanlan, Fr. Michael, TOR. *Inner Healing: Ministering to the Human Spirit through the Power of Prayer.* New York: Paulist Press, 1974.

Scanlan, Fr. Michael, TOR, and Randall Cirner. *Deliverance from Evil Spirits: A Weapon for Spiritual Warfare.* Ann Arbor, MI: Servant, 1980.

Sullivan, Fr. Francis, SJ. *Charisms and Charismatic Renewal: A Biblical and Theological Study.* Ann Arbor, MI: Servant, 1982.

Ward, Benedicta. *The Sayings of the Desert Fathers: The Alphabetical Collection.* Collegeville, MN: Liturgical, 1984.

Wigglesworth, Smith. *Ever Increasing Faith.* Mass Market Paperbacks, 2016.

Wilson, Julian. *Wigglesworth: The Complete Story.* Tyrone, GA: Authentic, 2002.

Wimber, John, and Kevin Springer. *Power Healing.* New York: HarperCollins, 1987.

Woodworth-Etter, Maria. *Signs and Wonders.* New Kensington, PA: Whitaker House, 1997.

Yocum, Bruce. *Prophecy: Exercising the Prophetic Gifts of the Spirit in the Church Today*. Ann Arbor, MI: Servant, 1993.

The WORD among us®
The Spirit of Catholic Living

This book was published by The Word Among Us. Since 1981, The Word Among Us has been answering the call of the Second Vatican Council to help Catholic laypeople encounter Christ in the Scriptures.

The name of our company comes from the prologue to the Gospel of John and reflects the vision and purpose of all of our publications: to be an instrument of the Spirit, whose desire is to manifest Jesus' presence in and to the children of God. In this way, we hope to contribute to the Church's ongoing mission of proclaiming the gospel to the world so that all people would know the love and mercy of our Lord and grow more deeply in their faith as missionary disciples.

Our monthly devotional magazine, *The Word Among Us*, features meditations on the daily and Sunday Mass readings, and currently reaches more than one million Catholics in North America and another half million Catholics in one hundred countries around the world. Our book division, The Word Among Us Press, publishes numerous books, Bible studies, and pamphlets that help Catholics grow in their faith.

To learn more about who we are and what we publish, log on to our website at www.wau.org. There you will find a variety of Catholic resources that will help you grow in your faith.

Embrace His Word, Listen to God . . .

www.wau.org